Emerging Powers and the UN

The post-2015 goals and the changing environment of development cooperation will demand a renewed and strengthened UN development system. In line with their increasing significance as economic powers, a growing number of emerging nations will play an expanded role in the UN development system. These roles will take the form of growing financial contributions to individual organizations, greater weight in governance structures, higher staff representation, a stronger voice in development deliberations, and a greater overall influence on the UN development agenda.

Emerging Powers and the UN explores in depth the relationship of these countries with, and their role in, the future UN development system. Formally, the relationship is through representation as member states (first UN) and UN staff (second UN). However, the importance of the non-public sector interests (third UN) of emerging economies is also growing, through private sponsorship and NGO activities in development. This book was originally published as a special issue of *Third World Quarterly*.

Thomas G. Weiss is Presidential Professor of Political Science, and Director Emeritus of the Ralph Bunche Institute for International Studies, at The City University of New York's Graduate Center, New York City, USA.

Adriana Erthal Abdenur is Professor of International Relations at the Pontifical Catholic University in Rio de Janeiro, Brazil, and General Coordinator of the BRICS Policy Center.

Thirdworlds

Edited by Shahid Qadir, University of London

THIRDWORLDS will focus on the political economy, development and cultures of those parts of the world that have experienced the most political, social, and economic upheaval, and which have faced the greatest challenges of the postcolonial world under globalisation: poverty, displacement and diaspora, environmental degradation, human and civil rights abuses, war, hunger, and disease. **THIRDWORLDS** serves as a signifier of oppositional emerging economies and cultures ranging from Africa, Asia, Latin America, Middle East, and even those 'Souths' within a larger perceived North, such as the U.S. South and Mediterranean Europe. The study of these otherwise disparate and discontinuous areas, known collectively as the Global South, demonstrates that as globalisation pervades the planet, the south, as a synonym for subalterity, also transcends geographical and ideological frontiers.

Terrorism and the Politics of Naming
Edited by Michael Bhatia

Reconstructing Post-Saddam Iraq
Edited by Sultan Barakat

From Nation-Building to State-Building
Edited by Mark T. Berger

Connecting Cultures
Edited by Emma Bainbridge

The Politics of Rights
Dilemmas for feminist praxis
Edited by Andrea Cornwall and Maxine Molyneux

The Long War – Insurgency, Counterinsurgency and Collapsing States
Edited by Mark T. Berger and Douglas A. Borer

Market-led Agrarian Reform
Edited by Saturnino M. Borras, Jr.

After the Third World?
Edited by Mark T. Berger

Developmental and Cultural Nationalisms
Edited by Radhika Desai

Globalisation and Migration
New issues, new politics
Edited by Ronaldo Munck

Domestic and International Perspectives on Kyrgyzstan's 'Tulip Revolution'
Motives, mobilizations and meanings
Edited by Sarah Cummings

War and Revolution in the Caucasus
Georgia Ablaze
Edited by Stephen F. Jones

War, Peace and Progress in the 21st Century
Development, Violence and Insecurities
Edited by Mark T. Berger and Heloise Weber

Renewing International Labour Studies
Edited by Marcus Taylor

Emerging Powers and the UN

What kind of development partnership?

Edited by

Thomas G. Weiss and
Adriana Erthal Abdenur

Routledge
Taylor & Francis Group

LONDON AND NEW YORK

First published 2016 by Routledge

2 Park Square, Milton Park, Abingdon, Oxon OX14 4RN
711 Third Avenue, New York, NY 10017, USA

Routledge is an imprint of the Taylor & Francis Group, an informa business

First issued in paperback 2017

British Library Cataloguing in Publication Data
A catalogue record for this book is available from the British Library

ISBN 13: 978-1-138-94732-0 (hbk)
ISBN 13: 978-1-138-08654-8 (pbk)

Typeset in Times New Roman
by RefineCatch Limited, Bungay, Suffolk

Publisher's Note
The publisher accepts responsibility for any inconsistencies that may have
arisen during the conversion of this book from journal articles to book chapters,
namely the possible inclusion of journal terminology.

Disclaimer
Every effort has been made to contact copyright holders for their permission to
reprint material in this book. The publishers would be grateful to hear from any
copyright holder who is not here acknowledged and will undertake to rectify
any errors or omissions in future editions of this book.

Contents

CONTENTS

Citation Information

The chapters in this book were originally published in *Third World Quarterly*, volume 35, issue 10 (November 2014). When citing this material, please use the original page numbering for each article, as follows:

Chapter 6
A changing world: is the UN development system ready?
Stephen Browne
Third World Quarterly, volume 35, issue 10 (November 2014) pp. 1845–1859

Chapter 7
South-South cooperation and the future of development assistance: mapping actors and options
Paolo de Renzio and Jurek Seifert
Third World Quarterly, volume 35, issue 10 (November 2014) pp. 1860–1875

Chapter 8
Emerging powers as normative agents: Brazil and China within the UN development system
Adriana Erthal Abdenur
Third World Quarterly, volume 35, issue 10 (November 2014) pp. 1876–1893

Chapter 9
Emerging powers and the UN development system: canvassing global views
Stephen Browne and Thomas G. Weiss
Third World Quarterly, volume 35, issue 10 (November 2014) pp. 1894–1910

Chapter 10
War-torn countries, natural resources, emerging-power investors and the UN development system
Graciana del Castillo
Third World Quarterly, volume 35, issue 10 (November 2014) pp. 1911–1926

For any permission-related enquiries please visit:
http://www.tandfonline.com/page/help/permissions

Notes on Contributors

Adriana Erthal Abdenur is Professor of International Relations at the Pontifical Catholic University, Rio de Janeiro, Brazil, and General Coordinator of the BRICS Policy Center. Her research focuses on development cooperation, international security and rising powers. Her recent publications include articles in *Trade & Integration, Third World Quarterly,* and *Revista CIDOB d'Afers Internacionals.* She has co-edited two recent books on BRICS, *A cooperação sul–sul e os BRICS* (2012), and *As Cidades e os BRICS* (2013). She was formerly a professor at Columbia University and the New School University, both New York City, USA, as well as a fellow of the India China Institute and Fulbright Research fellow.

Manaíra Assunção is a graduate student at the Institute of International Relations, Pontifical Catholic University, Rio de Janeiro, Brazil. Since 2011, she has also been a research assistant at the BRICS Policy Center. Her research focuses on international development cooperation principles and paradigms, particularly the question of ownership and changing donor and recipient relations, as well as on new development partners.

Stephen Browne is Co-director of the Future of the UN Development System (FUNDS) Project and Senior Fellow of the Ralph Bunche Institute for International Studies, The City University of New York, USA, and former Deputy Executive Director of the International Trade Centre, Geneva, Switzerland. He is the author of several books on development and the UN, including *United Nations Industrial Development Organization* (2012) and *The United Nations Development Programme and System* (2011).

Graciana del Castillo is Senior Fellow at the Ralph Bunche Institute for International Studies, The City University of New York, New York City, USA. She was Senior Research Scholar, Associate Director of the Center of Capitalism and Society, and Adjunct Professor of Economics and International Affairs at Columbia University, New York City, USA. She first worked with war-torn countries as the senior economist in the Office of the UN Secretary-General in the early 1990s, and then at the IMF. She is the author of *Rebuilding War-torn States: The Challenge of Post-conflict Economic Reconstruction* (2008) and of *Guilty Party: The International Community in Afghanistan* (2014).

Paolo de Renzio is Adjunct Professor in the International Relations Institute, Pontifical Catholic University of Rio de Janeiro, Brazil, where he researches BRICS and South–South cooperation. He is also a Senior Research Fellow at the International Budget Partnership (IBP) in Washington D.C., USA, where he coordinates a research programme on governance, fiscal transparency, and development. He has been a consultant for the World Bank, the OECD, the European Commission, various donor agencies, and international NGOs. His articles have appeared in such journals as *World Development*, *Governance*, and *Development Policy Review*.

Paulo Luiz Moreaux Lavigne Esteves is Director of, and Professor at, the International Relations Institute, Pontifical Catholic University of Rio de Janeiro, Brazil, and the General Supervisor of the BRICS Policy Center. His current research focuses on the intersections between international security, humanitarianism, and development, as well as on the role of Brazil and other rising powers within the international development field. In Portuguese he has edited *International Institutions: Security, Trade, and Integration* (2004) and *The BRICS and South–South Cooperation* (2010); and is author of *The Convergence between Humanitarian Aid and International Security* (2010). He has been a consultant for the UNDP, the State Government of Minas Gerais, CNPq, and CAPES, and he was founding partner, and director from 2005 to 2009, of the Brazilian International Relations Association.

Bruce Jenks is Adjunct Professor at the School of International and Public Affairs, Columbia University, New York City, USA; Lecturer at the University of Geneva, Switzerland; and Fellow at the Center on International Cooperation, New York University, USA, where he co-authored *United Nations Development at a Crossroads* (2013). He served at the United Nations for almost 30 years, most recently from 2000–10 as assistant secretary- general at the UNDP. He is currently senior advisor to the Hammarskjöld Foundation. In 2013 he became a member of the Council of the University for Peace, where he was elected vice-president.

Jurek Seifert is currently pursuing his Ph.D. at the University of Duisburg-Essen, Germany, and at the Pontifical Catholic University of Rio de Janeiro, Brazil. He is also enrolled in international development studies at the Ruhr University Bochum, Germany. His research focuses on the characteristics of South–South development cooperation against the background of global power shifts and changing patterns in international cooperation, as well as on Brazil as a new development partner in Africa.

Ramesh Thakur is Director of the Centre for Nuclear Non-proliferation and Disarmament, Crawford School of Public Policy, Australian National University, Canberra, Australia. He was formerly Senior Vice-Rector of the UN University. He is the author of *The Group of Twenty (G20)* (with Andrew F. Cooper, 2013) and co-editor, with Cooper and Jorge Heine, of *The Oxford Handbook of Modern Diplomacy* (2013).

John Toye is Chair of the Advisory Council of the Department of International Development, University of Oxford, UK. He began his career in the British Treasury in the 1960s. Since then he has been, successively, a Professor of Development Economics at the Universities of Wales, Sussex, and Oxford, all UK. He was Director of the Institute of Development Studies at the University of Sussex, Brighton, UK, from 1987 to 1997, and then Director of the UN Conference on Trade and Development from 1998 to 2000. He is co-author of *The UN and Global Political Economy* (2004). He is currently working on a history of UNCTAD.

Silke Weinlich is a political scientist specialising in international relations with a focus on international organisations and the United Nations (including peacekeeping, peace-building, development, and reform). In 2012 she joined the Centre for Global

Cooperation Research at the University Duisburg-Essen, Germany, where she heads the research unit on the (im)possibility of cooperation. Previously she worked at the German Development Institute in Bonn, Germany, on the reform of the UN development system.

Thomas G. Weiss is Presidential Professor of Political Science, and Director Emeritus of the Ralph Bunche Institute for International Studies, at The City University of New York's Graduate Center, New York City, USA. He is also a Research Professor at SOAS, University of London UK. He is Co-director of the FUNDS Project and of the Wartime History and the Future UN Project. He is a former president of the International Studies Association (2009–10) and chair of the Academic Council on the UN System (2006–09). His most recent single-authored books include *Governing the World? Addressing 'Problems without Passports'* (2014); *Global Governance: Why? What? Whither? (2013); Humanitarian Business* (2013); *What's Wrong with the United Nations and How to Fix It* (2012); and *Humanitarian Intervention: Ideas in Action* (2012).

Introduction: emerging powers and the UN – what kind of development partnership?

Thomas G. Weiss[a] and Adriana Erthal Abdenur[b]

[a]Ralph Bunche Institute for International Studies, The City University of New York, USA; [b]Institute of International Relations, Pontifical Catholic University, Rio de Janeiro, Brazil

Since the outset, in the aftermath of World War II, the United Nations development system (UNDS) has constituted an essential pillar of the world organisation's activities, along with those devoted to peacekeeping, humanitarianism, human rights and justice. Adaptations notwithstanding, serious questions remain about its effectiveness and capacity to represent adequately the aspirations of 'we, the peoples' – the opening words of the UN Charter – particularly in the global South. Although developing countries have joined forces at different stages in the international arena – including through the Non-Aligned Movement (NAM) and the Group of 77 (G77) – to increase their voices within the system, over the past decade a new twist has been added, the visibility of emerging powers. This reality not only reflects the latter's growing role as providers of development cooperation but also their criticism of the existing architecture for global economic governance. Both individually and through new alignments such as that of Brazil, Russia, India, China, and South Africa (BRICS), emerging powers are engaging more directly not only in the practices of development cooperation but also in key normative debates about how accelerated development and poverty alleviation could and should be carried out, and how major institutions could and should contribute. Recent research shows the extent to which Southern agency has been a source of global norms.[1] Whether or not the phenomenon of emerging powers reinforces the North–South divide or increases the diversity of positions and alignments within the international system, however, remains very much open to debate.

The essays in this volume address that debate and are the product of a fruitful collaboration between the Institute of International Relations at the Pontifical Catholic University in Rio de Janeiro (and its affiliated BRICS Policy Center) and the Future UN Development System Project (FUNDS) of the Ralph Bunche Institute for International Studies at The City University of New York's (CUNY) Graduate Center. In particular, this joint research effort sought to analyse the changing role of emerging powers in light of ongoing intergovernmental discussions about the UN's capacity to foster sustainable development. By bringing together a mix of practitioners from inside and outside the UN and academics specialising in development and in South–South cooperation, a conference held in Rio in April 2014 provided the opportunity to test analyses of these dynamics from a variety of perspectives and to foment debate about the politics and policies of development governance in the post-cold war era.

The moment was opportune. In 2015 the UN development system crosses an important threshold. It is the terminal year of the Millennium Development Goals (MDGS), drawn up at the UN Millennium Summit of 2000, and the start of a period in which new global development goals (including those from Rio+20) are expected to be agreed in a rapidly changing context of development cooperation. For the UN itself, and the more than 30 development organisations within it, the MDGS have set the agenda over the past 15 years. In addition to the momentous changes in the global landscape over that time (ranging from intensified globalisation to new technologies, from a growing middle class worldwide to increasing foreign direct investment and remittances[2]), the future holds new global challenges to be confronted by a widening array of development organisations with major new donors and partners emerging in the global South.

The post-2015 goals and the changing environment for development cooperation demand a renewed and strengthened UN development system. To repeat a theme from the FUNDS project's website: what is the UN we want for the world we want? Commensurate with their increasing economic significance, a growing number of emerging powers will undoubtedly play expanded roles in answering that query. These will take the form of growing financial contributions to individual organisations; greater weight in governance structures; higher staff representation; a stronger voice in development deliberations; and a greater overall influence on the UN development agenda.

This introduction begins by briefly reviewing some key concepts. It continues with an overview of the main issues that arise from the 10 articles in the issue. And it ends with a brief summary of the individual papers.

Some definitions

We can finesse the question about whether the USA or the West is declining, absolutely or relatively, while still being clear that the so-called unipolar moment was short-lived and that the American world order is under duress.[3] At a minimum we can point to what George Magnus has described as an 'uprising' to convey the notion that we are in the midst of an extraordinary change in the organisation and structure of the international system.[4] It is unnecessary to exaggerate either the shadow cast by the West, or what Amitav Acharya calls the 'hype of the rest',[5] to see that the role of emerging powers in global governance is changing the landscape for development cooperation, whether as conceived and implemented by the UN system or by bilateral donors and investors. Whether we toss aside the host of labels – including multipolar, a-polar, G-zero, the list goes on – it is clear that Acharya's depiction of a 'multiplex cinema' is an apt image with a choice of plots (ideas), directors (power) and action (leadership) available to observers under one roof.[6]

The label of 'emerging powers' is neither carved in stone nor uncontroversial. Our use of the term refers to countries whose policy elites are able to draw on economic and other sources of power to project influence both within and outside their immediate neighbourhood and regions, and which play a substantial role in the call for global governance reform. While this and other categories – including 'global South' or the 'North' or the 'Third World' – are deeply problematic and contested, they reflect specific perspectives on development and historical experiences. As such, these constructs have gained currency within UN development debates. In other words, despite the analytical flaws of such 'clumps', in political debates about development they matter. Hence these broad categories appear throughout the contributions in this volume. However, as with any project that seeks to shed light on an under-studied component of a broader phenomenon, we acknowledge that this collection of articles is by no means a complete or definitive treatment of current debates about the UNDS; here the category of emerging powers is in the forefront, with other developing countries and the North itself not receiving the same level of scrutiny.

For us, the emerging powers include not only BRICS but also Indonesia, Mexico, Chile, Argentina, South Korea, Turkey, the Philippines, Thailand and Nigeria, among others. This category has been 'expansive, fluid, and contested', writes Andrew Cooper. 'No one acronym has the field to itself'.[7] He had in mind of course not only 'BRICS' – anomalous in that they include two permanent members of the Security Council, one a former superpower and the other the world's second largest economy – but also a host of other abbreviations: BRIICS (BRICS plus Indonesia); BASIC (the BRICS minus Russia); IBSA (BRICS minus Russia and China); BRICSAM (BRICS plus Mexico); and MIST (Mexico, Indonesia, South Korea and Turkey). And we should not forget the G20 (South Africa, Canada, the USA, Mexico, Argentina, Brazil, China, Japan, South Korea, India, Indonesia, Saudi Arabia, Russia, Turkey, Australia, France, Germany, Italy, the UK, and the European Union),[8] or the 3G Coalition that exists as part of an informal variable geometry to get the G20 to be more inclusive of non-member views.[9] These structures lend new weight to long-standing critiques of Western dominance over the global governance of economic and financial affairs, including development, and perhaps provide a way to bridge the North–South chasm or the West-versus-the-Rest divide.

In focusing on the fluid category of emerging powers we recognise that they were once pigeonholed as part of the 'Third World' and the 'global South'. Indeed, many observers and diplomats argue that these countries are still members of that comprehensive grouping of over 130 developing countries, even if they have graduated from being recipients of official development assistance (ODA) to being net donors (or are close to doing so). Setting aside for the moment the cohesiveness of any category, all emerging powers have been important players within the field of international development – not only as beneficiaries of assistance and providers of cooperation, but also as contributors to initiatives and normative debates within the UN development system. During the Cold War configurations such as the G77 worked to address what developing countries perceived to be a highly unjust global economic system, a view that continues to characterise the position of all groups of developing countries. For instance, they put forth the New Economic International Order (NIEO), a set of proposals intended to address the deep asymmetries in international trade and to foster development within the Third World. However, the manoeuvring space available to these states was constrained not only by firm resistance from industrialised economies but also by the rigid bipolarity of that era.

In the post-cold war period, the importance of the emerging powers to the UNDS has both grown and become a topic about which it is harder to generalise in at least four ways. First, and structurally, the deep changes within the configuration of the international arena, with the possibility of a more multipolar order emerging, has emboldened some emerging powers and renewed debates about the need to update the architecture of global economic and financial governance.

Second, many emerging powers have become major providers of South–South cooperation, which they insist is distinct in principle and practice from more traditional development cooperation. Thus the relevance of these countries to international development has increased, but this has taken place primarily outside the parameters of the UNDS. That said, the rhetorical commitment to the United Nations remains in the headlines. In April 2011, for instance, BRICS issued the 'Sanya Declaration', which reiterated their collective 'strong commitment to multilateral diplomacy with the United Nations playing the central role in dealing with global challenges and threats'.[10]

Third, certain emerging powers have been working to enhance policy coordination and launch concrete joint efforts, for instance via BRICS. These initiatives include not only efforts to beef-up the UN's development pillar but also to resist the effectiveness agenda and aid procedures formulated by the Development Assistance Committee (DAC) of the Organisation for Economic Co-operation and Development (OECD). Rather than be subjected to norms that they perceive as being 'handed down' by traditional donors and international organisations dominated by industrialised economies, the emerging powers seek to actively participate in and even transform the global norms-setting process in the development cooperation arena. This shared desire has become more pronounced with efforts to define the post-2015 development agenda, although the positions of emerging powers within those debates are unclear as of this writing.

Fourth, emerging powers have not only engaged actively in the field of international development but have also diversified the forms of participation. Many providers of South–South cooperation deal with a wide variety of target governments, and some emerging powers have increasingly engaged in contexts marked by conflict or recurring political instability. Thus the role of emerging powers extends to ongoing debates within and outside the UN about how to balance security priorities with development initiatives in such settings.

However, and to state the obvious, the roles and positions of emerging powers are far from homogenous – their political regimes, development models, and geopolitical interests vary and frequently diverge. They point to differing motivations even when such states manage to make shared rhetorical claims. Thus, rather than treating them as an undifferentiated bloc, it is necessary to parse how their behaviours and interests vary, as well as how their approaches and strategies change over time, with particular reference in this volume to the UN development system. The UNDS includes over 30 agencies, funds and programmes that deal with some aspect of international development, but for our purposes it excludes the Washington-based international financial institutions – the World Bank and the IMF, which are *de jure* but not *de facto* part of the UN system – and the World Trade Organization. In keeping with the multi-stakeholder thinking that has animated development debates at the UN and elsewhere, we have framed the system not only in terms of intergovernmental relations – the '1st UN' of member states and the '2nd UN' of international civil servants – but also the '3rd UN' of non-state actors such as civil society organisations and private-sector firms.[11]

Key issues

Although the articles in this volume offer a wide variety of perspectives on the impact of emerging powers on the UN development system, several key themes run across them and may be useful in reframing old questions or raising new ones altogether. We offer our take on them as a guide for readers when they peruse the actual articles.

First, the set of articles addresses both continuity and change. Whereas some articles provide cross-sectional views of the role of emerging powers within the UNDS, others adopt a more overtly historical approach to show how, and to what extent, these powers' contemporary interests and positions within the UNDS were shaped by development experiences, whether through or outside of North–South development assistance. The identities, interests, and underlying motivations of emerging powers have not remained constant across time, but understanding their trajectories is valuable in avoiding an excessive emphasis on historical disjunctures.

Behind these macro-political changes lies a startling reality that was very much in evidence as the champagne flutes in New York were stored following the largest-ever global summit at UN headquarters in September 2005 on the occasion of the world organisation's 60th anniversary. Over 150 presidents, prime ministers and monarchs encountered the same problems that have restricted international cooperation since the launching of the current generation of global institutions that replaced the defunct League of Nations – indeed, since the beginning of modern experiments with multilateral cooperation in the 19th century.[12]

On the one hand, new challenges to international peace and security and human survival have arisen. New non-state actors have appeared on the world stage, and older ones have occasionally been transformed. New conventions and norms have proliferated. New intergovernmental initiatives and institutions have been established. Observers increasingly understand the links between security and development, and between human security and human development. And, indeed, the development landscape itself has changed dramatically. On the other hand, the dominant reality in world politics and international organisations consists of decision making by states. And the UN and its system of intergovernmental decision making have not changed substantially.

Hence nothing has altered the validity of an evaluation by Adam Roberts and Benedict Kingsbury in *United Nations, Divided World*: 'international society has been modified, but not totally transformed'.[13] The UN does not exist in isolation from the world that it is attempting to serve. Many scholars and practitioners resist the notion that there has been a fundamental change in world politics. Essentially they are right in claiming that the more things change, the more they stay the same. Certainly the fundamental units of the system – sovereign states – are here to stay. They are still organised to pursue their perceived national interests in a world without any meaningful overall authority.

Nothing in this collection indicates that states remain the main building block of the international system, and that the world thus still reflects what Hedley Bull and virtually all political scientists call 'anarchy',[14] or the absence of a central global authority. In spite of the construction of a seemingly ever-denser web of international institutions, there is nothing like a world government in the offing. Although it would be inaccurate to ignore the extremes – ranging from fractious political authority in many war-torn and failed states to the supranational integration of the EU – it still is accurate to point to a fundamental continuity: state sovereignty remains the core of international relations. That said, rule-setting processes matter, and emerging powers take them seriously.

Likewise the articles show the importance of keeping in mind the historical contingencies that enable and constrain the role of emerging powers within the international arena, including the UNDS. There have been other periods when emerging powers played highly visible roles within the system; and for broader structural reasons, these windows of opportunity narrowed or even closed. The G77-led NIEO led to proposals that floundered not only because of resistance by the industrialised states, but also because the oil crisis and ensuing indebtedness and structural adjustment programmes of the Washington-consensus era constrained the policy autonomy of developing countries, shifting agency away from the UNDS and towards the Bretton Woods institutions. The current salience of BRICS must be understood in light of the specific historical circumstances of the post-cold war period rather than treated as a phenomenon not subject to oscillations or even reversals. While the articles in this volume do not dismiss the BRICS category out of hand, they also do not overestimate the potential that these states have to reshape the development *problématique*, including via the UN. Indeed, recent research suggests that in some instances – eg China in the Democratic Republic of the Congo[15] – there may not be as clear a break as commonly thought from previous Western patterns. The interests of investors converge around stabilisation and market-driven economic activities.

Second, the articles shed light on how emerging powers view themselves in relation to the UN's development system. Voting patterns on development issues in the General Assembly confirm 'that BRICS never take opposing positions'.[16] At the same time, they may perceive the UN development system primarily from the perspective of consumers of development assistance and subsidies of various types – thereby viewing the agencies, programmes and funds that make up the UNDS as valuable resources to contribute to tackling their own domestic challenges. At other times, however, emerging powers may be willing to invest in the system, in the sense of boosting it – through financial contributions, participation in concrete initiatives and active engagement in normative debates – so that the system is better equipped to deal with challenges that are truly global. The specific case studies of emerging powers within this volume vary substantially as to whether the countries being analysed are more 'consumers' of than 'investors' in the UNDS. These perceptions and roles are not necessarily constant across the mechanisms of the UN's development system, nor across time.

Third, many of the analyses presented here address the role of emerging powers as normative actors in the field of international development. Such states have long desired to expand their participation in the rule-setting processes of global governance, unwilling to be mere 'rule-takers' but aspiring to be 'rule-makers'. To date, however, 'emerging economies appear to have preferred the status quo and working within existing institutions created by Western states', write David Held and Charles Roger. 'Yet, as they grow in power and seek to ensure that their needs and values are reflected at the global level, their assertiveness and dissatisfaction with existing institutions may rise'.[17] Robert Wade argues that 'the standard narrative about an emerging new global political order shaped by 'the rise of the South' is 'misleading…the primary responsibility for mobilizing cooperation around those global commons problems remains with the Western states, which continue to hold the commanding heights'.[18]

While the jury is still very much out, participation by emerging powers in normative debates related to development can take a variety of forms, from blocking normative proposals viewed as being promoted by developed countries – illustrated by BRICS's resistance to the OECD's effectiveness agenda – to altering existing norms and proposing new frameworks altogether. The proposed BRICS development bank, if it comes to fruition for example, may prove to be a platform for new levels of normative engagement by BRICS as a collective actor.

One key issue pertaining to BRICS's normative stance is the degree to which they espouse a revival of the idea of the developmental state. All of the countries that make up the BRICS grouping, to some extent, insist that the state plays a primordial role in socioeconomic development; that role varies considerably across the cases, as well as in other emerging powers. In addition, the centrality of the state as a promoter of development does not necessarily carry over into the country's cooperation initiatives abroad, particularly given that many emerging powers have tended to promote trade and the production of commodities through the distinct mechanism of South–South cooperation. While the charge that emerging powers promote neoliberalism with a veneer of the developmental state may be overstated, the articles in this issue suggest that there is a need to parse the degree to which their claims about the role of the state apply to their development cooperation strategies, both within and outside the UNDS.

Fourth, the articles prompt us to ask new questions about the representativeness of groupings like BRICS. Although this coalition is the parent of a strong rhetorical call to reform global economic governance, including making development cooperation more just and effective, the member states are also interested in opening up more space for themselves within the system. Their positions, even where they succeed in finding common ground, do not necessarily correspond to those of other developing countries, nor are they always willing or able to take on responsibility for claims by the broader group of developing countries. Other emerging economies may be more inclined to enter into a dialogue with traditional donors, even if such actions mean participating in the Global Partnership for Effective Development Cooperation (GPEDC) led by the OECD and the UN Development Programme (UNDP). More significantly, poorer countries may not perceive BRICS positions to be aligned with their own interests. In addition, there is considerable political contestation of BRICS's claims to leadership, including within their own regions, suggesting that there are limits on how far the grouping may mobilise support for its positions among other developing countries.

About this issue

The end of the Cold War altered many givens, but one thing remains remarkably fixed, namely the echo chamber for so many 'debates' in international relations, including those pertaining to development. They have consisted essentially of the North talking to the North, and the South talking to the South – with sparks flying when the two categories get together to negotiate or hammer out compromises. By shedding light on some of the pre-set positions and motivations of actors whose roles within these processes have not always been clear, this issue seeks to continue the dialogue begun in the pages of *Third World Quarterly* over recent years on the role of emerging powers.[19]

The individual articles contribute towards this bridge building in different ways. Part 1 is called 'Inequalities and multilateralism: revisiting the North–South axis'. It introduces the volume with three broad-brushed, historical overviews. First, John Toye begins by 'Assessing the G77: 50 years after UNCTAD I and 40 years after the NIEO'. While anniversaries are sometimes a useful human gimmick to focus attention, it was nonetheless significant to the organisers to look back over the past half century – more if we go back to the first gathering of the NAM in Bandung in 1955. In the following article Paulo Esteves and Manaíra Assunção take the next logical step and provide an overview of 'South–South cooperation and the international development battlefield: between the OECD and the UN', which probes the reasons why emerging powers are reluctant to be classified as 'donors' and to abide by the rules and procedures promoted by the traditional donors from industrialised countries. In the third and final contribution to the first part, Ramesh Thakur asks 'How representative is BRICS?'

The seven papers in Part 2 examine 'The changing development cooperation landscape'. They begin with Bruce Jenks's 'The financing of the UN development system and the future of multilateralism', which asks, among other key questions, the extent to which the binary categories of 'core' and 'non-core' (or earmarked) resources make sense within a world that has internationally agreed goals. Next Silke Weinlich's 'Emerging powers at the UN: ducking for cover?' probes the facts and figures behind Western calls for more financial contributions to the UNDS from the emerging powers. 'A changing world: is the UN development system ready?' is the next paper; Stephen Browne's answer is that the world has changed but the UN system remains remarkably fixed in its ways. Paulo de Renzio and Jurek Seifert trace the past and present range of efforts within developing countries in 'South–South cooperation and the future of development assistance: mapping actors and options'. Adriana Erthal Abdenur follows with a comparative analysis of two major powers in an underexplored UN arena in 'Rising powers and international development norms: Brazil and China at the United Nations'. Stephen Browne and Thomas G. Weiss tease out the range of views expressed in the spring 2014 FUNDS global survey, with specific attention to the countries in this issue, in their 'Emerging powers and the UN development system: canvassing global views'. Finally, in 'War-torn countries, natural resources and emerging-country investors', Graciana del Castillo examines what many see as an unexploited potential comparative advantage of the UN system, namely the UN's set of competences to work in conflict and post-conflict settings.

We hope that these articles help build bridges between the global South and North, leading to genuine and constructive conversations rather than the customary 'dialogue of the deaf'.

Acknowledgements

This volume and the deliberations leading to its quality control would not have been possible without the generous financial and administrative support of several sources. We begin with the financial backing from the governments of Sweden, Switzerland, Norway and Denmark that has nurtured steadily the work of the FUNDS Project; it would not have been possible to have commissioned and published this collection without these governments' generosity. We are also grateful to the Institute of International Relations, the Fundação de Amparo à Pesquisa do Estado do Rio de Janeiro (FAPERJ), and the Coordenação de Aperfeiçoamento de Pessoal de Nível Superior (CAPES) for funding the April 2014 conference in Rio de Janeiro. Moreover, for that conference the editors and authors gratefully acknowledge constructive comments by: Daniel Aragão, João Brígido, Fantu Cheru, Marta Garcia Moreno, Mônica Herz, Manuel Montes, Emma Mawdsley, Susan Myers, João Pontes Nogueira, Shahid Qadir, Annika Soder, Danilo Türk and Eduardo Viola. The co-sponsors, the Ralph Bunche Institute of the CUNY Graduate Center and the Pontifical Catholic University of Rio de Janeiro, supported the organisation and staffing of the session in April 2014 and the finalisation of this manuscript. Among the many helping hands necessary to bring the authors and commentators together, we would like to acknowledge especially the efforts by Geovana Zoccal Gomes and Paul Alois; for the final editing we are grateful to Danielle A. Zach.

Notes

1. Helleiner, "Principles from the Periphery," 359–481.
2. UNDP, *Human Development Report 2013*. For a discussion, see Wilkinson and Hulme, *The Millennium Development Goals and Beyond*.
3. Krauthammer, "The Unipolar Moment," 23–33.

4. Magnus, *Uprising*.
5. Acharya, *The End of American World Order*, 5, 59–78.
6. Ibid., 6–11.
7. Cooper, "Labels Matter," 76.
8. Cooper and Thakur, *The Group of Twenty*.
9. Cooper and Momani, "Re-balancing the G-20."
10. Indian High Commission, "Sanya Declaration."
11. Weiss et al., "The 'Third' United Nations."
12. Murphy, *International Organization and Industrial Change*.
13. Roberts and Kingsbury, "Introduction," 1.
14. Bull, *The Anarchical Society*. A more recent treatment is Jackson, *The Global Covenant*.
15. Curtis, "China and the Insecurity of Development in the Democratic Republic of the Congo."
16. Ferdinand, "Rising Powers at the UN," 387.
17. Held and Rogers, "Introduction," 6.
18. Wade, "Western States in Global Organizations," 81.
19. See recent special issues with guest editors Gray and Murphy, "Rising Powers"; and Cooper and Flemes, "Foreign Policy Strategies."

Bibliography

Acharya, Amitav. *The End of American World Order*. Cambridge: Polity Press, 2014.

Bull, Hedley. *The Anarchical Society: A Study of Order in World Politics*. New York: Columbia University Press, 1977.

Cooper, Andrew F. "Labels Matter: Interpreting Rising Powers through Acronyms." In *Rising States, Rising Institutions*, edited by Alan S. Alexandroff and Andrew F. Cooper, 63–82. Washington, DC: Brookings Institution, 2010.

Cooper, Andrew F., and Daniel Flemes, eds. "Foreign Policy Strategies of Emerging Powers in a Multipolar World." *Third World Quarterly* 34, no. 6 (special issue, 2013).

Cooper, Andrew F., and Bessma Momani. "Re-balancing the G-20 from Efficiency to Legitimacy: The 3G Coalition and the Practice of Global Governance." *Global Governance* 20, no. 2 (2014): 213–232.

Cooper, Andrew F., and Ramesh Thakur. *The Group of Twenty (G20)*. London: Routledge, 2013.

Curtis, Devon. "China and the Insecurity of Development in the Democratic Republic of the Congo." *International Peacekeeping*. Online November 27, 2013. http://dx.doi.org/10.1080/13533312.2013.853950.

Ferdinand, Peter. "Rising Powers at the UN: An Analysis of the Voting Behaviour of BRICS in the General Assembly." *Third World Quarterly* 35, no. 3 (2014): 376–391.

Gray, Kevin, and Craig N. Murphy, eds. "Rising Powers and the Future of Global Governance." *Third World Quarterly* 34, no. 2 (special issue, 2013).

Held, David, and Charles Rogers. "Introduction: Global Governance at Risk." In *Global Governance at Risk*, edited by David Held and Charles Rogers. Cambridge: Polity Press, 2013.

Helleine, Eric, ed. "Principles from the Periphery: The Neglected Southern Sources of Global Norms." Special section in *Global Governance* 20, no. 3 (2014): 359–481.

Indian High Commission. "Sanya Declaration." April 14, 2011. http://www.gov.cn/misc/2011-04/14/content_1844551.htm.

Jackson, Robert. *The Global Covenant: Human Conduct in a World of States*. Oxford: Oxford University Press, 2000.

Krauthammer, Charles. "The Unipolar Moment." *Foreign Affairs* 70, no. 1 (1990–91): 23–33.

Magnus, George. *Uprising: Will Emerging Markets Shape or Shake the World Economy?* London: Wiley, 2010.

Murphy, Craig. *International Organization and Industrial Change: Global Governance since 1850*. Cambridge: Polity Press, 1994.

Roberts, Adam, and Benedict Kingsbury. "Introduction: The UN's Roles in International Society since 1945." In *United Nations: Divided World*. 2nd ed., edited by Adam Roberts and Benedict Kingsbury. Oxford: Oxford University Press, 1993.

UNDP, *Human Development Report 2013: The Rise of the South – Human Progress in a Diverse World*. New York: UNDP, 2013.

Wade, Robert. "Western States in Global Organizations." In *Global Governance at Risk*, edited by David Held and Charles Rogers. Cambridge: Polity Press, 2013.

Weiss, Thomas G., Tatiana Carayannis, and Richard Jolly. "The 'Third' United Nations." *Global Governance* 15, no. 1 (2009): 123–142.

Wilkinson, Rorden, and David Hulme, eds. *The Millennium Development Goals and Beyond: Global Development after 2015*. London: Routledge, 2012.

Assessing the G77: 50 years after UNCTAD and 40 years after the NIEO

John Toye

Department of International Development, University of Oxford, UK

This article views the history of the Group of 77 through the lens of its relations with UNCTAD's establishment in 1964, its unsuccessful struggle for the NIEO in the 1970s, and the subsequent loosening of ties. The debt crisis of the 1980s, the Uruguay Round negotiations, and the arrival of the WTO are seen as crucial forces unravelling the previously close links. Growing differentiation among developing countries and the changing leadership of the G77 are also cited as important influences on its current relationship with UNCTAD.

The history of the Group of 77 (G77) is so intimately bound up with the history of the UN Conference on Trade and Development (UNCTAD) that it is hardly possible to narrate the history of the one without also narrating the history of the other. The G77's identity derives from its success in bringing UNCTAD to birth. UNCTAD's *raison d'être* has been to realise the G77's aims for international reconstruction. For many years, the two organisations worked extremely closely together. What follows is the story, laid out chronologically, of the relationship of the G77 and UNCTAD – how it started, what it achieved and how it unravelled.[1]

The call for a world trade conference

After the international community's failure to ratify the Havana Charter and establish the proposed International Trade Organization, many developing countries were dissatisfied with the interim arrangement for negotiating on world trade issues, namely the General Agreement on Tariffs and Trade (GATT). In 1957 the GATT commissioned a group led by Gottfried Haberler to report on the trade problems of developing countries. The report confirmed that developed countries' tariff and other barriers were causing these problems and made the complaints of developing countries harder to ignore.[2]

In the UN an Afro-Asian bloc began to operate in the 10th General Assembly after the Bandung conference of 1955, calling for an international trade conference. However, at the 1961 General Assembly, Latin American countries, with the notable exception of Brazil, still remained lukewarm to the idea of a new conference on trade and development.

In July 1962 the Conference on the Problems of Developing Countries was held in Cairo. Organised outside the auspices of the UN, 36 countries attended – not a large number but the significance lay in in their regional composition. The participants included African, Asian and Latin American countries. The willingness of Latin American countries to join the Afro-Asian group, notwithstanding the US attempt to co-opt them into the Alliance for Progress, was an event of great significance. The Cairo Declaration called for an international conference within the framework of the UN on 'all vital questions relating to international trade, primary commodity trade and economic relations between developing and developed countries'.[3]

Raúl Prebisch, the executive secretary of the UN Economic Commission for Latin America (ECLA, later ECLAC after the Caribbean was added to its name), was sceptical about launching a fresh international effort in the trade field, having watched many previous US–Latin American trade initiatives falter. Only the persistent urging of Wladek Malinowski, the Economic and Social Council's (ECOSOC) secretary, persuaded Prebisch to go Cairo. However, once there, Prebisch saw that cooperation between Third World countries across three continents had great potential to reshape global politics, if backed by discipline and good organisation.[4]

ECOSOC recommended in resolution 917 (XXXIV), and the General Assembly approved in December 1962 resolution 1785 (XVII) in favour of holding the first UN Conference on Trade and Development (UNCTAD I). The US permanent representative to the UN, Adlai Stevenson, reversed the USA's negative stance towards the conference. Since it could hardly be vetoed, he accepted it positively and hoped to influence its timing and content. Once Stevenson switched, other opposing countries followed suit. UNCTAD's existence in some shape or form was assured.

The developing countries that had voted for the General Assembly resolution authorising UNCTAD – the Group of 75, which did not include Cuba and the Ivory Coast but did include New Zealand – issued a Joint Declaration of the Developing Countries. While this declaration was clear about what signatories objected to, it lacked a clear vision for a new international trade regime and a positive agenda.

To strengthen the unity of the developing countries, Prebisch insisted that they should be compensated for past and future losses through deteriorating terms of trade, either through commodity agreements or compensatory financing. The second main incentive for unity was his demand for a system of preferences for all manufactures exported by developing countries to developed countries, and for developing country governments to be allowed to subsidise some of the marketing costs of their exporters of manufactures. Although only a few could benefit immediately from such preferences, they were in principle of general application and so less divisive than abolishing existing trade restrictions on particular industries, such as textiles.

The question of the design of a new UN trade and development institution was divisive. Some pressed for a new organisation to replace the GATT, while some wanted a small new think-tank on policy that would feed ideas into existing UN machinery. Prebisch, advised by Malinowski, supported a third option – a periodic conference with review responsibilities in the trade field.

The first UNCTAD conference

At the first session in Geneva, the US opening statement was candid to the point of harshness. The demands of the developing countries for $20 billion in financial or trade concessions risked, it said, their using UNCTAD as 'an escape from their own domestic responsibilities'. *Newsweek* reported that the US statement contained 'more than a hint of paternalism'.[5]

Developing countries voted on all resolutions as a caucus, ignoring conflicts of national interest to support the proposals in the conference report, thereby reinforcing Prebisch's position as the event's ringmaster. That tactic, initially very startling to developed countries, soon showed its limitations. It was futile repeatedly to out-vote developed countries if they remained unwilling to grant the concession on which they had been out-voted.

By the end of the conference, there was no agreement on any of the specific proposals in the conference report. The Final Act of the conference consisted of a series of agreed upon principles in those areas where appropriate wording had been negotiated, plus recommendations for action to be remitted to other existing bodies.

The question of future machinery to deal with issues of international trade and development was still on the table. Developed countries had dropped their initial opposition to any new UN institution for this purpose and were prepared to accept a new centre or institute, managed by the UN's Department of Economic and Social Affairs (DESA) in New York and reporting to ECOSOC. Developing countries were most unhappy with this proposal. They demanded that the new body be given its own staff and budget and that it be located elsewhere than in New York. They forced a vote in the Fourth Committee, but were met with warnings of non-cooperation from developed countries: any new machinery would have to be negotiated, not imposed by a majority vote.

The US representative, Richard N. Gardner, posed the central issue: since the top six countries transacted 70% of world trade, they should not be subject to majority vote on a one-country-one-vote basis. Accepting that the developing countries would have to compromise to avoid the conference collapsing, Prebisch proposed a threefold scheme. First, the conference should be reconvened every three or four years. Second, the conference should have a standing committee, the Trade and Development Board, representing groups of countries, to manage business between the conferences. Prebisch also recommended setting up a group system of negotiations on a permanent basis (with appropriate safeguards). Third, the conference should have its own secretariat, located outside DESA and New York, reporting directly to the UN secretary-general.

This proved acceptable to developed countries, but it was inconsistent with the developing countries' demand for a decision-making process of one country, one vote and majority voting. They gave Prebisch an angry and hostile reception when he presented his proposed compromise to them. They had achieved very few concrete concessions from the negotiations, and now they were being asked to abandon the voting system that had worked so well for them in the General Assembly. The radicals among them – including Che Guevara as a representative of Cuba, as well as Ismat Kitani (Iraq), U Maung (Burma), and Marcio de Rego Monteiro (Brazil) – were certainly not comfortable with the idea of compromising at the end of a long and expensive conference. In the end, however, Prebisch was able to convince them.

In a final assertion of unity 'The Joint Declaration of the Seventy-Seven Developing Countries', the enlarged Group of 75 (now minus New Zealand), pledged mutual cooperation in the common cause of a new world order. This joint statement smoothed over the evident fragility of the developing countries' group. The G77 was now a formal grouping of countries that operated within UNCTAD, although it was not yet constituted as an organisation. It was intended as a counterweight to the newly formed Organisation for Economic Co-operation and Development (OECD), which represented the common interests of the advanced industrial countries. However, the G77 lacked the OECD's research and organisational capacity, and this was to prove an enduring problem for it.[6]

Prebisch's key policies

The G77 still had no positive agenda of its own and relied on the agenda that Prebisch had laid out for UNCTAD. It had three central items. The first was a general framework for international commodity agreements. The second was new forms of supplementary finance – supplementary, that is, to the then new Compensatory Finance Facility of the IMF. The third was the demand for temporary preferences for the industrial exports that developing countries exported to developed country markets. All these policies were seen as alternative ways of tackling the balance of payments constraints that the developing countries faced. However welcome progress was in other areas, the credibility of UNCTAD with the G77 depended fundamentally on achieving one or more of these three central demands.

The strongest intellectual influences on UNCTAD's commodities policy were not technical analyses of commodity price regulation. They were nuggets of apparently practical wisdom. One was an inference from the international commodity regulation schemes of the 1930s that, whatever their technical difficulties, such schemes were feasible. The other was the inference drawn from the inclusion of a chapter on international commodity agreements in the abortive Havana Charter of 1948 that such schemes would be legitimate. The G77's interpretations of these two episodes became the drivers that influenced the UNCTAD secretariat's new commodity strategy. Unfortunately, both inferences were, for various reasons, flawed.

Advancing on a commodity-by-commodity basis quickly ran into difficulties. A cocoa commodity conference in August 1966, which was intended to approve the principle of a new UN-brokered Cocoa Authority, collapsed in disagreement. Bitter criticism, particularly from the African group, followed the G77's dashed hopes. Nevertheless, by October 1966, despite this setback and the warnings of commodity technicians, the UNCTAD secretariat had decided to embrace the policy of price stabilisation using buffer stocks, financed through a central fund, possibly to be provided by the World Bank.

The Final Act of the Geneva conference had instructed the World Bank to prepare a 'draft proposal on supplementary finance measures'.[7] In late 1965 a draft report was ready and George Woods, the World Bank's president, sent the study to UNCTAD. At the first meeting of UNCTAD's Committee on Financing, the so-called Woods report was well received among both developed and developing countries. Although the report linked supplementary finance to country performance – a forerunner of later loans that were conditional on policy changes – the G77 countries raised no objection. At the end of 1966 the Trade and Development Board endorsed the proposed supplementary finance agreement. All that remained was for a joint developed countries–G77 technical working group to agree on the final details. Yet, as with the failed conference on cocoa, it was not to be. Prebisch blundered by publicly highlighting policy differences between the World Bank and the IMF. He lost the backing of Woods, his erstwhile champion in Washington, and the World Bank withdrew its cooperation.

The G77 was frustrated and questioned Prebisch's credibility after so little progress had been made on the UNCTAD agenda. Meeting in Algiers in 1967, the ministers of the G77 constituted the group as a permanent organisation and, in the run up to the second UNCTAD conference in New Delhi, published its negotiating position as the Charter of Algiers. This proposed a short agenda of commodity agreements, supplementary financing, and trade preferences for manufactured products. Despite all the frustration and disappointment, it was the classic Prebisch agenda again.

At New Delhi developed countries refused further progress on commodities and supplementary financing, but in the committee on manufactures they agreed to the principle of a general system of non-reciprocal trade preferences (GSP), following Lyndon Johnson's acceptance of the idea at Punta del Este in 1967. However, controversy remained over the products that would be eligible, safeguards for domestic manufacturers, and the point of graduation from eligibility. The discussions aggravated disunity in the G77. The African regional grouping thought that the GSP was really a Latin American issue, while the Latin American countries resented the African group's attempt to retain the trade preferences that they already had with Europe. Tempers calmed down only when a special committee was approved to continue work on the GSP once UNCTAD II was over.

The main achievement at New Delhi was the GSP commitment, albeit with the need for follow-on negotiations. Privately Prebisch expressed disappointment at the limited results from his efforts and felt that UNCTAD was never likely to make decisive advances on the key policies of his and the G77's agenda. Settling for an incremental approach would have been realistic, but the attitudes of the more radical G77 states had left him little room to manoeuvre. In 1969 he resigned and returned to Latin America.

The G77 and the UNCTAD secretariat

The relationship between the G77 and the UNCTAD secretariat had from the start been intended to be symbiotic. However, developed countries upheld the concept of international officials working impartially in the interests of all UN member countries. They complained with some justification that in UNCTAD officials had become advocates on behalf of a particular group of member states

– the G77. Prebisch had publicly defended the secretariat, claiming that it was possible for it to be at the same time impartial and committed to his trade and development agenda, but this stance was hard to maintain in practice.

The negotiations around international monetary reform in the early 1970s represented a high point in UNCTAD's effort to achieve an international economic system that recognised the interdependence of trade, finance, and development. Manuel Pérez-Guerrero, Prebisch's successor, invested impressive resources in getting agreement on a common G77 position, sustaining internal support for it and lobbying for it externally.

The establishment in 1971 of the Group of Twenty-four (G24) in Washington was a major step in the G77's institutional evolution. Its purpose is to coordinate the G77's positions on issues of monetary and development policy that come before the International Monetary and Financial Committee and the Development Committee in Washington. Deciding which 24 countries would represent the remainder was a major feat, given the unease among some G77 members about being represented by others.

So the failure of the 1972–74 talks to secure a new multilateral agreement on international monetary reform was a serious blow. After UNCTAD III, held in Santiago in 1972, UNCTAD returned to its remaining core policy idea of commodity agreements with increased determination.

UNCTAD III endorsed a request from Mexican president Luis Echeverría that a working group be set up to draft a Charter of Economic Rights and Duties of States. The G77 had no institutional mechanism of its own to follow through on Echeverría's suggestion. Pérez-Guerrero to his credit had taken the initiative to devise a constitution for a G77 secretariat in 1971, but the G77 could not agree among themselves on a number of its key features. Was it to be located in the South or the North? From which continent was its chief executive to be recruited? Who was to pay for it? Larger developing countries feared that they would be expected to bear the costs, while the secretariat might be inclined to favour the viewpoint of the many smaller developing countries. The result of failure to solve their collective action problem was that the G77 remained totally dependent on UNCTAD to supply it with a policy agenda through the 1970s and beyond.[8]

Events now moved ahead quickly. A second Middle Eastern war in late 1973 was followed by an increase in the price of oil from $3.02 to $11.60 per barrel. A group of major oil-producing states in the Organization of the Petroleum Exporting Countries (OPEC) succeeded in using the price of oil as a weapon against an oil-dependent West already alarmed by warnings about rapidly depleting oil reserves. OPEC, as something close to a commodity cartel, used its ability to restrict supply successfully to raise its commodity price. Economically the effect was divisive. Those in the G77 that exported oil could benefit from the price rise, but those that imported oil – just like developed countries – suffered a large external shock to which they had to adjust either by policy change or by borrowing. However, at the same time the oil crisis had a politically unifying effect on the G77 because it was a demonstration of the power of collective action over a commodity's supply and price that gave hope that the price of other commodities could be influenced in similar ways if only collective unity was maintained.

At the Sixth Special Session of the General Assembly held in New York in April–May 1974 many developing country delegates expressed their view that UNCTAD III had betrayed their high expectations. Some coupled expressions of disappointment with praise for OPEC's use of the oil weapon.[9] Delegates from OPEC countries emphasised their own status as developing countries and their 'first and foremost duty to raise the standards of living of their peoples in all spheres'. Thus the steep rise in oil prices did not fracture G77 unity, as some expected, even though the majority of developing countries were oil importers. Instead it united them more strongly than before in pursuit of a New International Economic Order (NIEO).

Seeking a New International Economic Order

Just before the start of the Sixth Special Session, Gamani Corea of Sri Lanka took office as UNCTAD's third secretary-general. He immediately felt himself to be under immense pressure from the G77 to make UNCTAD something more than a debating house. They and he wanted it to be both a negotiating forum and a think-tank. The dramatic circumstances of the Sixth Special Session provided him with the opportunity to attempt this transformation, even though the UNCTAD secretariat had prepared no document for the session. Corea used the plight of the non-oil-producing developing countries to call not only for immediate short-term financial assistance – soon provided by the oil-exporting developing countries – but also for a long-term solution by means of official intervention in a range of core commodity markets.

Without having any mandate to do so, he presented the Trade and Development Board with a document 'Outline of an Overall Integrated Program' in August 1974, and UNCTAD committed itself to campaigning for the creation of a new international agency that would own a multi-commodity stockpile. However, the details of how such an agency would work were not clarified. The outline argued that, since individual commodity agreements (ICAs) were inadequate, a new agency should apply a wider framework of principles to a large number of core commodities and should own and manage stocks to influence prices. The target prices would be 'remunerative to producers and equitable to consumers'. The purchase of stocks would be financed from a central fund, the amount required being estimated at $6 billion. Oil producers were expected to invest their surpluses in the fund, which would pay them a return. Other investors were expected to be industrial countries and multilateral agencies.

Some time elapsed before the G77 reacted to the outline. Member countries were hesitant to commit to the project. Countries that were members of existing ICAs feared that the Common Fund would give other countries influence over the management of those commodities that were of special importance to them. Oil-producing countries had to import non-oil commodities and were reluctant to make any investment before it was clearer how the Common Fund would affect their prices. The G77 waited until 1976 and then moved in a direction that was inconsistent with the outline. When the G77 ministers met in Manila in early 1976 to agree upon a policy platform for UNCTAD IV, they adopted UNCTAD's Integrated Program for Commodities as their own proposal. At the same time they decided that all operations for market regulation by a common fund should be conducted through individual ICAS. The latter proviso was the price of agreement by the Latin American regional grouping, but it wrecked the plan for a common fund as an agency that could intervene directly in commodity markets. Now the Integrated Program could come into play only when individual ICAS turned to it as a source of finance.

When UNCTAD IV opened in Nairobi in May 1976, Corea had to correct the widespread belief, in relation to the Integrated Program on Commodities and the Common Fund, that the scheme would avoid a case-by-case approach to each commodity. After the G77 decisions in Manila all that the Integrated Program envisaged was 'a common frame of reference for the various case-by-case approaches'.[10] Although UNCTAD had hoped only to secure agreement to do further work on the Common Fund, a more militant mood animated the G77 delegations. They wanted to make the setting up of the Common Fund a precondition for negotiation on other parts of the Integrated Program. Although this was not acceptable to developed countries, they were divided. When Henry Kissinger, making the only appearance of a US secretary of state at UNCTAD, canvassed an alternative proposal for a new International Resources Bank, the European Economic Community was split between supporters and opponents of the Common Fund. With this degree of division, developed countries could not formulate a position and the G77 refused to negotiate further.

To avoid total breakdown of the conference, in a face-saving compromise, developed countries agreed to launch a post-Nairobi process of discussion and negotiation on a common fund, provided the Kissinger alternative proposal for the International Resources Bank was referred to the UNCTAD secretariat for further study. However, this compromise went badly wrong. After resolution 93 (IV) on further work on the Common Fund was passed without a vote, the G77 refused to support the second part – the study of the Kissinger proposal. The USA demanded a roll-call vote, on which it was defeated. Not surprisingly UNCTAD IV ended in sourness and recriminations.

G77 unity in favour of the NIEO was a façade behind which lay many different levels of commitment to the Common Fund. Some of the big oil producers, such as Saudi Arabia, did not want to do anything that would complicate their relations with the developed industrial world, which is where they wanted to invest the financial surpluses that they had accumulated after the oil price rise and where they wanted to be able to buy modern armaments to match those of Israel. Latin American countries that had established control over a commodity of special interest to them, such as coffee, did not want to see that control diluted when the Common Fund was established – hence their holding out in Manila for a fund operating through individual ICAS.

In the final analysis it was implausible to think that developed countries, which controlled the main global financial levers, would invest in a new fund that they did not control. If the G77 countries themselves had decided to invest more, the reluctance of developed countries would not have mattered; but at UNCTAD IV only 18 developing countries pledged voluntary contributions to the Common Fund and, most importantly, those that were oil-producers declined to play a decisive investment role. Eventually the developed countries that were willing to finance it could dictate the ultimate design of the miniscule Common Fund that finally emerged.

The end of confrontation

The main political change of the early 1980s was the arrival of a new wave of conservative leaders in the developed world (Margaret Thatcher, UK, Ronald Reagan, USA, Helmut Kohl, Germany, and Yasuhiro Namason, Japan), who quickly put an end to North–South dialogue. The main economic change of the early 1980s was the eruption of a debt crisis in Latin America and other developing regions that exposed them to pressures from their creditors to embrace neoliberal economic policies. The UN itself was put under financial pressure as a means to induce it to reform. UNCTAD, under its fourth secretary-general, Kenneth Dadzie, now encouraged developing countries to join GATT and participate actively in the Uruguay Round of negotiations (1987–94). This move recognised the fact that many G77 developing countries had by this time accepted structural adjustment programmes that precluded policy options other than trade liberalisation.

Developing countries did not adopt a unified negotiating position in the Uruguay Round, as they had in UNCTAD. Partly this reflected the fact that they were negotiating on a series of new issues that were highly variegated. However, it was also because of the absence of organised leadership from the G77. As Alister McIntyre recalled later: 'one of the things that has happened is that the leadership of the Group of 77 has evaporated'.[11] Fluid alliances spanning the North–South divide began to emerge. For example, the Cairns Group of 14 countries, accounting for around a quarter of global agricultural exports, formed a negotiating coalition in August 1986. Three were developed countries – Australia, Canada, and New Zealand – while the other 11 were developing countries. They pressed a common interest in bringing agriculture under the governance of trade subsidy rules. On other issues, such as intellectual property rights, a few large and powerful developing countries – in this case Brazil and India – took sole charge of the negotiations on behalf of developing countries.

The point here is not that developing countries had suddenly developed divergent interests. As the NIEO campaign revealed, these differences had always existed but previously they had been hidden behind a façade of unity. However, unity crumbled under the pressure of events. In 1962 it was the willingness of Latin American states to join the Afro-Asian bloc in a tri-continental alliance that created the G77 and solidarity among developing countries. Debt problems now pulled the Latin Americans and Africans apart because their crises followed very different trajectories.

Latin America's debts were mainly to private sector banks; the region's crisis was brought to a conclusion when creditor countries stopped pretending that the problem was one of liquidity and finally addressed it as a solvency issue. Under the Brady Plan of March 1989 creditors were allowed to choose one of two loans-in-exchange-for-bonds options, with the interest on the bonds being underwritten by the US Treasury. By contrast, African countries owed debts mainly to public sector financial institutions, so they felt little relief from the Brady Plan. Their economies continued to suffer from major debt over-hangs until after the Highly Indebted Poor Countries initiative of the IMF and World Bank began to provide debt relief in 1999. Different treatment of their debts by the international community effectively broke up the tri-continental alliance.

As one analyst put it, 'by the early 1990s, even G77 rhetorical unity had vanished'.[12] The G77's Tehran conference, in preparation for UNCTAD VIII, brought into sharp focus the increasing division between Latin American countries and the rest of the G77. The former went as far as agreeing with developed countries' criticisms of the UNCTAD group negotiation system. Although the unity of the G77 was weakened, developed countries continued to operate in groups such as the EU and OECD.

The process of differentiation

The G77 had been founded on the basis on suppressing national interests in favour of presenting a united front of developing countries within the United Nations. As a result, they viewed differentiation as potentially harmful to their overall unity. However, at UNCTAD II in 1968, it was agreed that special measures should be devised to enable the least developed among the developing countries to benefit from new policy measures being negotiated within UNCTAD. In relation to the distribution of new UNCTAD Special Drawing Rights, for example, the G77 wanted the least developed countries to benefit even more disproportionally to their IMF quotas than other developing countries.

The UNCTAD secretariat embarked on research into the typology of developing countries. On the recommendations of the UN Committee on Development Planning, the General Assembly approved a list of 'least developed countries' (LDCs) in 1971. The original defining criteria were threefold – per capita income of less than $900 in 1968 US dollars; a low manufacturing share of gross domestic product; and a high rate of illiteracy. Twenty-five countries, 16 in Africa, satisfied these criteria in 1971; under a changing set of criteria the list has continued to expand and the roll call now stands at 49, almost double the original number.

The result of UNCTAD's efforts to identify a group of LDCs has been to increase awareness of the special needs of these countries, and not least the needs of countries that are either landlocked or small islands. Donors have directed an increasing share of their aid to the LDCs and given them special measures of debt relief. GATT created a special category for the treatment of LDCs within its rules, and recognition of this status is now accorded to the 34 LDCs that have joined the World Trade Organization (WTO), although the nature of the 'special and differential treatment' they receive is somewhat limited.

At the other end of the scale of differentiation the 1970s saw a few developing countries growing rapidly, at more than 6% a year. Some of these were oil-exporting countries – Saudi Arabia, Libya, and Iran – but the others were the four Asian tigers of South Korea, Taiwan, Hong Kong, and Singapore, whose rapid growth was fuelled by exporting manufactures. Differentiation among developing countries was increasing and, though resisted in the interests of unity, it certainly had implications for the G77 and its ability to hold together in the longer run.

UNCTAD VIII in Cartagena showed that, despite advancing differentiation, developed countries could not unilaterally close down UNCTAD. Although the G77 was much weakened by the defection of the Latin Americans and the aid-dependence of the Africans, it still had enough leadership from the larger South and Southeast Asian countries (eg India, Malaysia, and Indonesia) to successfully resist its closure. Once the WTO was established in 1995, UNCTAD was radically downsized but still survived in diminished form.

The early 2000s saw the emergence of a new group of leading developing countries, consisting of Brazil, India, Russia in its post-cold war incarnation, China, and South Africa (BRICS). They were fast-growing, industrialising economies with considerable regional and global influence; but the last three were not G77 members. Together they have ambitions to reform global finance and have created the BRICS Forum and a calendar of summit meetings to promote these ambitions. On trade issues, however, their interests diverge, especially with reference to the liberalisation of trade in agricultural products. The very different land-to-labour ratios and agrarian technologies of Brazil and Russia, on the one hand, and India and China, on the other, place them in opposing camps in the WTO on this issue.

Brazil was already a member of the Cairns Group of agricultural countries, but wanted a stronger pro-liberalisation stance than was being taken by Australia. Before the 2003 WTO ministerial meeting in Cancun, Brazil took the initiative in organising the G20, a fluctuating group of developing countries that pressed the EU and the USA for greater liberalisation of agriculture than they were willing to concede. The G20 effectively turned the free trade argument against those European and North American countries that preached it and yet at the same time heavily protected their agricultural sectors. It echoed the original North–South confrontation but gave it a novel twist, challenging developed countries to live up to the principles that they urged on others. By contrast, India (like China, not a member of the G77) has pressed for strong safeguards against surges of food imports that could ruin the livelihood of millions of small-scale cultivators. Despite the G20's activism and pressure, little progress was made in reducing agricultural subsidies and market access barriers.

On industrial market access, India (again like China) has been unable to agree with the USA on the depth of reciprocal reductions in their bound tariffs on manufactured goods. This, rather than the deadlock over agricultural trade, appears to stand in the way of the completion of the Doha Development Round as envisaged in its work programme.

States with lower trade involvement and poorer negotiating capacities have joined together, for example the Africa regional group inside the WTO. This began as a simple voluntary agreement between some African countries to exchange information about their proposed negotiating positions. It soon broadened into a more institutionalised arrangement with states offering to act as the group's convener for a set period of regular meetings, where countries' positions on key issues were not only discussed but proposed actions were also mutually coordinated.

The Africa coalition scored one notable success – the legitimisation of the trade in generic rather than branded medicines under certain circumstances. The WTO's Agreement on Trade-Related Aspects of Intellectual Property Rights (TRIPS) allowed countries to infringe the patents only of domestic manufacturers for the home market. Countries that did not have any domestic manufacturing capacity were thereby obliged to import branded drugs at market prices, because trade in generic drugs was prohibited – even in the event of epidemics. The Africa coalition was able to get the support of potential generic drugs exporting countries like India and Brazil, and secured a temporary waiver of this prohibition at the Cancun ministerial meeting in 2003. Then in 2005 they secured the first ever amendment to TRIPS that made the temporary waiver permanent. One commentator has dubbed the WTO's developing country members as 'the awkward newcomers'.[13] They had different objectives from the organisation's founder members and were able to make them count in negotiations.

The G77 and UNCTAD in the recent decade

Because the G77 had supported Panitchpakdi Supachai's candidature so strongly in the 1999 WTO leadership contest against Mike Moore, it was assumed that his appointment as UNCTAD secretary-general would have their backing. In fact, the G77 was unhappy with this unprecedented move – an ex-WTO director-general leading UNCTAD. The upshot was that, on arrival at UNCTAD, Supachai had to adapt quickly. He was now in charge of the organisation about whose statements and actions he had received almost daily complaints while at the WTO, and he did not find this comfortable. He quickly distanced UNCTAD from the Doha Round debates and chose to emphasise investment as a major priority subject for the organisation.

In October 2005 Supachai established a panel of eminent persons to advise him on UNCTAD's development role and impact. The panel reported in June 2006. It gave credit to UNCTAD for a number of past achievements but made no reference to UNCTAD's work on macroeconomics and finance, despite the fact that in this area UNCTAD had also succeeded in 'highlighting and analyzing issues that often became salient in international policy-making later on'. Although the G77 highly appreciated this area of UNCTAD's work, the panel excluded it from its discussions, an omission that was in line with Supachai's initial intention to emphasise investment as the leading priority.

The G77 reacted nervously when Supachai realised that the panel's report would have little impact unless introduced into intergovernmental discussions. Neither the G77 nor the developed country group had requested the panel of eminent persons, and the report contained many suggestions that one group or the other disliked. Eventually the most benign proposals found their way into the negotiating text for UNCTAD XII in Accra in 2008.

There UNCTAD's broad mandate was reaffirmed. The Accra Accord noted reassuringly: 'Trade and development will remain a core preoccupation in the ongoing reforms of the United Nations, and UNCTAD will have a distinct role to play in carrying forward the trade and development mission of the United Nations'. However, when the G77 and China proposed a new Commission on Globalization and Development Strategies, developed countries did not agree. Instead, in a compromise, it was agreed that a regular item on globalisation and development strategies be placed on the agenda of the Trade and Development Board's annual meeting.

Although there was a fleeting reference in the Accra Declaration to 'the onset of current difficulties', the conference seemed to assume that the continuing growth of newly emerging economies would offset them, and that these economies would become the new engine of global growth. The arrival of the financial and economic crisis of 2007–08 led UNCTAD to take up lines of research and advocacy that were more independent of the views and wishes of developed countries than had been the case in the previous four years. Supachai was able to relate the crisis to his own experiences of being on the receiving end of IMF lectures during the 1997–98 Asian crisis, and he became very vocal on the shortcomings of leading industrial countries. The sudden exposure of the failings of deregulated financial markets and the macroeconomic policies of the leading industrial countries seemed to embolden UNCTAD to shake off any remaining vestiges of neoliberal economic doctrines and strengthen its commitment to neo-Keynesian ideas.

Inevitably UNCTAD's more independent stance was not well received by the leading developed countries. They had contested UNCTAD's mandate in relation to international monetary issues right from the establishment of the G77. They wanted monetary issues to be dealt with in international institutions with voting systems weighted in their favour, rather than the one-country-one-vote system that the G77 favoured. The G77 supported UNCTAD's right to analyse macroeconomic and financial issues and to make recommendations that the IMF and World Bank were free to adopt or reject. Developed countries were never fully reconciled to this arrangement, and over the next 50 years they made sporadic attempts to close down this part of UNCTAD's mandate. After the debacle of 2007–08 exposed their poor stewardship of the international financial system, UNCTAD had pointedly underlined their many failures, and developed countries again tried to shut off this source of criticism and alternative policy options. Their opportunity came at UNCTAD XIII in Doha, Qatar, in December 2012.

The secretary-general's report to UNCTAD XIII was an eloquent denunciation of the unevenness, instability, and unfairness produced by finance-driven globalisation. At the same time it explained how certain countries had been able to achieve strong economic growth. It called for an agenda of rebalancing in order to move towards more development-led globalisation. This would involve efforts to build developmental states; making international institutions capable of more robust collective responses; and strengthening South–South cooperation. This document inspired and invigorated the G77, as it represented the coherent alternative vision that it wanted UNCTAD to advocate.

Developed countries came to Doha in militant mood. They made the case that UNCTAD's macroeconomic and finance work was duplicating the ongoing work of the IMF and the World Bank and was therefore a waste of resources. In fact, UNCTAD's analyses were very different from those of the Bretton Woods institutions, whose analyses had become contaminated by the group-think of the Western private-banking industry. Although developed countries conceded that UNCTAD had been ahead of the intellectual curve before the financial collapse of 2007–08, they argued that by 2012 the IMF had completely revised its thinking and thus the existence of this new and wiser IMF made the continuation of UNCTAD's work in this area redundant.

Since 1987 all UNCTAD conferences have had to end with an accord, agreed by consensus, specifying the next four years' work programme.[14] Developing countries struggled to find an outcome that would not undermine UNCTAD's finance work. With developed countries adamant in their demands, for most of the conference it seemed that for the first time since 1987 no consensus accord on the next mandate would be reached. The negotiation turned on whether the new accord should 'build on' or 'reaffirm and build on' the Accra Accord. The first phrase would have allowed part of the previous mandate to be cut out, while the second would prevent that.

At the very last moment the trade ministers of India and South Africa – who had prioritised a BRICS meeting in Mexico over the long-arranged UNCTAD XIII in Doha – arrived and took charge of making the final deals on wording with the EU and the non-EU OECD groups. The final Doha Accord contained the key phrase 'reaffirm and build on', thanks to the late intervention of the BRICS heavyweights on the side of the G77.

Conclusion

The events of Doha in 2012 illustrate four ways that the G77's relation with UNCTAD has evolved since its inception. First, there has been the estrangement of UNCTAD and the G77. In the early years the G77 shaped UNCTAD's general mission, but relied on the UNCTAD secretariat for the construction of its detailed policy agenda. In terms of negotiating this agenda, the G77 consistently favoured more confrontational tactics than the secretariat. This difference produced tensions between the G77 and the secretariat when, as often happened, negotiations failed or agreed policies were implemented half-heartedly. These tensions were managed until the early 1990s. Although secretaries-general from Pérez-Guerrero to Dadzie kept close relations with the G77, it is noteworthy that, since the latter's tenure, no regular meetings have taken place between the G77 and the UNCTAD secretary-general.

Second, UNCTAD has been downsized. Part of the reason for the estrangement is that at UNCTAD VIII the organisation was deprived of its powers of negotiation on trade issues, leaving the field to the WTO. As a result, UNCTAD became less important to the G77 as an instrument to pursue its international objectives.[15] Meanwhile, the G77 has broadened its outreach within the UN and set up chapters to liaise with other UN agencies – in Rome for the Food and Agriculture Organisation, the International Fund for Agricultural Development, and the World Food Programme; in Vienna for the UN Industrial Development Organization; in Nairobi for the UN Environment Programme; and in Paris for the UN Educational, Scientific and Cultural Organization.

Third, there are new resources for the G77. Whereas the G77 used to be totally reliant on UNCTAD for support in Geneva, the establishment of the South Centre in 1995 and of the International Centre for Trade and Sustainable Development in 1996, both located in Geneva, has provided the G77 with a wider range of sources of advice and assistance. UNCTAD no longer has a monopoly as the G77's adviser.

Fourth, BRICS are no longer leaders of the G77. Since 2000 the most powerful developing countries – Brazil, India, China, and South Africa – have downgraded their relations with both the G77 and UNCTAD. They have been more concerned with building links among themselves and Russia, and constructing their own BRICS initiatives, than with leading the G77. Their absence from Doha until the last moment signals where their priorities lie, but their ultimate intervention on the side of the G77 is testimony to their continuing practical solidarity with the group, even if the leadership of the G77 now rests with smaller and weaker developing countries.

The G77 provided a façade of unity for developing countries in their search for a more equitable regime of international regulation of trade, finance, and development. UNCTAD's system of group negotiations reinforced and preserved it. A doctrine of inclusiveness justified it. The G77's claim to represent the developing world depended on recognising that there are many and diverse paths to development, and that each country had a right to follow its own development path without external interference. Somewhat paradoxically this recognition of diversity became the bulwark of unity because unity in diversity always trumped particular conflicts of national interest when constructing the G77 negotiating platform.

After 50 years, however, the very different growth trajectories of the group's countries have made it so disparate that it cannot hold together in the same way that it did in the past. Its former leaders have graduated into a widening circle of elite developed and emerging economies, while many of its economically unsuccessful members have been officially recognised as least developed countries or even as failed states. Even this increasing differentiation might not have been decisive if the strategies pursued by the G77 in its first two decades had been more unifying, both internally and for the world in general. That, however, was not the reality of the past half-century.

Notes

1. Williams took this approach in his *Third World Cooperation*, 2–3. He wrote: 'The central assumption of this study is that an investigation confined to the G-77 in UNCTAD will provide an adequate explanation of the nature and behavior of the wider coalition'.
2. For more on the findings and influence of the Haberler Report, see Toye and Toye, *The UN and Global Political Economy*, 215.
3. United Nations, *The History of UNCTAD*, 10.
4. Dosman, *The Life and Times of Raul Prebisch*, 378–379, 381–382.
5. "In Geneva: Global Collective Bargaining." *Newsweek*, April 6, 1964, 28.
6. See Williams, *Third World Cooperation*, 71, 88, 166.
7. Quoted by Dosman, *The Life and Times of Raul Prebisch*, 420.
8. 'Much of the so-called agenda of the G-77 was articulated by the UN secretariats rather than by the G-77 itself...Whatever we put down as the course of action on any issue, whether on commodities, the Common Fund, the transfer of technology, shipping – you name it, that was taken by the G-77 and made into their own platform.' See Ralph Bunche Institute for International Studies (RBI), "Oral History Interview of Gamani Corea."
9. The delegate from Guinea praised OPEC for 'its brilliant victories in bringing about a just and more harmonious equilibrium in international economic relations'. See General Assembly, *Oral Records*, 5–6.

10. "A Report of the UNCTAD IV Encounter for Journalists, 29–30 April, Nairobi, Kenya." Judith Hart Papers, 8/37.
11. Weiss et al., *UN Voices*, 262.
12. Lavelle, "Ideas within a Context of Power," 45.
13. "The Awkward Newcomers" is the title of Chap. 5 of Cable, *The Storm*, 93–114.
14. Boucher and Siebec, "UNCTAD VII."
15. This point is extended in Williams, *Third World Cooperation*, 167.

Bibliography

Boucher, Carlston B, and Wolfgang E. Siebec. "UNCTAD VII: New Spirit in North-South Relations?" *Finance and Development* 24, no. 4 (1987): 14–16.

Cable, Vince. *The Storm: The World Economic Crisis and What it Means*. London: Atlantic Books, 2009.

Dosman, Edgar J. *The Life and Times of Raul Prebisch 1901–1986*. Montreal: McGill-Queen's University Press, 2008.

General Assembly, *Oral Records, Sixth Special Session*. 2211th Plenary Meeting, April 11, 1974.

Judith Hart Papers. "A Report of the UNCTAD IV Encounter for Journalists, 29–30 April, Nairobi, Kenya." People's History Museum, Manchester, UK: Labour History Archive and Study Centre (reference GB 394 HART).

Lavelle, Kathryn C. "Ideas within a Context of Power: The African Group within an Evolving UNCTAD." *Journal of Modern African Studies* 39, no. 1 (2001): 25–50.

Ralph Bunche Institute for International Studies (RBI), "Oral History Interview of Gamani Corea, 1 February 2000." 30 in *Oral History Collection of the United Nations Intellectual History Project*. CD-Rom. New York: RBI, 2007.

Toye, John, and Richard Toye. *The UN and Global Political Economy*. Bloomington: Indiana University Press, 2004, 215

United Nations. *The History of UNCTAD 1964–1984*. New York: United Nations, 1985.

Weiss, Thomas G., Tatiana Carayannis, Louis Emmerij, and Richard Jolly. *UN Voices: The Struggle for Development and Social Justice*. Bloomington: Indiana University Press, 2005.

Williams, Marc. *Third World Cooperation: The Group of 77 in UNCTAD*. London: Pinter, 1991.

South–South cooperation and the international development battlefield: between the OECD and the UN

Paulo Esteves and Manaíra Assunção

Institute of International Relations, Pontifical Catholic University, Rio de Janeiro, Brazil

This article discusses the transformation in development architecture, focusing on the role of emerging powers and the growing relevance of South–South cooperation (SSC). Drawing on a conceptual toolkit based on the work of Pierre Bourdieu, it aims to approach SSC as a narrative and to understand the processes of contestation that have turned international development into a battlefield since the end of the 1990s. The article argues that the emergence of SSC has contributed to decentring the field of international development, both in terms of the agents authorised to play and the practices considered legitimate. Within this process the Global Partnership for Effective Development Cooperation, led by the OECD's Development Assistance Committee, and the United Nations Development Cooperation Forum have become two sites on the battlefield on which the borders of international development are being redrawn.

After the 2011 Fourth High Level Forum (HLF-4) on Aid Effectiveness in Busan, South Korea, many analysts have emphasised the significance and the fast pace of the changes within the development community. Some of them suggest that 'the old aid land is in existential crisis',[1] while others try to understand the process as a constructive destruction in the 'aid industry'.[2] Rosalind Eyben and Laura Savage, among others, identify the emergence of a more complicated and diverse landscape.[3] This growing complexity raises questions about the future of development architecture, which over the past 40 years has encompassed leading institutions like the IMF, the World Bank, the OECD and its Development Assistance Committee (DAC), and several UN organisations, as well as bilateral agencies in developed and developing countries.

Drawing on a conceptual toolkit based on the work of Pierre Bourdieu, this article addresses these transformations with a focus on the role of South–South cooperation (SSC) in remaking the international development field. The Busan HLF is taken as a vantage point from which, in a field monopolised by developed countries, competing practices can be historically traced. Hence the historical reconstruction of SSC practices allows us to understand the processes of contestation which, since the end of the 1990s, have turned international development into a battlefield.

The article argues that the emergence of SSC has contributed to decentring the field of international development, both in terms of the agents authorised to play and the practices considered legitimate. Within this process the Global Partnership for Effective Development Cooperation (GPEDC) led by DAC and the UN Development Cooperation Forum (DCF) became two sites on the battlefield on which the borders of the international development field are being redrawn. The article begins with a discussion of the development field's constitution and SSC's emergence. The second section addresses the field's dynamics during the first decade of the twenty-first century, the birth of the effectiveness agenda, and the rise of SSC providers as protagonists within the field. Finally, it concludes with the decentring process that took place at the end of the 2000s and after the Busan HLF.

The international development field and the birth of South–South cooperation

The field of international development emerged as a result of at least two distinct political processes in the shadow of the Cold War: Europe's reconstruction and the final disintegration of colonial empires. The European Recovery Programme, known as the Marshall Plan, constituted the first experiment of massive and systematic technical and economic assistance to independent national states.[4] Indeed, the Marshall Plan allowed the articulation of a set of practices, such as the permanent peer review of policies, programmes, and projects, and the harmonisation of procedures, which would later become routine practices in North–South cooperation (NSC). Moreover, when the OECD was established officially in 1961, it took over directly from the Organisation for European Economic Co-operation created in 1948 to help administer the Marshall Plan.

The dismantling of European colonial empires opened up new areas for competition between the two superpowers. Foreign assistance (technical, economic and, in most cases, military) was widely used as a tool for building so-called spheres of influence. Nevertheless, foreign assistance progressively gained autonomy in relation to the field of international security and to the geostrategic interests of the superpowers. Eventually this process had two effects: first, the constitution of an autonomous field; and, second, the re-hierarchisation of the international system in terms of the cleavage between developed and what were first labelled 'underdeveloped' countries.

The first effect is related to the establishment of a common understanding about the ultimate meaning of development and the legitimate ways to achieve it. Bourdieu called intersubjective and commonsensical understanding 'doxa',[5] which refers to 'the inter-subjectively shared, taken for granted, values and discourses of a field'.[6] Hence, talking about an international development doxa means assuming that agents engaged with development practices share common beliefs and vocabulary. Agents share a practical sense structured within a given field by doxic practices, which turns these particular understandings into a self-evident and naturalised truth.[7] In the case of development practices, even though their origins in the aftermath of the Second World War were related to super-power competition, a development community arose and established a common understanding about the legitimate practices of development cooperation. This particular understanding was enacted through the concept of official develop-ment assistance (ODA) within DAC between 1969 and 1972:

> ODA consists of flows to developing countries and multilateral institutions provided by official agencies, including state and local governments, or by their executive agencies, each transaction of which meets the following test: a) it is administered with the promotion of the economic development and welfare of developing coun-tries as its main objective, and b) it is concessional in character and contains a grant element of at least 25 per cent.[8]

Despite its technical and perhaps anodyne vocabulary, the definition had politi-cal significance for several reasons. The definition underscores the ultimate social purpose of international development: 'the promotion of the economic development and welfare of developing countries'. It also establishes ODA as the way through which development and welfare should be fostered. The social pur-pose and a set of practices considered legitimate constitute the field's doxa. The definition also indicates what international development cooperation is not: trade, investment, and military aid. Hence, while discriminating ODA from other official flows, the definition established a clear boundary between international development practices and other political initiatives within the international sys-tem. In the field of international development, ODA became a doxic practice that established its borders and stabilised its meanings.

For Bourdieu a field is a structured social space in which agents are articu-lated as such, and in which social struggles occur;[9] it is a space of structured positions. As suggested by the ODA definition, the international development field is structured along two positions: developing and developed countries, or donors and recipients. This dyadic structure, established in the early 1970s, would be kept stable for four decades, consolidating not only donor and recipi-ent positions but also the rules of mobility governing the ways through which one developing country could graduate to become a developed country. As a club the DAC was the perfect institutional niche both to gather the donors and to actively reinforce the field's boundaries. Its role (along with that of the Bretton Woods institutions) in establishing and consolidating the international develop-ment field is undisputed. Within and throughout DAC, two puzzles were solved: how to create a common understanding about the role of donors in fostering international development (the 'donor puzzle'), and how donor and recipients should relate to each other (the 'donor–recipient puzzle').

The donor puzzle comprises two dimensions – domestic and international. The domestic dimension is related to the social processes through which agents are authorised to act (and spend economic, symbolic, and social resources), pro-moting development abroad. In fact, and as mentioned above, during the Cold War development assistance was, in many cases, domestically authorised as part of a broader strategy of containment. The second dimension of the donor puzzle relates to the ability of developed countries to shape a common understanding about their roles within the field. The structured position is abstract and ascribes particular patterns of behaviour to the agents that partake in it. Despite many changes over the past decades, the donor site was consolidated, and its ability to impose a particular set of goals for development practices was strengthened.

Once they occupied the donor position, development agencies were authorised to speak and act on behalf of international development – that is, to lead recipient countries in the global South along a common development path. Although economic asymmetries were a sine qua non for the establishment of such a dyadic structure, the donor position was to be recognised by the recipients as an authoritative site in order to be consolidated. Donors should be able to rule the field and ascertain what to do and how to do it in order to achieve development and welfare.

The relationship between donors and recipients comprises a second puzzle that was solved at the international development field's genesis. Donors' legitimate leadership (donorship) over recipient countries was the final condition for the consolidation of international development as a field of practices. Although this condition was eventually achieved, countries of the global South articulated their own strategies in order to reach a less dependent status both within the field and in the international system as a whole. One of these strategies was the promotion of ssc as a way of playing within the rules on the field, as well as to challenge its doxa and to exert some pressure over its boundaries.

It is common to identify the emergence of ssc with the Bandung conference in 1955 and the Non-Aligned Movement (NAM). The Bandung communiqué distinguishes cooperation among countries inside the Afro-Asian region 'on the basis of mutual interest and respect for national sovereignty', and between them and developed countries.[10] Cooperation within the postcolonial region was a strategy not only to strengthen the capacities of the newly independent states individually (national self-reliance) but also to build collective capabilities (collective self-reliance).

In Bandung economic and political cooperation were part of the broader context of coalition building among newly independent states, which would unfold in the following decades with the 1964 creation of the United Nations Conference on Trade and Development (UNCTAD) and the Group of 77 developing countries (G77), and later with the 1974 Declaration on the Establishment of a New International Economic Order (NIEO).[11] After Bandung the idea that the formal independence of states in the postcolonial world had led to actual economic dependency was consolidated.[12] The emphasis on the discourse of economic self-reliance and the postcolonial claim for *de facto* political autonomy transformed the divide between North and South into open confrontation within the UN General Assembly and other international forums. Such confrontation would have an institutional unfolding, with Southern countries emphasising the organisational structure related not only to the UN General Assembly or Economic and Social Council (ECOSOC), but especially to UNCTAD. For Southern countries the universal-membership United Nations was the natural and main institutional setting for contestation.

Within the postcolonial world there was a growing perception that the principles established within the DAC would perpetuate enduring inequalities. Yet from the point of view of the North, as discussed above, these demands were captured by the concept of ODA, to be managed by the emerging bilateral cooperation agencies, or multilateral organisations such as the IMF or the World Bank. Nevertheless, the Southern coalition saw the focus on ODA as reproducing the asymmetries within the international system. Indeed, the donor–recipient dyad was a way to transform economic asymmetries into political hierarchy. Such hierarchy was embedded in most international organisations, such as DAC or the World Bank. Created as clubs, their governance structures and decision-making mechanisms reproduced the dividing lines between North and South.

While the emerging field of international development was structured along-side the donor–recipient dyad, the Southern coalition questioned the legitimacy of such a hierarchy and advocated structural reforms that could create the necessary conditions for autonomous decisions on development policies in the global South. Moreover, the NIEO and the creation of the G77 brought the field's emerging doxa to the fore, contesting its fundamental assumptions and its positions. The NIEO provided a way for many Southern governments to engage in a doxic battle in which they could 'strive to gain the power to impose the legitimate version of the social world and its division'.[13]

Meanwhile, two modalities of SSC were institutionalised within the UNCTAD secretariat and inside the G77: Technical Cooperation and Economic Cooperation among Developing Countries (TCDC and ECDC, respectively). Subsequently, the emphasis in SSC fell on technical cooperation. During its 32nd Session the General Assembly discussed the principles of TCDC, thus defining its main objectives: furthering the national and collective self-reliance of developing countries and enhancing their creative capacity to solve problems of economic development. At the end of the 1978 Global South Conference on TCDC, 138 countries adopted the Buenos Aires Plan of Action (BAPA), which reinforced principles that indirectly recovered the results of the Bandung conference, and argued that TCDC should strengthen the creative capacity of developing countries to solve their problems through self-reliance. The BAPA employed, for the first time, the expression 'horizontal cooperation', which would become a key to characterising SSC and a synonym for cooperation among developing countries. Moreover, in addition to the reference to mutual benefits, 'horizontal cooperation' would be used to distinguish and contrast South–South cooperation with the 'vertical' North–South cooperation fostered by the OECD.[14]

Despite expectations for strengthened SSC generated by the BAPA, the debt crisis of the 1980s negatively affected all forms of development cooperation, but particularly the practices of SSC. By then SSC had lost most of its revisionist impetus, allowing the consolidation of the international development field through the defeat of the NIEO programme. Southern countries were, then, playing at the field of international development as recipients. SSC became a strategy through which they posited themselves as both recipients (vis-à-vis Northern donors) and partners (in the face of other developing countries). During this period the United Nations High Level Conference on Economic Cooperation among Developing Countries, held in Caracas, Venezuela, was responsible for creating a programme of action for ssc practitioners. It maintained the articulation between development cooperation and the NIEO, and recognised the relevance of ECDC resulting from the complementary nature of Southern economies. Nevertheless, ssc only gained new impetus in the 2000s, when emerging powers became protagonists within the field. In April 2000 the G77 held the first South Summit in Havana, Cuba. Its final declaration emphasised the importance of ssc in the new millennium and advocated greater participation of countries from the global South in the mechanisms of international decision making.[15]

From the above it is possible to recognise the emergence of ssc as both a set of practices for promoting development among developing countries, and as a strategy for advancing a revisionist effort through the claim for reform of the international system. Moreover, as a collective strategy, ssc helped to cement the political coalition that had resulted in the creation of NAM and the G77. However, an analysis of the action plans, declarations, and communiqués from post-cold war conferences and meetings indicates the waning of this revisionist impetus inherited from the Bandung conference, so as to adjust to the wider underpinnings of the international system. In fact, even if it remained in the discourses of many ssc agents, the revisionist claim now lived alongside impulses for the technical and political adequacy of these practices to broaden the frameworks of the international development field consolidated under the DAC.

During the 1990s this transformation would appear not only in assertions about the complementary character of ssc in relation to NSC, but also in the attempts to increase standardisation of practices of ssc vis-à-vis those of NSC. Thus, if claims for the revision of the international order were still part of the discourse of the agents of ssc, they were now constrained by a development model and a set of practices based on 'official development assistance' that had become hegemonic. The tension between the revision of the international order and adaptation to a hegemonic model of development is perhaps the distinguishing feature of ssc in the twenty-first century.

Ten years' crisis: international development as a battlefield

The new century started with the convergence of two parallel processes that, ultimately, rearranged the entire field of international development: the exhaustion of market-oriented reforms and the pro-poor approaches embodied within the Millennium Development Goals (MDGs). The 'Battle for Seattle', alongside the World Trade Organization Ministerial Conference of 1999, brought the Washington consensus's promises to the fore, while questioning the asymmetric structure of the economic governance machinery and its iniquitous effects.[16] The demonstrations against the proceedings of trade and financial institutions contributed to eroding the legitimacy of market-oriented reforms; they also had an impact on the international development field, with a growing awareness of the negative and exclusionary effects of economic integration under the Washington consensus. Furthermore, the legitimacy of the donor-centred structure of the international development field started to be disputed by developing countries' governments and transnational social movements. Understood as a coercive tool, the conditionalities embedded in development assistance deepened the gap between donors and recipients and emphasised the differences between them. For many Southern governments conditionalities were seen as interference in domestic affairs and as a way to advance donors' interests instead of fostering recipients' development. Parallel to these struggles the MDGS and the Millennium Declaration formed the culmination of a decade of UN conferences, which mobilised governments, transnational social movements, and NGOs around the social costs of economic globalisation.

Hence, at the beginning of the 2000s, development agents had to deal with an increasingly contested field. Both the donor positions and the practices of donorship were disputed. In addition, the fundamental goals of development policies and the ways to achieve them became problematic. The struggles in Seattle were only one episode in a deeper crisis or in an enduring doxic battle that continues today. All the pieces of the puzzle that constituted the international development field since the Cold War were, again, scrambled. The donor puzzle opened up the question of how agents were authorised to act as 'donors'. Taking into account the growing budget deficits of developed economies, the main question was 'how do we justify the use of scarce domestic taxpayer money for external development assistance as governments face growing fiscal austerity?'.[17] As for the relationship between donors and recipients, or the donor–recipient puzzle, considering that aid programmes were increasingly perceived as benefiting donors as much as recipients, the fundamental question became how development processes could be, at the same time, controlled by recipient countries and consistent with donors' principles. This doxic battle had a germane effect on the field, since it drew attention to its borders, problematising what would be considered legitimate practices within the international development field.

Taken together, these questions led to the re-articulation of the field's doxa in terms of a renewed partnership between donors and recipients established throughout the aid effectiveness agenda. As Richard Manning later elaborated, this shift was necessary in order 'to rebalance relations, moving from the highly conditioned donor mindset of the structural adjustment era'.[18] Facing a legitimacy crisis, Northern donors intended to re-establish their relations among themselves and with recipient countries. Allegedly donors were considering passing major control over development projects and programmes to recipient countries. This move was supposed to end the conditionalities that disrupted the domestic affairs of developing countries.

From 2001 to 2005 this broad agenda was codified in a set of principles established during the Second High Level Forum (HLF-2). In an attempt to rebuild their position, donors and the DAC gathered multilateral agencies and representatives from the developing world. The final declaration was endorsed by 61 bilateral and multilateral donors as well as by 56 recipients. These Paris Principles assembled a managerial perspective of 'aid effectiveness' with a political arrangement founded upon the ideas of country-led partnerships and co-responsibility. The 'reform' encompassed five principles: ownership over the development agenda by the recipient country; alignment between donors with a partner country's priorities and goals, and greater confidence in their country systems; coordinated, simplified, and harmonised actions between multiple donors; 'mutual accountability'; and 'management for results'.

The dominant narratives in the field were established around the Paris Declaration and the Paris Principles. The latter soon became a hallmark because they promised to address the multiple puzzles that were shaking the structures of the field at the beginning of the decade. Indeed, the managerial perspective underpinning both the principles of 'mutual accountability' and 'management for results' were supposed to answer the donor puzzle, at least regarding legitimacy before their own constituencies. The call for harmonised, transparent, and collectively effective actions among donors addresses the second dimension of the puzzle, namely the relationship among donors. Harmonisation and transparency were conditions for establishing a coherent monitoring framework, which would provide consistency for their position as donors.

The principle of ownership, the fundamental pillar of the declaration, put recipients in the 'driving seat' and transformed traditional asymmetries in the field. Furthermore, the Paris Declaration assumed that development aid should be oriented towards poverty reduction and towards the achievement of the MDGS. Thus the Paris Principles seem to align the field of international development cooperation with the broader agenda within the United Nations. In terms of bilateral and multilateral cooperation, this alignment would be materialised with the requirement that ODA should be provided to nationally owned strategies.[19]

While traditional donors were struggling to rearticulate the field through the Paris agenda, SSC gained momentum with the growing presence of emerging powers as protagonists of development cooperation. Although traditional donors still provide the bulk of development cooperation, the increasing activism of emerging providers, particularly in the past decade, is indisputable and has changed the conversation.

From the traditional donors' perspective, however, the growing relevance of development cooperation provided by emerging powers breaks the dominant aid logic and belies a unified epistemic donor community.[20] This reality became even clearer after the 2008 economic crisis. ODA and other forms of official flows were affected by packages of fiscal austerity in Northern donors and by the indebtedness of developing countries.[21]

For Southern providers the financial crisis was an opportunity to highlight the differences between traditional ODA and SSC, as well as to establish new positions within the international development field. As discussed above, since its origins the boundaries of the field have been conceived by a structured set of positions defined under the dyad 'donor' and 'recipient'. Emergent providers from the global South are challenging this long-lived structure, scrambling once again the pieces of the puzzle. At odds with the traditional donor position, these actors assert themselves as 'partners'. Southern providers refuse either to identify themselves as donors or to support the past practices of donorship, considered to be interference in domestic affairs. Instead, these agents position themselves as equal partners and claim the possibility of establishing a relationship based on the principles of horizontality and mutual benefits.[22]

Despite what Southern actors are claiming, the partner position and the practices of partnership are also intricate political puzzles with their own dilemmas, which are unfolding domestically and internationally. At home Southern providers must get support from their own constituencies. Nevertheless, they claim neither to be part of nor to represent the interests of the group of developed countries. In fact, most of these governments are still dealing with poverty and growing domestic inequalities. Having to justify public expenditures in development projects abroad, these agents very often face domestic resistance, increasing the costs of building a solid position as a partner. Moreover, in order to manufacture the partner position within the international development field, emerging donors need to agree upon common principles and goals, which seems an even more complex dimension of the partner puzzle: SSC providers not only have to differentiate themselves from DAC donors but also to negotiate and coordinate their practices. In this respect there might be a split within the global South along two axes. While South Korea and Mexico, for instance, have established a dialogue with the DAC, Brazil, India, and China have refused DAC principles. While the former consider SSC complementary to ODA, the latter reject that developed-country donor position. For them SSC practices are inconsistent with the structure of the field.

In a context of financial crisis, the impact of Southern providers over that of DAC donors has been germane. While the latter have focused on good governance and institutional capacity building during the past two decades, they are now re-examining economic growth paradigms as a means to promote poverty reduction. SSC providers, however, are debating sustainable and inclusive development vis-à-vis the promotion of economic growth. These debates, in the absence of a common doxa, reinforce the assumption that the stakes in the field are being revaluated and that the traditional ODA-oriented doxa can no longer be maintained.

Facing a new doxic battle, DAC has made major efforts to restore some consensus among donors, recipients, and newly recognised partners in development cooperation. The Working Party on Aid Effectiveness (WP-EFF),[23] for example, is seen as a major expression of the 'inclusiveness' move undertaken by DAC, stimulating a multi-stakeholder process that included 80 members by 2009 (out of which 24 were recipient and 31 donor countries). The WP-EFF created the Task Team on South–South Co-operation to review South–South experiences regarding the Paris agenda, having recognised the issue of diversity in development practices.[24] However, the ties between DAC and the WP-EFF remained unclear, and many saw the task team as DAC's latest attempt to sustain the current doxic field.[25]

The general perception among SSC providers is that DAC reforms still maintain traditional power asymmetries, and that a new forum would be the best way to ensure greater influence.[26] Many identify the DCF (established after the UN World Summit in 2005 as a G77 initiative) as the most inclusive development forum for reviewing trends and progress in international development cooperation – clear evidence of the G77's opposing DAC's dominant role in the evolving development landscape.[27] Because of strong similarities between the mandates and agendas of the DCF and DAC, both forums are frequently evaluated in terms of increasing and diminishing roles and influence.[28] Especially in relation to the debate about whether DAC is a suitable forum for discussing SSC in light of its Northern origins, the DCF is presented as a viable and legitimate alternative. Its potential importance is suggested by the fact that some analysts are suggesting that the WP-EFF and the whole effectiveness agenda could be passed on under a UN umbrella, ie to the DCF.[29] Thus it is not surprising that the forum is seen as an attempt to challenge the primacy of DAC and the WP-EFF in this context, having been established just before Accra.

Despite the fact that the DCF is still viewed as fledgling and faces criticism because of its loose working arrangements,[30] many Southern partners are attracted by its more inclusive space, especially when compared with other development institutions. Brazil, Russia, India, China, and South Africa (BRICS), for instance, have confirmed their engagement and clearly recognise it as a preferable locus to strengthen and modernise SSC.[31] Thus, the DCF is a direct response to the perception of the donors' status.

The crisis in international development, which started with the contestation of Washington consensus policies, reached its most acute point at the end of the first decade of the twenty-first century with the dual impact of the global financial crisis and the rise of emerging powers as providers of development cooperation. At that point the structured positions within the field and the practices that they authorise were contested from inside and outside developed countries. The doxic battle became a ubiquitous condition in a field whose borders had become increasingly blurred.

Scrambling the pieces: the Busan High Level Forum

Among the series of forums organised by DAC to assess aid effectiveness and restructure the field, the 2011 HLF-4 has been considered another landmark within the international development field. The HLF-4 was to review the progress made since HLF-2. Nonetheless, as discussed above, the puzzles' pieces were, once again, scrambled.

On the donor side, with the outbreak of the financial crisis and the consequent recession and austerity policies adopted by developed countries, public support for aid disbursements was increasingly debated. In addition, the continual assessment of the effectiveness of donor practices (in 2006, 2008, and 2011) showed that very little overall progress had been achieved in relation to the 12 targets set in 2005. Donor agencies were, once again, under scrutiny from their own national constituencies and, at the same time, starting to support practices beyond the strict definition of ODA. The donor position thus encountered tensions from two sources – domestic and international.

Moreover, with countries of the global South exploring distinct modalities of cooperation inconsistent with but not captured by ODA definitions, another source of pressure emerged. Accordingly Southern partners offered alternatives for both the dyadic structure of donorship and for the relationship partners were supposed to establish. Instead of reinforcing the donor–recipient dyad, the new protagonists claimed that their practices established horizontal partnerships among Southern countries. In addition, SSC assumed that development cooperation should be based on mutual benefits, instead of aid or assistance. Since the principle of mutual benefits encompasses practices such as trade and investment, alien to the strict definition of development assistance, the engagement of Southern countries with cooperative arrangements ended up exerting pressure to enlarge the field's borders. Suddenly, developing and poor countries became both recipients (according to DAC vocabulary) and equal partners (following SSC principles).

In a practical sense increasing the pool of donors and partners (including ssc providers and the private sector) has at least three potential positive effects for 'recipients'. First, developing and poor countries may have additional leverage and be in a better position to negotiate their preferences for particular aid and cooperation projects or programmes. Second, the potentially competitive logic among agents may reinforce the doxic battle, creating the necessary conditions for a 'race to the bottom' dynamic.[32] Third, in a doxic battle, developing and poor countries might play competitors off against one another.

Facing these renewed challenges, DAC could not host another HLF to assess the effectiveness agenda. Busan is constantly described as a turning point thanks to its singular character in challenging dominant positions and divisions within the field through the recognition of diverse practices, and in pointing to the limits of DAC structures within the multilateral arena.[33] Furthermore, it proposed a different approach from that of former HLFs, which were criticised for their highly technical nature.[34]

The Busan Outcome Document presents two key innovations: the recognition of other development cooperation actors besides the traditional DAC donors (especially ssc providers and the private sector), and the consequent call for a new GPEDC. A better balance between representativeness and inclusiveness was viewed as a solution to major legitimacy problems because it would permit newcomers to participate in setting the development agenda. The GPEDC initiative suggests a double compromise: between the aid effectiveness agenda and development cooperation (the 'beyond aid' movement), on the one hand, and between DAC donors and Southern providers, on the other hand.[35] According to GPEDC supporters, the initiative has the double merit of opening a dialogue on development cooperation paradigms and models, while recognising ssc providers and the private sector – the sources of non-ODA flows – as equal partners, having a stake in development.[36]

Synthetically four major innovations from Busan are noteworthy: the concept of development effectiveness; the recognition of ssc as a legitimate modality; the recognition of private actors as legitimate partners; and the call for a renewed institutional arrangement, to include all partners and modalities. Nevertheless, instead of establishing a common understanding about meanings, goals, and ways to foster international development, Busan inaugurated a period of intense contestation. The concept of development effectiveness, potentially Busan's most important product, turned out to be the newest buzzword within the field, having its meaning increasingly disputed.[37] While for traditional donors the concept emphasises both development outcomes as well as the continuity of the 'aid effectiveness' agenda, for emerging partners development effectiveness means the enlargement of the field's boundaries. Hence, for the latter, the concept weakens the role of traditional donors, opening a renewed space for ssc practices, whereas for the former it does the opposite.

The shifting focus towards emerging partners in general, and their engagement based on ssc principles in particular, reinforces the dichotomy between donors and providers. Inscribed in the North–South divide, it reproduces the symbolic battle over principles and better practices. The archetypical call by emerging partners in Busan for 'common principles but differentiated responsibilities' reinforces the lines separating North and South.[38] Moreover, the dispute between traditional donors and emerging providers is currently allowing SSC practitioners to enter the field as if they could actually solve ODA's past failures – despite the evidence and contrary views from donors, recipients, and researchers.[39]

The growing recognition of the importance of the for-profit private sector within the field was another important step. Both traditional donors and emergent providers are increasingly advocating alternative public and private blends of partnership as a way to foster development.[40]

Finally, the shape of institutional arrangements remains a contentious issue. While the OECD and traditional donors support the GPEDC as a 'coalition of the willing' focused on mutual learning and improvement of development cooperation practices,[41] some emerging partners characterise it as 'old wine in new bottles'.[42] Indeed, the GPEDC's Steering Committee is still replicating the dyadic structure of the field. Although current proposals aim to better represent the entire spectrum of agents within the field, it still maintains the dyad donor–recipient at the centre.

Conclusion

Instead of ending the enduring doxic battle, the Busan process and the GPEDC are probably its most visible front. Indeed, what was at stake in Busan was the most stable concept in the field of international development: official development assistance. Hence, while problematising the very concept of ODA, Busan also creates a vantage point from which to understand the field of international development as a battlefield. The concept of ODA articulated the field in terms of its positions and doxic practices. It allowed Northern countries to raise domestic support for extending financial resources in development programmes abroad and to create a common 'donor' position among like-minded sources of external financing. This donor position, fostered and represented by DAC, solved what was called the 'donor puzzle'.

Additionally, the concept secured the boundaries of the field for some four decades. Accordingly, during the Cold War the concept and the practices of ODA were able to contain the revisionist impulse of Southern countries expressed by the NIEO and other NAM and G77 demands. The practices of ODA helped defeat these demands and turned revisionist agents into ODA recipients, solving what was called the 'donor–recipient puzzle'. As recipients developing countries recognise, even tacitly, the legitimacy of ODA practices (donorship) and of the field's boundaries. Nevertheless, the victory of ODA practitioners did not mean full acceptance of either the donor–recipient dyad, or the practices of donorship. South–South cooperation comprised a set of practices presented as either complementary or supplementary to ODA. Although development outcomes resulting from SSC might be considered lacklustre until the end of the 1990s, SSC continued as a viable strategy, which ultimately contributed to foster and indeed strengthen a political coalition among countries of the global South; it also served to interrogate the structured positions and boundaries of the international development field.

Nevertheless, since the end of the 1990s, the entire field's structure has been contested. However, even after 10 years of crisis and with the renewed impulse of the Paris agenda, the practices of ODA have remained central to the field, maintaining its boundaries and conventional positions. The outbreak of the financial crisis, along with the impact of SSC providers' growing advocacy, suggested the exhaustion of the Paris agenda. After a decade of severe tensions inside the donor position and of growing pressures from outsiders (Southern countries, recipients, civil society, and the private sector), development agents arrived in Busan to discuss whether the concept of ODA was still appropriate to keep together the variety of practices of development cooperation. Thus the HLF-4 made clear that the attempts to organise the entire field of international development around the single concept of ODA would be futile vis-à-vis the heterogeneity of practices espoused by traditional donors, Southern providers, the private sector, and civil society organisations.

The concept of a doxic battle facilitates an understanding of the nature of this struggle. The doxic battle means that different agents were struggling to impose particular meanings for the goals of development and the legitimate means to foster it. Doxic battles comprise struggles upon the structured positions in the field as well as its boundaries. The concept of doxic battles allows us to approach the international development field as a battlefield – a space in which enduring struggles turn positions into puzzles, allowing agents to interrogate how legitimate such authorised positions and practices actually are.

While the 2000s are aptly characterised as a doxic battlefield, it was only in Busan that the concept of ODA, the donor position, and the practices of donorship came under a more general attack. However, the partner positions (or puzzles) and the so-called practices of partnership, supported by many Southern countries, were also attacked by domestic constituencies, traditional donors, and recipients and partners. In short, every position in the field now confronts a situation in which its authority is challenged.

Busan underscores how decentred the field of international development currently is. Not only are multiple practices now recognised as legitimate, but also a variety of positioning strategies (ranging from the donor–recipient dyad to horizontal partnerships or public–private partnerships) are now in direct competition. While traditional donors are trying to maintain the OECD's DAC as the symbolic centre of the field, many Southern providers support the UN's DCF as the legitimate arena for realignment, coordination, and norm setting. The DAC-led GPEDC and the DCF have become the two sites of the doxic battlefield on which donors and partners are struggling to draw the new borders of the international development field.

Funding

This work was supported by "Conselho Nacional de Desenvolvimento Tecnológico" and "Fundação Carlos Chagas Filho de Amparo à Pesquisa do Estado do Rio de Janeiro".

Notes

1. Gore, "The New Development Cooperation Landscape," 770.
2. Kharas and Rogerson, *Horizon 2025*.
3. Eyben and Laura, "Emerging and Submerging Powers."
4. Woodward, *The Organisation for Economic Co-operation and Development*.
5. Bourdieu, *Outline of a Theory*.
6. Leander, "Thinking Tools," 9.
7. Villumsen, "Capitalizing on Bourdieu."
8. Führer, *The Story of Official Development Assistance*," 24.
9. According to Bourdieu, the definition encompasses two dimensions: it 'is a field of forces, whose necessity is imposed on agents who are engaged in it, and…a field of struggles within which agents confront each other, with differentiated means and ends according to their position in the structure of the field of forces'. Bourdieu, *Practical Reason*, 32.
10. Final Communiqué of the Asian–African Conference, Bandung, April 24, 1995.
11. The Sixth Special Session of the UN General Assembly, April 9 to May 2, 1974, adopted, on May 1, 1974, the "Declaration on the Establishment of a New International Economic Order," A/RES/3201 (S-VI); and the "Programme of Action on the Establishment of a New International Economic Order," A/RES/3202 (S-VI).
12. Shaw, "The Non-Aligned Movement."
13. Villumsen, "Capitalizing on Bourdieu."
14. United Nations, *Buenos Aires Plan of Action for Promoting and Implementing Technical Co-operation among Developing Countries 1978 Documentation*, 1978.
15. Group of 77 South Summit, "Declaration of the South Summit," Havana, Cuba, April 10–14, 2000.
16. Raghavan, "After Seattle."
17. Chin and Qadir, "Introduction," 496.
18. Manning, *The DAC*, 3.
19. Dijkstra, "The PRSP Approach"; Gottschalk, "The Macro Content"; Gottschalk, "The Effectiveness"; and Lavers, *The Politics of Bilateral Donor Assistance*.
20. Mawdsley et al., "A 'Post-aid World'?," 29.
21. United Nations, *World Economic Situation and Prospects*.
22. For DAC the emergence of Southern providers implied rearranging the classification schemes and creating new hybrid categories such as 'donor–recipient' agents. The terminology of 'hybrid actors' points to emerging taxonomies, which are disputed by the actors within the field, at the same time as previous categorisations – including 'developed' and 'developing' countries – lose their interchangeable character and applicability. See Davies, "Towards a New Development Cooperation Dynamic."
23. The WP-EFF was responsible for managing the Paris Meeting and the process of high-level meetings, as well as the Open Forum for CSO Development Effectiveness. In 2003 the working group started as a DAC subsidiary.
24. The Task Team on South–South Cooperation (TT-SSC) was created in 2009 and derived from the Accra Agenda for Action commitment to partnerships. WPF-EFF and DAC consider it a Southern-led platform. Its main achievement was the mapping of 110 cases of South–South and triangular cooperation presented at the Bogotá High-level Event on South–South Cooperation and Capacity Development in 2010.
25. Killen and Rogerson, "Global Governance."
26. Mawdsley, *From Recipients to Donors*, 76.
27. Three years later the DCF was established and became operational as a new ECOSOC function. Its structure embraces biennial cycles of high-level meetings and a final DCF meeting held at UN headquarters. See Kindornay and Samy, *Establishing a Legitimate Development Co-operation Architecture*.

28. Verschaeve, "Is the Development Assistance Committee?"
29. Glennie, "Who should Lead the Aid Effectiveness Debate in the Future?"
30. Verschaeve, "Is Development Assistance Committee?"
31. Molina, "Can the UN Development Cooperation Forum?"
32. Indeed, the doxic battle is eroding the main principles of both modalities, NSC and SSC. Assessed from the Southern position, aid practices, as predicted by the effectiveness agenda, are still hiding under the principle of ownership, the structural hierarchy of the field, and the customary conditionalities. Nevertheless, while evaluating Southern practices, Northern donors consider that SSC is either complementary to NSC or a new colonial enterprise.
33. Kharas, *The Global Partnership*.
34. Already in the WP-EFF the idea was to move away from previous HLFS, which were criticised for their highly technical nature. See Kindornay and Samy, *Establishing a Legitimate Development Co-operation Architecture*.
35. Kim and Lee, "Busan and Beyond."
36. Atwood, "Creating a Global Partnership."
37. Eyben, "Struggles in Paris," 88.
38. Busan Outcome Document, *Busan Partnership for Effective Development Co-operation*, Fourth High-Level Forum on Aid Effectiveness, Busan, South Korea, December 1, 2011, §2.
39. Eyben and Savage, "Emerging and Submerging Powers."
40. Verschaeve, "Is Development Assistance Committee?"
41. Atwood, "Creating a Global Partnership."
42. There are different views among middle-income countries and SSC providers. While some countries, like China, Brazil, and India, are highly critical of the GPEDC process, others, like Mexico, Turkey, and Indonesia, identify it as the right forum for standardising principles on SSC. Within the GPEDC's Steering Committee, three distinct constituencies were established (recipient countries, donor countries, and providers and recipients of development cooperation, among others), drawing on WP-EFF's member categories: ODA recipient countries; recipients and providers of assistance; and donor countries reporting to DAC. See Kharas, *The Global Partnership*; and Assunção and Esteves, "The BRICS and the GPEDC."

Bibliography

Assunção Manaíra, and Paulo Esteves. "The BRICS and the GPEDC." *BPC Policy Brief* 4, no. 3 (2014). http://brics policycenter.org/homolog/arquivos/SSCMONITOR.pdf.

Atwood, Brian J. "Creating a Global Partnership for Effective Development Cooperation." Paper prepared for the University of Minnesota's Center for Integrative Leadership conference on Creating Public Value in a Multi-sector, Shared-Power World, September 20–22, 2012.

Bourdieu, Pierre. *Outline of a Theory*. 16th ed. Cambridge: Cambridge University Press, 2002.

Bourdieu, Pierre. *Practical Reason: On the Theory of Action*. Stanford, CA: Stanford University Press, 1998.

Chin, Gregory, and Fahimul Qadir. "Introduction: Rising States, Rising Donors and the Global Aid Regime." *Cambridge Review of International Affairs* 25, no. 4 (2012): 493–506.

Davies, Penny. "Towards a New Development Cooperation Dynamic." Draft Background Paper, North–South Institute, June 2011. http://www.nsi-ins.ca/content/download/Davies2011.pdf.

Dijkstra, Geske. "The PRSP Approach and the Illusion of Improved Aid Effectiveness: Lessons from Bolivia, Honduras and Nicaragua." *Development Policy Review* 29, no. S1 (2011): 110–133.

Eyben, Rosalind. "Struggles in Paris: The DAC and the Purposes of Development Aid." *European Journal of Development Research* 25 (November 2013): 78–91.

Eyben, Rosalind, and Laura Savage. "Emerging and Submerging Powers: Imagined Geographies in the New Development Partnership at the Busan Fourth High Level Forum." *Journal of Development Studies* 49, no. 4 (2012): 457–469.

Gore, Charles. "The New Development Cooperation Landscape: Actors, Approaches, Architecture." *Journal of International Development* 25, no. 6 (2013): 769–786.

Gottschalk, Ricardo. "The Effectiveness of the Macroeconomics Frameworks of the PRSPS for Growth and Poverty Reduction." In *Poverty Reduction and Policy Regimes*. Geneva: UNRISD, 2007–2010.

Gottschalk, Ricardo. "The Macro Content of PRSPS: Assessing the Need for a More Flexible Macroeconomic Policy Framework." *Development Policy Review* 23, no. 4 (2005): 419–442.

Führer, Helmut. *The Story of Official Development Assistance: A History of the Development Assistance Committee and the Development Co-operation Directorate in Dates, Names and Figures*. Paris: OECD, 1996. http://www.oecd.org/dac/1896816.pdf.

Glennie, Jonathan. "Who should Lead the Aid Effectiveness Debate in the Future?" Speech at the first ODI Busan Debate, House of Commons, London, July 6, 2011.

Kharas, Homi. *The Global Partnership for Effective Development Cooperation*. Policy Paper 2012-04. Washington, DC: Brookings Institution, 2012. http://www.brookings.edu/~/media/research/files/papers/2012/6/06%20global%20partnership%20kharas/06%20global%20partnership%20kharas.pdf.

Kharas, Homi, and Andrew Rogerson. *Horizon 2025: Creative Destruction in the Aid Industry*. London: ODI, 2012.

Killen, Brenda, and Andrew Rogerson. "Global Governance for International Development: Who's in Charge?" OECD Development Brief Consultation Draft, Issue 2, June 2010. http://www.oecd.org/dac/45569897.pdf.

Kim, Eun Mee, and Jae Eun Lee. "Busan and Beyond: South Korea and the Transition from Aid Effectiveness to Development Effectiveness." *Journal of International Development* 25, no. 6 (2013): 787–801.

Kindornay, Shannon, and Yiagadessen Samy. *Establishing a Legitimate Development Co-operation Architecture*. Working Paper. Ottawa: North–South Institute, May 14, 2012. http://cso-effectiveness.org/IMG/pdf/2012wp_kindornay_samy_devarch.pdf.

Lavers, Tom. *The Politics of Bilateral Donor Assistance: Combating Poverty and Inequality*. UNRISD Flagship Report. Geneva, September 2008. http://www.unrisd.org/80256B3C005BCCF9/%28httpAuxPages%29/7F5D440F4E1E0C71C1257A5D004BFD0C/$file/LaversWeb.pdf.

Leander, Anna. "Thinking Tools: Analyzing Symbolic Power and Violence." In *Qualitative Methods in International Relations: A Pluralist Guide*, edited by Audie Klotz and Deepa Prakash. Basingstoke, UK: Palgrave Macmillan, 2008.

Manning, Richard. *The DAC as a Central Actor in Development Policy Issues: Experiences over the Past Four Years*. Discussion Paper 7/2008. Bonn: German Development Institute, 2008.

Mawdsley, Emma. *From Recipients to Donors: Emerging Powers and the Changing Development Landscape*. London: Zed Books, 2012.

Mawdsley, Emma, Laura Savage, and Sung-Mi Kim. "A 'Post-aid World'? Paradigm Shift in Foreign Aid and Development Cooperation at the 2011 Busan High Level Forum." *Geographical Journal* 1, no. 1 (2014): 27–38.

Molina, Nuria. "Can the UN Development Cooperation Forum Replace the OECD DAC as the Place for Global Aid Negotiations?" European Network and Debt and Development, July 17, 2008. http://eurodad.org/2560/.

Raghavan, Chakravarthi. "After Seattle, World Trade System faces Uncertain Future." *Review of International Political Economy* 7, no. 3 (2000): 495–504.

Shaw, Timothy M. "The Non-Aligned Movement and the New International Economic Order." In *Transforming the World-economy?* ed. Herb Addo, 138–162. London: United Nations University, 1984.

Verschaeve, Joren. "Is the Development Assistance Committee Still Calling the Tune in International Development? A Comparative Analysis of the Legitimacy of the OECD-DAC and the UN-DCF." Paper prepared for the 8th Pan-European Conference on International Relations, Warsaw, September 18–21 2013. http://www.eisa-net.org/be-bruga/eisa/files/events/warsaw2013/Verschaeve_Is%20the%20DAC%20still%20calling%20the%20tune%20in%20international%20development.pdf.

Villumsen, Trine. "Capitalizing on Bourdieu: Boundary-setting, Agency, and Doxic Battles in IR." Paper presented at International Studies Association Annual Convention, Montreal, 2006.

United Nations, *World Economic Situation and Prospects*. New York, 2012. http://www.un.org/en/development/desa/policy/wesp/wesp_archive/2012wesp.pdf.

Woodward, Richard. *The Organisation for Economic Co-operation and Development*. New York: Routledge, 2009.

How representative are BRICS?

Ramesh Thakur

Crawford School of Public Policy, Australian National University, Canberra, Australia

The five countries known as BRICS, while not homogeneous in interests, values, and policy preferences, do have a common interest in checking US/Western power and influence through collaboration with non-Western powers. They vary considerably but all are ahead of other developing countries on population, military power, economic weight, geopolitical clout, and global reach and engagement. They are unrepresentative of the typical developing country in terms of interest, capacity, and resources, but they can represent the interests and goals of developing countries as a group on those issues for which the North–South division is salient. The diversity within BRICS, their differences from other developing countries, and their potential to reflect and represent the global South are explored with respect to climate change, finance, trade, aid, human rights and intervention, and development. It remains unclear whether BRICS can morph from a countervailing economic grouping to a powerful political alternative.

The world may have made the transition from one in which the most salient divide during the Cold War was between the US- and Soviet-led blocs to one in which the most relevant and potent divide is between the global rich and poor.[1] The *2013 Human Development Report* began with the dramatic sentence: 'The rise of the South is unprecedented in its speed and scale'.[2] While the UK and the USA took 150 and 50 years, respectively, to double their output with industrialisation, China and India achieved that feat in less than 20 years. Moreover, 'For the first time in 150 years, the combined output of the developing world's three leading economies – Brazil, China, and India – is about equal to the combined gross domestic product (GDP) of the long-standing industrial powers of the North – Canada, France, Germany, Italy, the United Kingdom and the United States'.[3] Thanks to their weight in the global economy, emerging powers have both the opportunity and the responsibility to ensure the peaceful rise and anchor the economic development and prosperity of Asia, Africa, and Latin America.

Any attempt to define and specify the identity of 'emerging powers' could quickly become esoteric, idiosyncratic and not particularly helpful for the central issue under analysis in this article. Instead, a simpler option of substituting the five countries that make up BRICS – Brazil, Russia, India, China, and South Africa – is adopted. Although not quite as disparate as the open-ended 'emerging powers', BRICS are far from homogeneous in interests, values, and policy preferences. On some issues they will have common interests, while on others they will compete, and will even collaborate with some Western and industrialised powers. For example, New Delhi might join Washington in a hedging strategy against China's rapidly growing military footprint and assertive behaviour across Asia and the Pacific, even while teaming up with Beijing against Europe and the USA on greenhouse gas emission targets.

This article proceeds as follows. First, it briefly describes the BRICS grouping. Next, it examines whether this can represent developing countries on the issue areas of climate change, trade and finance, and the responsibility to protect (R2P). The final section takes a specific look at development and the UN development system.

BRICS

BRICS form a diplomatic grouping following the coining of the acronym by a private sector analyst.[4] The grouping is not the product of diplomatic negotiations based on shared political values or common economic interests. Yet it serves as the key tag of the major emerging countries. BRICS are among the confetti of 'G' groups that dot the contemporary international political, security, and economic landscape. In the constellation of 'G groups', the G7 is the body that brings together the big rich economies; BRICS brings together the big emerging powers; the G77 is the international trade union of the poor developing countries; and the G20 tries to ensure that the big countries from the global North and South work collaboratively rather than confrontationally to address common global challenges. In its logic the G20 is meant to be the forum of the countries of the world with global clout: all countries with global clout and only those countries with clout.[5] BRICS comprise those emerging powers whose rapidly growing economies, substantial populations, military capabilities, and expanding diplomatic reach translate into rising power profiles.[6] Thus BRICS is an important grouping because it brings together the big emerging markets whose economic growth is predicted to outstrip and indeed anchor the rest of the world, and because of the diversity and spread of continents, political systems and values, and economic models that they span.

Yet it is also of uncertain unity, coherence, and staying power because the diversity hides the reality of a lack of unifying values, principles, goals and even interests among the group's members, which leaves them open to the dismissive comment of being 'bricks in search of cement'.[7] BRICS are totally different countries with separate histories, contexts, political and economic systems, needs, opportunities and futures. In all of them domestic priorities and problems trump club solidarity. They are riven with rivalries over borders, resources, and status. With long and not always settled borders, India and Russia have problems with China. In an environment of growing energy and food demand, China's and India's anxiety about rising energy prices must be set against Russia being a beneficiary, while Brazil is both a cause and beneficiary of rising food prices. China's highly competitive exports inflict material harm on Brazil. Two of the five are authoritarian states. The three democracies have their own subset called IBSA (India, Brazil, and South Africa),[8] although they too have a tradition of reticence in global democracy-promotion efforts. Many also seem at present to be stuttering economically, which would undercut the very basis of their recently added global clout. Investors have begun to flee the fragile and uncertain emerging markets to return to the USA. This is especially hard on economies like Brazil and India, whose imports exceed exports, as the gap must be filled by overseas borrowing. All five retain deep and specific ties with the pivotal Northern countries in the general context of complex interdependence vis-à-vis the global economy.

The two heavyweights in BRICS are China and India. How China develops domestically and behaves internationally are among the two most critical questions for the future. Because of the sweeping expansion of its comprehensive national power, China has seen an exponential increase in its weight in the global economy, in Asian and global power balances, and regional and global governance institutions. In its growing international relations to date, China has reaffirmed Westphalian norms of state sovereignty and responsible international behaviour such as non-aggression, non-intervention, and non-interference in internal affairs. But it remains reticent and reluctance to shoulder the managerial responsibilities of world order traditionally associated with being a great power. China's currency manipulation has imposed significant economic costs on its fellow BRICS. Brazil has complained that China's sharp practices include damaging Brazilian prospects in third markets, dumping exports diverted from Europe in Brazil, and erecting steep tariff barriers to Brazilian imports.[9] China is now Africa's biggest trading partner, and this has raised concerns among some Africans, including former South African president Thabo Mbeki,[10] about a new colonial relationship in which Beijing contributes to Africa's deindustrialisation and underdevelopment through consumption of African raw materials, followed by cheap Chinese manufactured goods flooding Africa.[11]

India is at once a country with a very large number of very poor and vulnerable people, whose natural allies are the other poor developing countries, especially in sub-Saharan Africa; and a big emerging market with a rising global profile with many interests in common with the other rapidly industrialising countries. The G77 is the natural home for the poverty-stricken in India, BRICS the abode of the wealthier part of the population. India's international role also is hampered by the paradox of being a 'premature power', one whose global reach is outstripped by national indicators of development.[12] There is an ambivalence in India's often defensive and rarely entrepreneurial response, rooted in its transitional identity as a rising power with growing economic weight that is translating into greater political clout, but also as a hugely poor and underdeveloped country with a multitude of serious policy challenges – at the same time 'a rising power and a vulnerable nation'.[13] At best it is a hesitant rule shaper that is shedding the past pathology of rule breaking (eg on nuclear issues), is too big and powerful to be a mere rule taker, but lacks capacity and will to be a rule maker.

The most significant potential source of BRICS cohesion is geopolitical: the common interest in checking US/Western power and imperialist impulses by leveraging collaboration with the other non-Western powers. All five members have a strong vested interest in protecting strategic autonomy vis-à-vis the USA in global affairs, and the BRICS summits have been vocal on this point. All five generally take an instrumental approach to international governance. China and Russia are instinctively suspicious of the very notion of global governance as a self-serving Western concept, preferring informal gatherings of big powers and regional institutions to formal multilateral machinery.[14] They are divided on reform of the UN Security Council, with China's interest lying more in a bipolar than a genuinely multipolar global order, and on the global economic effects of China's currency value. Nor do they always act as a concerted bloc within other institutional settings. In 2012 they failed to mount a united campaign for either the Nigerian or Colombian candidate against the ultimately successful US nominee for president of the World Bank. Relative gains calculations may promote competition as much as cooperation among BRICS, and between BRICS and the rest of the developing world. Although many countries are strong enough to veto Western action, 'none has the political and economic muscle to remake the status quo'.[15]

BRICS *are highly atypical of developing countries*

More crucially, if ironically for the theme of this article, BRICS are different from other countries in the global South, with each being either too big or uncomfortable in its immediate neighbourhood. All have demonstrated an impressive continental and global reach in terms of their diplomatic profile. On the basis of purchasing power parity GDP, China, India, Russia, and Brazil are all in the top 10. South Africa is substantially out of line with the other group members in population, economy, size, and growth rate. These are offset, however, by its resource endowments, infrastructure, and corporate and financial footprints in the rest of Africa,[16] which explain why it retains a pivotal status as a diplomatic actor and a regional economic powerhouse.

BRICS' global reach and influence will be determined by the interplay between their economic weight, geopolitical clout, the number and quality of personnel in the foreign policy and trade bureaucracies, the resources allocated to these departments, the technical expertise of their officials, the soft power of universities, research institutes and think-tanks supporting officialdom, and the personal engagement and leadership qualities of their heads of government and foreign ministers. On the one hand, these countries vary quite considerably among themselves on these measures. On the other hand, they are well ahead of most other developing countries on such measures. They are anything but representative of the typical developing country in terms of interest, capacity, and resources. But they do have the ability and may have the will to represent the interests of developing countries on those issues where the global North–South division is among the most salient.

BRICS' natural international constituency is the global South. Economic weight, geopolitical clout, and normative skills backstop the ability and willingness to contribute to the advancement of the developing countries' interests and goals as a group. Many developing countries remain worried that the forces of globalisation impinge adversely on their economic sovereignty, cultural integrity, and social stability. 'Interdependence' among unequals can mean the dependence of some on international markets that function under the dominance of others in norm setting and rule enforcement. To the extent that the United Nations is the central coordinating agency of the global commons, developing countries need to be drawn into its key management bodies so as better to protect their interests.

From Table 1 it becomes immediately clear that BRICS are anything but representative of developing countries with respect to population size, GDP, military power, etc. Of the five, only India has typical levels of poverty, illiteracy, low life expectancy and health. But what BRICS can do and have done is to reflect and represent the interests and priorities of most developing countries, and leverage their atypical attributes of market power and geopolitical clout to negotiate with the developed countries on many global challenges. Few non-BRICS developing countries can match BRICS in their market size and power, or legal, scientific, research and technology base. In other words, it is precisely the attributes that make them atypical – size of population, GDP, military power, diplomatic reach, intellectual infrastructure – that give them the capacity to represent the views, interests, and concerns of the typical developing countries in international forums like the UN.

BRICS can represent developing countries

The combination of the diversity within BRICS and the features that set them apart from other developing countries means that the viability, credibility, and relevance of BRICS will depend not simply on the growth trajectories of individual group members, but also on the extent to which, in global discourse and decisions, they can individually and collectively represent the worldviews, interests, and policy priorities of the mass of developing countries. Can BRICS use their newfound clout to secure greater democracy and justice for the world's poor, for example by exploiting the emergent new 'emancipatory multipolarity'?[17] On many global issues they share a common interest in securing a broad array of economic, political, and security interests relative to the dominant industrialised states. BRICS share concerns about the financial and geopolitical dominance of the US-led West. They were among the opponents of the strikes by the North Atlantic Treaty Organization (NATO) on Serbia and of the US-led invasion of Iraq in 2003. While South Africa initially voted for Security Council resolution 1973 on Libya in 2011, all five expressed unhappiness with NATO's exceeding the 1973 mandate.

Looking at various BRICS summit declarations, as well as statements from the five countries individually, their common position on a number of trouble spots can be distilled into four elements on which they are highly representative of the South:

- o BRICS support a rebalancing of the current global trade and financial system to reflect developing-country concerns and interests. They are at the forefront of demanding changes to both the institutions and the rules regulating the global economic order, including greater voice and vote in writing the rules and designing and controlling institutions.
- o BRICS are sceptical of the morality and efficacy of sanctions. They are generally opposed to the use of sanctions as a tool of international policy to enforce compliance on states flouting global norms, for example in Iran and Syria. They do so both on principle (sovereignty) and for reasons of

Table 1. BRICS in a comparative context

	Pop (mn) (rank)	Military personnel (mm)	Military exp $ bn	Military exp % of GDP	GDP $bn nominal (rank)	GDP p/capita, PPP (rank)	Avg % annual GDP growth 1990–2000	Avg % annual GDP growth 2000–2012	% share of export trade Merchandise (rank)	% share of export trade Com serv (rank)	% share of import trade Merchandise (rank)	% share of import trade Commercial services	% of pop < $1.25/day	HDI (rank)
Brazil	198.7 (5)	0.71	33.14	1.6	2252 (7)	11,716 (74)	2.7	3.7	1.3 (22)	0.9 (29)	1.3 (22)	1.9 (17)	6.1	0.73 (85)
Russia	143.5 (9)	1.36	166.1	3.9	2022 (8)	23,501 (43)	-4.7	4.8	2.9 (8)	1.3 (22)	1.8 (16)	2.5 (14)	0.0	0.79 (55)
India	1236.7 (2)	2.65	46.12	2.7	1841 (10)	3813 (127)	6.0	7.6	1.6 (19)	3.4 (6)	2.6 (10)	3.0 (7)	32.7	0.55 (136)
China	1350.7 (1)	2.94	90.75	2.1	8358 (2)	9083 (92)	10.6	10.6	11.2 (1)	4.4 (5)	9.8 (2)	6.8 (3)	11.8	0.70 (101)
South Africa	51.2 (25)	0.08	4.47	1.3	384 (28)	11,255 (77)	2.1	3.6					13.8	0.63 (121)
World	7046.4	28.02	1745	2.4	72,440	10,103	2.8	2.7	100	100	100	100		0.69
LDCS	846.5	3.93		1.7	504	1346	2.8	5.6						0.45
S Asia	1649.2	4.53	56.1	2.5	2286	3241	5.6	7.2					31.0	0.56
E Asia Pacific	1991.6	7.15	330.2	1.9	10,329	6616	8.5	9.2					12.5	0.68
SSA	910.4	1.86	22.7	1.5	1,289	2094	2.4	5.4					48.5	0.47
LAC	581.4	2.31	74.5	1.4	5,344	10,429	3.1	3.5					5.5	0.74

Sources: Population ranking from World Bank, http://wdi.worldbank.org/table/2.1; HDI ranking from UNDP, *Human Development Report*, http://hdr.undp.org/sites/default/files/reports/14/hdr2013_en_complete.pdf; GDP nominal ranking from World Bank, http://data.worldbank.org/data-catalog/GDP-ranking-table; and GDP per capita ranking from World Bank, http://data.worldbank.org/indicator/NY.GDP.PCAP.PP.CD.

pragmatism (ineffectiveness-cum-harm to innocent civilians).

o BRICS are far from homogeneous in their domestic political systems on democracy, human rights, and the rule of law. But they are surprisingly similar in their resistance to democracy promotion and human rights monitoring and enforcement by external state, intergovernmental, and nongovernmental actors.

o BRICS reject militarisation of disputes and conflicts,[18] promote political resolution through diplomatic talks, work to soften the West's interventionist impulse in the internal affairs of independent states (typically developing countries), and are strongly opposed to infringements of territorial integrity and sovereignty. In part they are motivated by historical memories of being invaded and colonised by the major European powers, and in part by fears of Western interference in their own internal affairs (Kashmir, Chechnya, Tibet, etc).

On these issues in general and over time BRICS' positions and votes (for example in UN bodies) are more closely aligned to one another than to those of the G7. When BRICS act collectively to oppose the G7's policies and deepen the latter's diplomatic discomfort on these issues, they are indeed often representative of the developing world's global policy preferences. But this is not always the case, with climate change (discussed below) being a prominent example where the interests of the major BRICS countries diverge from each other and from those of several developing countries. On some issues, including the Doha round of trade talks and climate change discussions, BRICS – either collectively or through their most powerful members – have disrupted and stalled international negotiations. On others they have worked effectively to dilute UN resolutions or agreed conference outcomes to produce suboptimal collective decisions, rendering multilateralism less effective.

BRICS, especially when united, can represent all developing countries in protecting many interests shared in common against the North. This is true, for example, with respect to environmental, labour, and human rights standards 'infecting' trade relations, which almost all developing countries view as disguised non-tariff barriers to protect uncompetitive Western agricultural and manufacturing sectors. On intellectual property, whether it be with respect to generic life-saving drugs, seeds for agriculture, or traditional medicine, BICS (BRICS minus Russia) can team up to take on the lobbying power of Big Pharma (eg Pfizer) and global agribusiness (eg Monsanto) to robustly protect the rights of poor people to affordable medicines, of poor farmers to affordable seeds, and of indigenous peoples to retaining ownership of their traditional knowledge. A typical developing country is much too vulnerable to sustained pressure from the rich and powerful countries acting to promote the interests of their commercial sectors. At the same time the private sector coalition of trade associations representing US copyright industries estimated losses from piracy and copyright theft to total nearly $10 billion in China and $3.3 billion in India in 2012.[19]

That BRICS can represent developing countries may be illustrated with four recent examples. First the grouping offers both China and Russia a forum for creating a buffer zone between themselves and the West and for drawing influential nonaligned countries into their orbit.[20] Thus, with respect to the extra-UN sanctions imposed on Iran by the West, the day before the fourth BRICS summit in New Delhi in March 2012, India's Commerce and Industry minister, Anand Sharma, noted pointedly that 'We respect UN resolutions', while China's trade minister insisted that Beijing was 'not obliged to follow any domestic laws and rules of any particular country'.[21] Second, Brazilian president Dilma Roussef cancelled her scheduled trip to the USA and a meeting with President Barack Obama in September 2013 in a very public protest over the US National Security Agency's surveillance of Brazilian targets, including the president herself. Third, in January 2014 India got caught in a very public row over a diplomat in its New York consulate who was arrested, handcuffed, and strip-searched over alleged visa and minimum wages fraud.[22] Because 'Few governments in the world have the geopolitical heft' that India has, says Kishore Mahbubani, 'virtually every other government in the world was quietly cheering on the Indian government as it insisted on total reciprocity in the treatment of Indian and American officials'.[23] Fourth, in February the Indian government directed its officials not to meet a visiting delegation from the US International Trade Commission, a quasi-judicial body investigating the impact of India's patents, trade, and investment regulations on the US economy. New Delhi took the view that such policies are governed by multilateral agreements and the proper dispute resolution forum is the World Trade Organization (WTO), not an extra-territorial application of US laws.[24]

BRICS are all active participants in and significant beneficiaries – if to varying degrees – of the major post-1945 rules-based liberal global economic and political order, from the UN to the World Bank, IMF, and WTO. This situation runs counter to the historical trend: 'Few rising powers in history have been as fully invested in the institutions of global politics and economics' as China and India, note George Gilboy and Eric Heginbotham.[25] The global rebalancing underway embraces military, geopolitical, economic, and even moral adjustments to the shifts in power, wealth, influence, and ideas of good governance and civic virtue. Westerners have lost their previous capacity to set standards and rules of behaviour for the whole world. As Mahbubani argues, the minority West must find some accommodation with the 88% majority rest based on common principles and the equal moral worth of all human beings.[26] The rest of the world is increasingly converging in average income with the West on the backs of a burgeoning middle class that takes its major lifestyle cues from the Western middle class, producing a parallel convergence in values and aspirations. This accelerating convergence heightens the urgency of the need to redress global governance deficits: the principles of democracy, power sharing, equity, and accountability, as well as geopolitical realignments. But the West is proving singularly reluctant and obdurate in exporting democratic structures and procedures to international governance institutions, in ceding power in order to share it, in assuming equitable costs of managing the global commons, and in general in supporting a universal rules-based order in which one law applies to all. One illustration of this is in the cosy arrangement by which Europe and the USA have monopolised the leadership of the IMF and World Bank, respectively. The chutzpah with which the current leaders of these two institutions were chosen was breathtaking.[27]

Western powers, 'concerned about the decline of their influence and the norms and values that are espoused by them in global diplomacy', are motivated primarily to ensure that Beijing will 'abide by the rules set by the US and Europe after World War II'.[28] BRICS resent calls for 'responsible' stakeholder policies as efforts to subjugate their worldviews to the global North's priorities and have begun instead to challenge the West's stranglehold on control of many of these institutions and to trim its capacity to pursue its interests and agendas. While all five have an interest in a relatively open international trading system, they 'seek to adjust the way global wealth is generated and shared',[29] and all have a significant stake in placing greater limits on the international exercise of US national power.

Climate change

For poor countries, development, poverty reduction, and climate change require inseparable policy settings. With the exception of South Africa, the other countries in the grouping have massive populations and land areas and are rising economic powers. Their development imperatives cut across the need to reduce emission targets in order to limit the potential damage from climate change. The negative impacts of global warming will be felt most acutely by small and poor developing countries, in particular island states like those in the Caribbean and the South Pacific. The two groups also have variable domestic capacity to understand the science of climate change, to adapt and mitigate, and to develop the policies best suited to their individual circumstances. Their interests are thus fundamentally misaligned, and it is hard to see how BRICS can represent the smaller developing countries and island states in any meaningful sense of the term on what is generally acknowledged to be one of the gravest and most pressing policy challenges of our time. This became clear at the disastrous Copenhagen climate change conference in December 2009 and was reaffirmed in the follow-up Durban conference in November 2011.[30]

Trade, finance, and aid

BRICS' biggest common interest is in global economic governance. There are multiple disconnects – for instance between the highly indebted but politically dominant industrialised economies and between the distribution of decision-making authority in existing international financial institutions and the realignment of economic power equations in the real world. To put it another way, in the emerging new global balance of power the old global political imbalances need to be readjusted to the new global economic imbalances. BRICS have been calling for increased voice and vote on issues of global finance. The 2011 summit in Sanya, China, was followed by a stronger insistence in New Delhi in 2012 on the need to reform international financial governance structures.[31] Yet, even with the reforms of 2008 and 2010, the advanced economies retain a 55.3% voting share in the IMF, with countries of the EU by themselves accounting for 29.4%.[32] The primary beneficiaries of increased IMF voting shares for developing countries were China and India.

After the Asian financial crisis of 1997–98, and as China's economy began its dramatic climb, Beijing started to invest a growing amount of diplomatic resources in building alternative institutional options to the Bretton Woods rules. These included strengthening regional development banks across the global South.[33] Since the 2008 global financial crisis, Beijing has given new emphasis to re-engaging the Bretton Woods institutions. Amid the global financial crisis low-income countries learned that the new powers were not yet able or willing to supplant these existing global institutions and take on global crisis management responsibilities, especially global lender-of-last-resort functions. The rising states did, however, provide support by pushing for more responsive, flexible, and rapid financing for low-income countries to help them ward off the contagion effects of the crisis and shore up their national developmental objectives. They also called for reform of the international monetary system, consideration of diversifying beyond the dollar as the de facto global currency, and gradual steps in expanding the role of the IMF's Special Drawing Rights as a supplemental global reserve asset option.

Developing countries have also noted that Europe was treated much differently during the Eurozone crisis from the harsh medicine meted out to Asia, Latin America, and Eastern Europe in earlier crises. As a Bloomberg columnist notes, G7 officials have failed to walk the talk since 2008 on rebalancing the global economy, giving developing countries more say in collective decision making, lowering trade and capital barriers, letting markets set currency rates, and increasing transparency. BRICS's move to set up their own development bank is explained as a reaction to the West's doublespeak.[34] At the 2013 Durban summit South Africa's finance minister, Pravin Gordhan, remarked that the 'roots of the World Bank and the IMF still lie' in the post-1945 equations.[35] BRICS agreed in principle to create a development bank to finance infrastructure projects worth $4.5 trillion. However, the five have yet to agree on the amount of seed money to start the bank and on its location. Because China's economy is bigger than the other four combined, there will be pressure not to locate the new bank in China, so as to assuage concerns about Beijing's dominance. South Africa has put in a strong bid based on physical and financial infrastructure strengths, including corporate governance, auditing, and accounting.[36]

Fahimul Quadir has shown how South–South cooperation breaks from the West-dominated paradigm of development assistance. BRICS have broken from aid conditionality, whether it be with respect to Brazil's technical cooperation, India's horizontal partnerships or China's silence on policy reforms and structural adjustments. Although there is no uniform approach by BRICS donors, all accept a definition of development and the agenda and priorities set by the recipients themselves.[37] In addition, developing countries, and in particular sub-Saharan African countries, have benefited from the ending of the West's monopoly on power, knowledge, and benevolence.[38]

Human rights and the responsibility to protect

There is little basis for expecting China to assume a leadership role in the promotion and defence of human rights in the foreseeable future. Yet evidence-based research can puncture some intuitive beliefs. In one study China was found to engage in arms transfers to democracies more than to autocracies, with the USA being the opposite. The same was true when the human rights records of recipients were examined. And China's arms transfers to countries experiencing civil wars were much lower than US transfers.[39] Even the democratic rising powers – Brazil, South Africa and, especially, India, with its more than six decades of constitutional democratic governance – do not demonstrate a high priority for hard or soft human rights promotion as an integral element of their foreign policy. 'India has integrated both democracy promotion and human rights into its foreign policy, but carefully chooses form, forum and messages on these topics'.[40]

The majority of armed conflicts involve challenges to national integration (calls to self-determination by sub-groups within existing territorial borders) or to the government's authority (wars over government without attempted secession). That is, they are ethno-national conflicts over national territorial borders or internal political arrangements in countries that have recently emerged from colonial rule. Most Western leaders are incapable of comprehending the framework within which their developing country counterparts must cope with such challenges; most developing country leaders can empathise with one another on this point. The May 2009 climax of the Sri Lankan civil war, when the government mercilessly crushed the ruthless Tamil Tigers, raised troubling questions about the limits to the authority of the legitimate government to use force when confronted with armed challenge. The debate in the Human Rights Council in Geneva showed that most developing countries, to the shock of Westerners, back a government's right to suppress armed insurgencies and terrorist groups with military force.[41]

The debate over R2P is not really a North–South issue. Although BRICS have all been extremely cautious about the new norm, their caution is not representative of either the need or the policy preferences of most developing countries. Many non-Western societies have a historical tradition of reciprocal rights and obligations that bind sovereigns and subjects. As argued by Mohamed Sahnoun, in many ways R2P is a distinctly African contribution to global human rights.[42] R2P helps to shift the balance towards interventions – an enduring fact of international life long before R2P – that are rule-based, multilateral, and consensual, without guaranteeing good outcomes. Such an equation is very much in the interests of developing countries. The key questions are shared understandings and expectations about the circumstances in which the use of international force across sovereign borders is both legal and legitimate, and the authorising and implementing agency. Because of their mediating role between developing countries and the global North, the emerging powers – more than any other group of states – will, through global governance mechanisms and international accountability instruments, have to ensure that: vulnerable groups are protected from predations by brutish rulers domestically; weak countries are protected from the predations of regional or global major powers; and violators of both sets of norms on the use of force are made to answer for their transgressions.[43]

In Libya all BRICS objected strongly to the shift from the politically neutral posture of civilian protection to the partial goal of assisting the rebels and pursuing regime change. On Syria China and Russia remain resolutely opposed to any resolution that could set in train a sequence of events leading to Resolution 1973-type authorisation for outside military operations; they emphasise an inclusive, Syrian-led political resolution. India and South Africa have vacillated between opposition and support for the various draft resolutions, feeling uncomfortable about the use of violence by rebels and the regime.

Brazil offered a paper on 'Responsibility while Protecting' with the potential to bring in some agreed parameters on the conditions that will govern the use of UN-authorised R2P operations. Contrary to common belief, China too has been trying for the past dozen years to engage with the R2P principle. In 2012 Ruan Zonge, vice president of the foreign ministry-affiliated China Institute of International Studies, wrote on 'responsible protection', which will help China build 'a just and reasonable new international political order'.[44] The surprising omission from the list of major emerging powers trying to improve the implementation of R2P without questioning its underlying value is India, which has the longest democratic pedigree in the group. As with the Brazilian and Chinese examples, critics should engage with R2P actively; if they remain more concerned with consolidating their national power aspirations than developing global norms and institutions,[45] they will remain incomplete powers, limited by their own narrow ambitions, with their material grasp being longer than their normative reach.

Economic development

Can some among BRICS represent the future to which other developing countries may aspire with respect to the paths to and destination of development? Lacking the size of these big emerging markets, others may never acquire matching geopolitical weight. But success in development goals will greatly increase the quality of life of their peoples and immeasurably enhance their self-esteem and international reputation. Developing countries found it convenient to place the primary blame for their underdevelopment on colonialism, and looked therefore to technical assistance, financial transfers, and concessional terms of trade from the West as the panacea for their economic ills. Rich nations and the international financial institutions they control have provided contradictory advice to poor states, despite the fact that no significant economy has ever developed successfully via free trade and deregulation from the beginning. Yet the most successful region on virtually all development indicators has turned out to be Northeast Asia (Japan, Taiwan, and South Korea), which followed outward-looking policies in which the state drove and the market followed. Their state-led industrialisation first targeted internal land reforms and then protected (in the domestic market) and subsidised (to offset competitive disadvantages in overseas markets) export-oriented manufacturing firms.[46]

China, India, and Brazil see themselves as developing countries still making the transition to major global players. They perceive their national interests as tied to exporting a variation of 'the developmental state' as a new model. Their views on how to encourage stable and sustained national growth, while recalibrating the balance between citizens, states, and markets have gained traction of late. All three offer some development lessons for others as strong proponents of purposive state intervention to guide market development and national corporate growth, rather than relying solely on market-led growth. They have promoted the principles of increased state intervention for market regulation, greater balance between the real economy and the virtual economy, and between reliance on the national versus international markets.

Brazil and India were among the leading countries to practise import-substitution industrialisation. China's continuing rise and the more recent successes of

Brazil and India, combined with a global financial crisis that began in the USA, have revived interest in the notion of a developmental state with differing needs, strategies, and growth trajectories from those of the so-called 'Anglo-American' model. With the statist model the goals of strengthening state capacity, promoting social cohesion, maintaining territorial integrity and political independence, resisting encroachments on national sovereignty, achieving economic growth to bankroll material progress, and advancing the indicators of human development (eg GDP per capita, maternal and infant mortality, life expectancy, literacy) receive top priority over human rights, democracy, and unregulated markets.

Some developing countries were tempted by the recipe for faster growth and greater stability of the 'Beijing Consensus' comprising a one-party state, government-guided development, strictly controlled capital markets and an authoritarian decision-making process that can think strategically for the long term, make tough choices and long-term investments, and not be distracted by daily public polls. Yet the idea of 'a' China model is questionable, with the country being too diverse in terms of regional and related cultural differences to amount to a single coherent model. Nor can other countries adopt a Chinese economic model, with its unique path dependence, without also establishing a communist party or similar political system.[47]

China also offers a salutary counter-narrative to the liberal peace paradigm, favoured by the UN and the World Bank, whose track record in building stable, peaceful, and prosperous democratic orders in societies coming out of conflict is patchy.[48] A government that had won power by military means after more than a century of foreign humiliations, attacks, invasions, and a bitter civil war – in other words, a post-conflict country par excellence – has demonstrated peace-building skills and success on a scale that is both unrivalled and unimaginable. In the three decades from 1980 to 2010, 80% of the world's total poverty alleviation took place in China, a one-party state ruled by a communist party. It provided authoritarian but stable and orderly government. Yet there are few references in the literature to and theorisation about a China model of peace building. In 2013 Eric Lee, a Shanghai entrepreneur, observed that the three dominant assumptions of the liberal democratic governance paradigm are that one-party states are politically closed, operationally rigid, and illegitimate. Instead, he argues, China's one-party system has proven, over six decades, the political virtues of meritocracy, adaptability, and legitimacy. There is debate about levels of support, but he argues that the people are generally optimistic about the country's future and that the government and regime, unlike those in most contemporary Western democracies, enjoy impressive levels of popular support.[49]

Conclusion

BRICS are far from being united in interests and policy preferences. Rather, the argument is that, on those issues where there is a shared view among them (financial norms, trade rules, non-interference in internal affairs, etc), they can exert more significant leverage together than separately. They can help to shape a new, post-2015 global development agenda of poverty alleviation, sustainable development, and inclusive growth. They can also give voice to developing country interests and concerns on new rules for health care, pharmaceuticals, intellectual property rights, etc. They can share and learn from one another's more relevant development experience, from China's successes in reducing poverty and developing infrastructure to Brazil's in clean fuel generation. And they can act as a counterweight to the West's excesses in the UN, WTO, World Bank, and the IMF.

BRICS profess a shared vision of inclusive global growth and the rapid socio-economic transformation of their own nations in which no village is left behind. They come to the global governance table with a mutually reinforcing sense of historical grievances and claims to represent the interests of all developing countries.[50] They share a neo-Westphalian commitment to state sovereignty and non-intervention. Their resource endowments show many complementarities. They proclaim the need for a rules-based, stable, and predictable world order that respects the diversity of political systems and stages of development. As one scholar put it:

> One of the *advantages* of the BRICS process is that it remains a loose association of states with somewhat disparate interests, so no effort is made to force a common position when the BRICS states cannot agree on one. But these states have also found a way to disagree on some key issues…without torpedoing the entire enterprise.[51]

The challenge for BRICS is in working from economic reality to a tighter sense of normative and ideational identity among its members. It is tempting to dismiss BRICS as 'more a way station than a summit',[52] because of the lack of commonality, existing tensions and squabbles, and potential serious conflicts that divide more than unite them. Yet the grouping has tried to put pressure on the West to facilitate and accommodate rather than block the rise of the emerging economies.[53]

Is 'BRICS' a construct of the social media-driven marketplace of ideas – an attention grabbing glib phrase in which speed is a substitute for and trumps quality and depth of analysis? It may also be the case that the deceleration in the countries of the grouping's growth rates reflects the fact that the advantages of cheap labour – especially surplus labour from the countryside – and imported technology are levelling off as they exhaust the rapid, investment-intensive, catch-up model of growth. A particularly good reality check is offered by Ruchir Sharma, Morgan Stanley's head of emerging markets, who emphasises the exceptional features of the past decade, during which BRICS grew so fast in unison. The decade itself was exceptional in the wide scope and fast pace of global growth. BRICS began from a low base and so their growth story was exaggerated.[54] Sharma notes that, typically, high growth rates are sustained only for a decade. In any one decade about one-third of developing economies manage to grow at 5% or higher, fewer than one-quarter manage it for two decades, and only one-tenth can sustain it for four decades. The momentum stalls for most once they reach middle-income status. As the global economy returns 'to its normal state of churn'[55] – with moderate growth in the developing world, a return of the boom-bust cycle, and an end to the herd behaviour of emerging market countries – the per capita income gap between the developed and developing economies could again begin to widen just as it did from 1950 to 2000.

All countries will be buffeted by unanticipated and new political environments, competitors, and technologies.

Similar stances on a few contentious international issues are not enough to offset the crisis of identity caused by differing and sometimes clashing national priorities. Can BRICS morph from a countervailing economic grouping to a powerful political alternative? Their record of collective action thus far leads to three conclusions. First, they have been increasingly successful at 'norm spoiler-ship', defeating proposals they dislike and blocking previously dominant US ability to form winning coalitions to achieve its preferred outcomes in multilateral forums. But, second, they have shown less inclination and capacity to engage in norm entrepreneurship, forming successful winning coalitions to achieve their own preferred outcomes, for example with respect to the choice of World Bank and IMF chief executives. In consequence, third, they have become more interested in joining the struggle to rewrite the rules of many multilateral institutions to embed their developing country-cum-emerging power interests and policy preferences.

Notes

1. Thakur, *Towards a Less Imperfect State.*
2. UNDP, *Human Development Report 2013*, 11.
3. Ibid., 12–13.
4. O'Neill, *The World needs Better Economic BRICs*; and Wilson and Purushothaman, *Dreaming with BRICs.*
5. Cooper and Thakur, *The Group of Twenty (G20).*
6. Cooper and Thakur, "The BRICS."
7. Gillespie, "BRICS Highlight Skewed Nature."
8. Al Doyaili et al., "IBSA."
9. Pearson and Leahy, "Cheap Asia Imports."
10. Pant, "The BRICS Fallacy," 99.
11. "Sanusi: China is Major Contributor."
12. Dubash, "Of Maps and Compasses," 272.
13. Ibid., 275.
14. Grant, *Russia, China and Global Governance.*
15. Bremmer, *Every Nation for Itself*, 10.
16. Landsberg and Moore, "BRICS."
17. Gray and Murphy, "Introduction."
18. This might seem an odd statement after the Ukraine crisis. The contradiction is more apparent than real. None among BRICS is pacifist; all have powerful military forces that they are prepared to use for self-defence and other core security interests. BRICS regard Crimea as falling within Russia's core security zone, as did Cuba 'for the US' in 1962; therefore the situation is qualitatively distinct from using force away from one's own borders in others' quarrels, as the West did in Kosovo, Iraq, and Libya. See Thakur, "Geopolitics through the Ukrainian Looking Glass."
19. Gilboy and Heginbotham, "Double Trouble," 131.
20. Mandel and Lin, "NATO's New Neighbors"; and Weitz, "Russia's Asia Play Mustn't be Ignored."
21. "China leads, BRICS backs Iran."
22. Thakur, "Rogue States Behaving Badly."

23. Mahbubani, "Two Shades of Immunity."
24. Sidhartha, "India hardens Trade Stance against US"; and Kumar, and Rajesh Kumar Singh, "New Delhi vs Washington: India hardens stance against US protectionism."
25. Gilboy and Heginbotham, "Double Trouble," 128.
26. Mahbubani, *The Great Convergence.*
27. Thakur, "Wealth and Power trump Good Governance."
28. Desker, "Can Europe Prevent Asia's Rise?"
29. Gilboy and Heginbotham, "Double Trouble," 136.
30. Dubash, "Of Maps and Compasses," 268.
31. "BRICS Summit – Delhi Declaration." Ministry of External Relations, Government of India, New Delhi, 29 March 2012.
32. http://www.imf.org/external/np/sec/pr/2010/pdfs/pr10418_table.pdf.
33. Chin and Stubbs, "China, Regional Institution-building."
34. Pesek, "The BRICS expose the West's hypocrisy."
35. Quoted by Smith, "BRICS eye Infrastructure."
36. Since this article was written, at the July 2014 summit in Brazil, all these questions were answered. The New Development Bank will be headquartered in Shanghai and the inaugural president will be Indian. The bank is to be capitalized initially at $50 billion (and subsequently at double that amount), with each country contributing $10 billion. See Thakur, 'Not Just Another Brick in the Geopolitical Wall'.
37. Quadir, "Rising Donors." See also Sidiropoulos et al., *Development Cooperation.*
38. Carmody, *The Rise of the BRICS*; and Brautigam, *The Dragon's Gift.*
39. de Soysa and Midford, "Enter the Dragon!"
40. Malone, "Soft Power in Indian Foreign Policy," 39.
41. Philp, "Sri Lanka forces West to Retreat."
42. Sahnoun, "Africa." For another African perspective supportive of R2P, see Atuobi, *The Responsibility to Protect.*
43. Thakur, "R2P after Libya and Syria."
44. Zongze, "Responsible Protection."
45. Acharya, "Can Asia Lead?"
46. Studwell, *How Asia Works.*
47. Chin, *China's Automotive Modernization*, 22–47.
48. Paris, *At War's End.*
49. Lee, "A Tale of Two Political Systems."
50. The claims to developing-country representation are widely contested within their own respective regions; see Vieira and Alden, "India, Brazil and South Africa."
51. Gvosdev, "The Realist Prism" (emphasis added).
52. Baru, "BRICS in Search of Cement."
53. Amsden, *The Rise of 'The Rest'.*
54. Sharma, "Broken BRICS." See also van Agtmael, "Think Again."
55. Sharma, "Broken BRICS," 3.

Bibliography

Al Doyaili, Sarah, Andreas Freytag, and Peter Draper. "IBSA: Fading out or Forging a Common Vision?" *South African Journal of International Affairs* 20, no. 2 (2013): 297–310.

Acharya, Amitav. "Can Asia Lead? Power Ambitions and Global Governance in the Twenty-first Century." *International Affairs* 87, no. 4 (2011): 851–869.

Amsden, Alice. *The Rise of 'The Rest': Challenges to the West from Late-Industrializing Economies.* New York: Oxford University Press, 2003.

Atuobi, Samuel. *The Responsibility to Protect: The Time to act is Now.* KAIPTC Policy Brief 1. Accra: Kofi Annan International Peacekeeping Training Centre, July 2009.

Baru, Sanjaya. 2011. "BRICS in Search of Cement." *Business Standard* (Delhi), April 18.

Brautigam, Deborah. *The Dragon's Gift: The Real Story of China in Africa.* Oxford: Oxford University Press, 2009.

Bremmer, Ian. *Every Nation for Itself: Winners and Losers in a G-zero World.* New York: Penguin, 2012.

Carmody, Pádraig. *The Rise of the BRICS in Africa: The Geopolitics of South-South Relations.* London: Zed, 2013.

Chin, Gregory. *China's Automotive Modernization: The Party-state and Multinational Corporations.* Basingtoke, UK: Palgrave Macmillan, 2010.

Chin, Gregory, and Richard Stubbs. "China, Regional Institution-building and the China–ASEAN Free Trade Area." *Review of International Political Economy* 18, no. 3 (2011): 277–298.

"China leads, BRICS backs Iran." 2012. *Times of India*, March 29.

Cooper, Andrew F., and Ramesh Thakur. "The BRICS in the New Global Economic Geography." In *International Organization and Global Governance*, edited by Thomas G. Weiss and Rorden Wilkinson, 265–278. London: Routledge, 2014.

Cooper, Andrew F., and Ramesh Thakur. *The Group of Twenty (G20)*. London: Routledge, 2013.

de Soysa, Indra, and Paul Midford. "Enter the Dragon! An Empirical Analysis of Chinese versus US Arms Transfers to Autocrats and Violators of Human Rights, 1989–2006." *International Studies Quarterly* 56, no. 4 (2012): 843–856.

Desker, Barry. "Can Europe prevent Asia's Rise?" *PacNet Newsletter*, no. 65, October 23, 2012. http://csis.org/publication/pacnet-65-can-europe-prevent-asias-rise.

Dubash, Navroz K. "Of Maps and Compasses: India in Multilateral Climate Negotiations." In *Shaping the Emerging World: India and the Multilateral Order*, edited by Waheguru Pal Singh Sidhu, Pratap Bhanu Mehta, and Bruce Jones. Washington, DC: Brookings Institution Press, 2013.

Gilboy, George G., and Eric Heginbotham. "Double Trouble: A Realist View of Chinese and Indian Power." *Washington Quarterly* 36, no. 3 (2013): 125–142.

Gillespie, Paul. 2012. "BRICS highlight Skewed Nature of Global Power." *Irish Times*, March 31.

Grant, Charles. *Russia, China and Global Governance*. London: Centre for European Reform, 2012.

Gray, Kevin, and Craig N. Murphy. "Introduction." In *Rising Powers and the Future of Global Governance*, edited by Kevin Gray and Craig N. Murphy. London: Routledge, 2013.

Gvosdev, Nikolas. 2012. "The Realist Prism: What the US can learn from the BRICS." *World Politics Review*, June 22.

Landsberg, Chris, and Candice Moore. "BRICS, South–South Cooperation and the Durban Summit: What's in it for South Africa?" *Portuguese Journal of International Affairs* 7 (Spring/Summer 2013): 3–14.

Lee, Eric X. 2013. "A Tale of Two Political Systems." *Shanghai*, July 3. https://www.youtube.com/watch?v=ebXA1lRqDfM.

Malone, David M. 2011. "Soft Power in Indian Foreign Policy." *Economic and Political Weekly*, September 3.

Mandel, Seth, and Christina Lin. 2012. "NATO's New Neighbors." *National Review Online*, May 17. http://www.nationalreview.com/blogs/print/299791.

Mahbubani, Kishore. *The Great Convergence: Asia, the West, and the Logic of One World*. New York: Public Affairs, 2013.

Mahbubani, Kishore. 2014. "Two Shades of Immunity." *Indian Express*, January 12.

O'Neill, Jim. *The World needs Better Economic BRICS*. Global Economics Paper 66. New York: Goldman Sachs, October 2001.

Pant, Harsh V. "The BRICS Fallacy." *Washington Quarterly* 36, no. 3 (2013): 91–105.

Paris, Roland. *At War's End: Building Peace after Civil Conflict*. Cambridge: Cambridge University Press, 2004.

Pearson, Samantha, and Joe Leahy. 2011. "Cheap Asia Imports hit Brazil's Industries." *Financial Times*, April 20.

Pesek, William. 2013. "The BRICS expose the West's hypocrisy." Bloomberg, March 28. http://www.bloombergview.com/articles/2013-03-28/the-brics-expose-the-west-s-hypocrisy.

Philp, Catherine. 2009. "Sri Lanka Forces West to Retreat over 'War Crimes' with Victory at UN." *The Times*, May 28. https://www.timesonline.co.uk/tol/news/world/us_and_americas/article6375044.ece?.

Quadir, Fahimul. "Rising Donors and the New Narrative of 'South–South Cooperation'." In *Rising Powers and the Future of Global Governance*, edited by Kevin Gray and Craig N. Murphy, 139–157. London: Routledge, 2013.

Sahnoun, Mohamed. 2009. "Africa: Uphold Continent's Contribution to Human Rights, urges Top Diplomat." allAfrica.com, July 21. http://allafrica.com/stories/printable/200907210549.html.

"Sanusi: China is Major Contributor to Africa's De-industrialisation." 2013. *This Day*, March 13. http://www.thisdaylive.com/articles/sanusi-china-is-major-contributor-to-africa-s-de-industrialisation/142029/.

Sharma, Ruchir. "Broken BRICS: Why the Rest Stopped Rising." *Foreign Affairs* 91, no. 6 (2012): 2–7.

Sidhartha [sic]. 2014. "India hardens Trade Stance against US, wants Disputes to go to WTO." *Times of India*, February 22.

Sidiropoulos, Elizabeth, Thomas Fues, and Sachin Chaturvedi, eds. *Development Cooperation and Emerging Powers: New Partners or Old Patterns?* London: Zed Books, 2012.

Smith, David. 2013. "BRICS eye Infrastructure Funding through New Development Bank." *Guardian*, March 28.

Studwell, Joe. *How Asia Works: Success and Failure in the World's most Dynamic Region*. New York: Grove Press, 2013.

Thakur, Ramesh. "Not Just another Brick in the Geopolitical Wall." *Tehelka Magazine* 11, no. 31 (2014): 36–40.

Thakur, Ramesh. "Geopolitics through the Ukrainian Looking Glass." *Tehelka Magazine* 11, no. 19 (2014): 38–41.

Thakur, Ramesh. "R2P after Libya and Syria: Engaging Emerging Powers." *Washington Quarterly* 36, no. 2 (2013): 61–76.

Thakur, Ramesh. "Rogue States Behaving Badly." *The Diplomatist* (January 2014): 39–42.

Thakur, Ramesh. *Towards a Less Imperfect State of the World: The Gulf between North and South.* Dialogue on Globalization Briefing Paper 4. Berlin: Friedrich Ebert Stiftung, April 2008.

Thakur Ramesh. 2012. "Wealth and Power trump Good Governance." *The Australian*, April 18.

UNDP. *Human Development Report, The Rise of the South – Human Progress in a Diverse World*, 2013. New York: Oxford University Press, 2013.

van Agtmael, Antoine. "Think Again: The BRICS." *Foreign Policy*, November 2012. http://www.foreignpolicy.com/articles/2012/10/08/think_again_the_brics.

Vieira, Marco Antonio, and Chris Alden. "India, Brazil and South Africa (IBSA): South–South Cooperation and the Paradox of Regional Leadership." *Global Governance* 17, no. 4 (2011): 507–528.

Weitz, Richard. 2012. "Russia's Asia Play Mustn't be Ignored." *The Diplomat*, May 17. http://the-diplomat.tumblr.com/post/23238257235/russias-asia-play-mustnt-be-ignored.

Wilson, Dominic, and Roopa Purushothaman, *Dreaming with BRICS: the Path to 2050*. Global Economics Paper 99. New York: Goldman Sachs, October 2003. www.gs.com/insight/research/reports/99.pdf.

Zongze, Ruan. "Responsible Protection: Building a Safer World." *China International Studies* (May–June 2012): 19–41.

The Economist. "Seeking Protection," January 14, 2012.

Kumar, Manoj, and Rajesh Kumar Singh. "New Delhi vs Washington: India hardens stance against US protectionism," *Times of India*, March 4, 2014.

Financing the UN development system and the future of multilateralism

Bruce Jenks

School of Public and International Affairs, Columbia University, New York, USA

This article seeks to accomplish four tasks. It explores the historical relationship between the financing instruments that dominated different phases of the evolution of the UN development system and the understanding of the concept of multilateralism. Bearing in mind this historical context, it seeks to analyse the defining characteristics of multilateral finance in the context of the UN, in particular the characteristics that make a financial instrument more or less multilateral. It then explores a number of new financial instruments and their possible impact on the future shape multilateralism takes in the UN system. The article concludes with some thoughts on financing for a new multilateralism. In order to go beyond the core/non-core stalemate, it is necessary to develop a new variable geometry based on function, which brings into play assessed, negotiated pledges, voluntary core and non-core instruments.

This article seeks to accomplish four tasks after providing a quick snapshot of the overall United Nations development system (UNDS). The first is to explore the historical relationship between the financing instruments that dominated different phases of the UNDS and our understanding of the concept of multilateralism. The second task is to analyse the defining characteristics of multilateral finance in the UN context. What makes a financial instrument more or less multilateral? The third is to examine a number of new financial instruments and their possible impact on the future shape of multilateralism in the UNDS. There follow some concluding thoughts on financing for a new multilateralism.

An overview

In 2011 overall contributions to the entire UN system amounted to just under $40 billion. Some $2.5 billion is provided for the UN's regular budget, another $8 billion for peacekeeping and $6.5 billion for normative and standard-setting activities. That leaves $23 billion for operational activities. The breakdown of operational activities is presented in Table 1. The definition of operational activities includes both development and humanitarian but excludes peacekeeping and normative activities.

For this article it is important to distinguish between four types of financing. 'Assessed budgets' refer to arrangements whereby countries are assessed a fixed amount calculated by means of an agreed formula that represents the cost of membership. 'Negotiated pledges' refer to an agreement that is legally binding on the member states that have assented to the particular scale in question. The only case in the UN system (excluding the World Bank and its International Development Authority, [IDA]) is the International Fund for Agricultural Development (IFAD). 'Voluntary/regular resources' refers to strictly voluntary contributions that are non-earmarked; these are sometimes referred to also as 'core resources'. Finally 'voluntary/earmarked resources', also referred to sometimes as 'non-core resources', refers to voluntary contributions that are earmarked, either to a theme or to a country or region.

The evolution of the UNDS, its financial architecture and the concept of multilateralism

Four periods are helpful markers within the history of financing for the UN's development system. The four phases are: the origins; the move away from communities of interest; service for member states; and the goal-setting era.

Phase 1: origins

The UN system was designed around the concept of communities of practice that would create the building blocks to peace through their pursuit of common goals and interests.[1] The International Labour Organization (ILO) had already been established in 1919 as a forum for issues related to labour and social justice. The Food and Agriculture Organization (FAO), the UN Educational, Scientific and Cultural Organization (UNESCO), the World Health Organization (WHO), and a succession of other agencies were all created to allow communities of practice to build networks. Each of these agencies has its own governance structure that is accountable for its activities. The Economic and Social Council (ECOSOC), one of the UN's six principal organs, was given loosely defined coordination functions; in practice, however, autonomous organisations work within the overall framework of a common system. The UN secretary-general has no ultimate authority over these agencies.

At the heart of this design is the idea that each organisation is supported by its own constituency. These constituencies may align more with the international communities of practice embedded in each organisation than with the foreign ministries of their own countries. This was precisely the intention of the functionalist founders of the system.[2] Functionalist thinking was deeply suspicious of the tension between a policy process vested in foreign ministries and building global communities of interest.

The mission and values of the system being constituted revolved around the application of expertise and skills in different areas of work. The wartime and immediate postwar periods witnessed numerous expert meetings and a plethora of expert reports. Their roles were to transfer skills and fill gaps. Universal principles were advocated and shared.

Each of the agencies established was financed through assessed budgets. As the cost of membership, countries were required to invest in organisations whose purpose was to build communities of interest that would create the building blocks for peace and help bind countries together. Purpose and financial instrument came together in support of a multilateral vision.

In 1949 the Expanded Program for Technical Assistance (EPTA) was launched and envisaged as an effort that would provide support through the established communities of practice. At the outset financing for the EPTA represented a very small percentage of the total. Nonetheless, the principles underlying the overall vision were applied to the EPTA – hence the financing available for it was distributed on the basis of percentage shares to the different specialised agencies.

Phase 2: the transition from communities of interest

The convergence of the Cold War with the emerging needs of developing countries arising from decolonisation led to a new sense of purpose and a new financial instrument. The Cold War's division of the world into two camps also redefined the rationale for technical assistance. Affiliation with one side and not development performance was the criterion for financial support. With the acceleration of decolonisation the international development agenda became focused on the fundamental process of national development. International organisations were to play the role of facilitating the transfer of resources from one state to another. There was a deep sense that the newly independent countries were entitled to such transfers. Throughout the UN system a shift took place from supporting communities of practice to one of service to member states.

Hence Inis Claude contended that the UN's function had actually become to support the 'capacity of states to stay in business'.[3] The core vision for the mission of the UN development system had been turned upside down: from drawing on communities of practice to bring states closely together to building the capacity of individual states to develop and exercise their prerogatives as states.

The 1966 establishment of the United Nations Development Programme (UNDP), and in particular the 1970 approval in General Assembly resolution 2688 (XXV) of the so-called indicative planning framework (IPF) system for the allocation of the UNDP's resources, marked the highpoint for the transformation of the system from functionalist to country-based principles.[4] With the introduction of the IPF framework, the allocation of development assistance moved for the first time from an agency-based system to a country-based system. Whereas previously each agency had been allocated a fixed share of total resources, countries themselves were allocated resources based on a number of objectively defined criteria. The system had moved from 'agency entitlement' to 'country entitlement'.

Table 1. Contributions for operational activities for development, by entity and type of funding (core and non-core), 2005-2011.

Entity	2005 Core	2005 Non-core	2006 Core	2006 Non-core	2007 Core	2007 Non-core	2008 Core	2008 Non-core	2009 Core	2009 Non-core	2010 Core	2010 Non-core	2011 Core	2011 Non-core
UNDP a/	955	3 341	941	3 836	1 182	3 649	1 171	3 816	1 104	3 878	1 037	4 289	974	4 040
UN-Women	..	..	..	..	..	..	..	..	..	..	..	..	124	101
UNFPA	364	141	362	156	420	241	433	336	472	259	498	340	449	445
UNICEF	796	1 946	1 043	1 710	1 090	1 889	1 067	2 273	1 055	2 178	965	2 685	1 078	2 604
WFP	294	2 646	242	2 455	257	2 452	888	4 144	321	3 779	352	3 520	445	3 172
UNHCR	258	876	246	862	262	1 003	308	1 324	288	1 468	307	1 550	445	1 627
IFAD	127	30	223	37	291	197	143	136	399	144	354	94	238	99
ITC	13	33	14	31	23	18	16	31	16	31	17	41	19	43
UNAIDS	135	53	220	38	236	47	250	35	249	26	227	34	238	22
UNCTAD	1	35	1	29	1	37	0	31	2	32	2	32	2	41
UNEP	60	70	58	58	70	95	89	119	85	114	81	139	80	116
UN-HABITAT	10	99	10	92	18	119	18	73	7	126	7	161	17	191
UNODC/UNDCP	32	72	30	94	35	190	33	257	32	195	38	234	10	239
UNRWA	396	167	368	222	431	216	502	262	522	378	552	296	527	469
FAO	191	348	195	503	195	654	237	833	274	807	260	862	259	866
ILO	198	177	222	176	222	219	238	233	193	262	219	242	247	255
UNESCO	183	341	183	335	192	355	189	292	193	275	196	287	214	278
UNIDO	79	156	94	90	95	143	115	144	106	139	99	189	101	121
WHO	334	1 559	347	1 447	347	1 625	448	1 232	452	1 232	475	1 405	478	1 294
Other Specialized agencies b/	116	138	120	172	126	192	268	180	181	262	176	247	182	263
UNOCHA	59	81	65	95	68	106	77	190	77	94	96	104	128	98
UNDESA	7	86	5	48	8	82	5	53	7	71	11	58	11	62
OHCHR	12	35	20	34	26	35	41	35	42	33	38	32	36	35
Regional commissions c/	10	55	8	40	12	44	13	48	14	73	8	57	9	60
Total	4 630	12 484	5 019	12 559	5 607	13 609	6 548	16 079	6 092	15 856	6 016	16 898	6 311	16 539

Source: United Nations, *Report of the Secretary-General: Analysis*.

Table 2.   Lead agencies, ministries, or departments for allocation decisions made by 22 DAC member countries.

	Foreign	Development	Finance	Health	Agriculture	Environment	Economy	Education	Combination of different Ministries / Departments
UNDP	14	9	-	-	-	-	-	-	-
UNDPKO	18	1	-	-	-	-	-	-	2
GAVI	9	7	1	1	-	-	-	-	-
Global Fund	12	8	-	2	-	-	-	-	-
UNICEF	16	7	-	-	-	-	-	-	-
WHO	6	2	-	9	-	-	-	-	6
FAO	7	3	-	-	9	-	-	-	4
Global Environment Facility (GEF)	6	6	7	-	-	2	-	-	2
Clean Technology Fund	3	3	4	-	-	3	-	-	1
Climate Investment Funds	4	4	4	-	-	2	1	-	1
UN-REDD	5	3	-	-	-	2	-	-	1
Education for All — Fast Track Initiative	7	10	-	-	-	-	-	-	1
UNESCO	14	2	-	-	-	-	-	4	3
Global Agriculture and Food Security Program	3	7	2	-	-	-	-	-	-
UNHCR	16	7	-	-	-	-	-	-	-
WFP	12	7	-	-	2	-	-	-	2
TOTAL	157	91	22	12	11	9	1	4	24

Source: Bruce Jenks and Bruce Jones, *United Nations Development at a Crossroads*. New York: Center on International Cooperation, 2013, 116.

For over three decades the vision underlying the UN development system's work was marked by a duality that was increasingly difficult to reconcile. On the one hand, from the 1950s onwards, there was a deep shift to a mission of service for member states. On the other hand, there was still a commitment to the original concept of a UNDS as an actor that had value as a 'system'. Hence, with the progression to country programming, the responsibility for prioritising projects was transferred to governments; but implementation was still reserved for the agencies and programmes that constituted the system. Since each UN organisation had a specific mandate, in practice governments could decide which projects to do, but they had a very limited choice, if any, as to which member of the UNDS would implement the project.

Phase 3: service for developing countries

By the late 1980s the unresolved tensions between the concept of national ownership and ultimate accountability for programme results, on the one hand, and the privileged status of UN agencies which continued to be entitled to do implementation, on the other hand, was reaching breaking point. A situation had been created in which the UNDP, as the central funding agency to which donors entrusted their resources, could not exercise credible accountability for implementation performance, either to programme countries or to the donors.

The inevitable consequence of this was increasing UNDP assertiveness in protecting its reputation as it saw it, leading to gradual disintegration of the system, in time coming back to question the UNDP's role in the system. It was in 1990 for the first time that UNDP's Governing Council decision 90/34 established a number of priorities for the organisation.

The logical consequence of asserting national ownership was that countries needed to be able to choose their own implementation arrangements. In the early 1990s a radical change resulted in the method chosen for the implementation of the system's operational activities. In the 1970s and 1980s, the specialised agencies undertook the great bulk of project implementation. In 1990, however, member states requested a major review of the arrangements that supported the implementation of operational activities.[5] Whereas in the 1960s and 1970s agencies often had services to provide that were not accessible in the market, the study noted that reality was different. It recommended that agencies revert to being centres of excellence, and that the system as a whole move towards the use of national execution. National capacities, both public and private, had increased substantially and were now often in a position to take responsibility for actual implementation.

The 1990s witnessed a transformation in the system's political economy: the long-standing proportions of core to non-core funding were reversed. During the 1970s and 1980s the UNDP had provided around 75% of the total technical assistance funds through the UN system, and 90% of UNDP's funding came in the form of voluntary and regular contributions. In the mid-1980s the six biggest agencies (WHO, ILO, FAO, UNESCO, the UN Industrial Development Organization [UNIDO], and the UN itself) accounted for 58% of total programme delivery financed from the UNDP, while national execution accounted for only 6%. By 1995 the figures were 15% and 58%, respectively. There was no longer a

UN-wide funding system. Moreover, the funding of operational activities was overtaking assessed as well as regular budgets as a funding source for individual organisations. As a consequence, the system went in the opposite direction from that envisaged by the study. Each agency developed its own funding strategies. Technical cooperation became a high priority, and the competition for resources led down the road of taking on the role of contractors focused on implementation and the delivery of services.

Simultaneously the Cold War's end and the acceleration of globalisation changed the entire rationale for the allocation of aid. By the mid-1990s the UN development system was rapidly fragmenting. Activities increasingly became oriented to the delivery of services in a competitive market. It could be argued that both the focus of activities and the financing instruments were beginning to lose their distinctive multilateral character.

Phase 4: the goal-setting era

In the early 1990s the international development community anticipated enormous growth in aid budgets as a result of the 'peace dividend' that would accompany the end of the Cold War. In reality the end of the primary foreign policy rationale for foreign aid led to its rapid decline – by 2000 global aid in nominal terms was almost exactly the same as it had been around 1990 ($54 billion). This meant a substantial decrease in real terms instead of the doubling during the decades of the Cold War.[6]

Against this background the mission and rationale for development cooperation had to be radically redefined. The series of global conferences held during the 1990s culminated in the 2000 Millennium Summit, which crystallised the emergence of a new common development agenda. A key document was authored by the Organisation for Economic Co-operation and Development's Development Assistance Committee (OECD-DAC), *Shaping the 21st Century: The Contribution of Development Cooperation.*[7]

The most important element that bound together the conferences in the 1990s was the desire to define clear goals and objectives towards which the international community of states would commit itself. The shift to defining clear goals and setting measurable targets was the inevitable consequence of the need to provide a new rationale for development cooperation.

The alignment of the system behind a set of clear goals had radical implications for the way it was to be financed and for the UNDS's institutional shape. In the mid-1990s earmarked (non-core) funding took off, the logical expression of a rationale for aid that focused on clear goals and measurable targets. If the case for aid was going to be constructed around achieving specific goals, it was inevitable that the system of financing the achievement of those goals would measure success against the stated goals.

The result is clear in Figure 1. The graph demonstrates that in less than a decade the funding base of the UN development system was transformed from reliance on regular contributions to a strong bias to earmarked financing.

This reorientation fit well with the emerging 'goals' and 'results' culture that put pressure on each organisation to identify its specific comparative advantage and value proposition. Insisting on value for money from each institution made

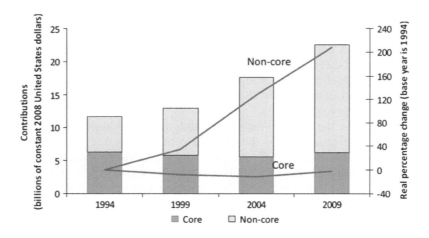

Figure 1. Trends in total contributions for operational activities for development, 1994–2009.
Source: United Nations. *Report of the Secretary-General: Analysis of the Funding of Operational Activities for Development of the United Nations System for 2009*. UN document A/66/79. May 6, 2011, 25.

absolute sense. The value of development cooperation was to be measured against specific benchmarks and targets. Donors would go to their parliaments and secure budgetary provisions for aid on this basis.

The explosion of non-core resources as the financing instrument of choice was the source of major fragmentation at two levels. At the country level it led to massive fragmentation and a concomitant loss in national ownership. It was particularly evident for finance ministers, who lost effective control of large parts of their budgets, which resulted in the inevitable reaction that the allocation of development resources had to be overseen and indeed decided upon by national authorities. It is not accidental that the ensuing process was led by DAC and the World Bank. The counter reaction to the victory of vertical funding achieved its pinnacle with the Paris Declaration in 2005.[8] This committed the international development community to a set of principles whose core purpose was to control the multiplication and proliferation of vertical programming and funding. Government ownership, alignment with national priorities, simplification, and harmonisation were seen as critical to the future of development effectiveness.

In addition, the explosion of non-core funding has led to fragmentation within UN organisations, which has in turn led to a sense of loss of control over overall budgets and a serious decline in the willingness of the international community to invest in the overall purposes of individual organisations. The financing of operational activities takes priority over the funding of normative activities, which is directly reflected in the performance-measurement systems put in place. The financing instrument becomes a vehicle for achieving specific results – in reality the case for assessed and regular contributions becomes increasingly flimsy.

Where does that leave the UNDS today? The general consensus is that the system is facing a 'bilateralisation' of funding through earmarked donations from wealthy countries, making the system less multilateral and weakening the influence of poorer countries. The correct response is seen to be a rebalancing of regular and earmarked resources. Is this a correct analysis?

Reflections on financing and multilateralism

What are some of the characteristics that determine whether or not the design of a financing system is more or less 'multilateral'? There is an extensive literature on the definition and meaning of multilateralism, but the intention here is not to enter into that dialogue. Rather this article explores four specific aspects that have particular relevance for ongoing debates at the United Nations.

Control of the allocation system vs purposes for which finance is provided

Historically there has been a real tension between the idea that multilateralism is a function of where control of the allocation system lies, on the one hand, and that multilateralism is about the purposes for which financing is provided, on the other hand. It is useful to trace the evolution of this tension through the four historical phases explored above.

In the original design phase the allocation of resources lies firmly within intergovernmental machinery (through objective criteria) and within each organisation (for the use of the allocation). In the second transition phase the allocation of overall resources again lies within intergovernmental machinery, and programme countries take the lead in the use of the resources made available but are obliged to use UN agencies for implementation. In the third phase, of service for developing countries, the overall allocation remains multilateral (still through objective criteria) and project selection and implementation are nationally owned. Today, in the fourth phase, control of the resources allocation process is largely outside the multilateral framework. With 70%–80% of the income of many UN organisations and programmes being non-core, the allocation of these resources often lies at the mercy of bilateral negotiations. Hence, the criticism heard often is of the contemporary trend towards the 'bilateralisation' of development cooperation.

The purpose of the system in the original design was to establish the building blocks for peace by creating and supporting communities of interest that would transcend national boundaries. In the subsequent phase the purpose changed course, focusing on service to member states. Over time the idea of ensuring national ownership became the dominant principle, but this reality raised some interesting questions. Within the framework of decolonisation and the emergence of newly independent states, a powerful argument could be made that supporting them to develop the capacities to exercise their sovereignty demonstrated a vision of global solidarity. At the same time, how should one characterise transferring resources for purposes incompatible with multilateral goals and purposes?

In today's era of goals the use of earmarked resources to finance global goals endorsed universally by the international community of states could be considered very much compatible with multilateral principles. However, from the perspective of the control of the allocation process, this type of financing instrument is considered by many to represent a serious deterioration of the multilateral system. This 'bilateralisation' can take place both at the supply end (donors acting unilaterally) or at the demand end (governments acting without reference to goals endorsed by the international community of states).

To argue that the use of earmarked resources to finance the achievement of specific internationally endorsed goals is inherently contrary to multilateral principles is to support the following: multilateralism is a function of where the control of the allocation system lies. This proposition trumps one where multilateralism is about the purposes for which the financing is provided.

An interesting footnote to this discussion lies in DAC's statistical treatment of earmarked funding for the UN development system. At the request of member state donors, their earmarked funding to the UN system is reflected in their bilateral portfolios. DAC statistics thus did not reflect non-core allocations made to the UN system. The consequence was that the 75% of total UN system operational resources – that is, those earmarked – were not reflected in DAC's tables about relative contributions to multilateral and bilateral organisations.

At the same time, in the governing boards of individual UN entities, both donors and secretariats provided assurances that earmarked funding did not distort the principles of multilateralism. The issue was only addressed at the time of DAC's first multilateral report, when UN representatives pointed out that the statistics in the report were close to meaningless if the purpose was to understand the complete picture of the UN system. A number of DAC tables continue only to capture regular resources as UN system resources. Clearly tension and confusion still exist around the relationship between the practice of donor earmarking and the concept of multilateralism.

Coherence

Another important question is whether the design of a financing system supports the growth of a coherent UNDS, or whether it leads to competition and fragmentation. If one believes that the coherence of the system is integral to the credibility of multilateralism as an effective instrument, then whether the design of the financial system promotes or undermines coherence is significant.

Clearly the architecture embedded in the original design gave rise to a high degree of coherence in so far as the financing instrument, the EPTA, directly supported the entities of the system. This fact held true also in the transition phase as UN organisations remained the service providers of choice. The evolution of the system to a mission of service to developing country member states, in which UN agencies were just one of many possible choices to receive the allocation of UNDP funds, seriously undermined the coherence of the system. For the first time it introduced real competition. This reality gave rise to a major unresolved tension that still lies at the centre of debates about financing, which relates to the contradiction between calling for a division of labour and allowing for healthy competition to determine the best entity for any given task. A system that is built on the idea that tasks are allocated according to mandate and not performance is not one to generate much confidence. A system that allows market competition to allocate resources is one that should not have undue concern about duplication and mission creep. But if the UN's objectives include the provision of services that are under-provided and thus under-financed, not to mention the pursuit of goals and values that are fundamental to its mission, then being competitive in the market may not represent the success indicator that member states are seeking.

In today's era of universal goals prospects for coherence are ambiguous. Clearly the practice of vertical funding gives rise to a highly competitive market place. In the long run individual organisations may prosper but multilateralism may be marginalised if it becomes just another route to successful contracting. By contrast, it is possible that a new form of coherence aligned to the achievement of specific goals may come to define a new way of looking at multilateralism.

Consumption vs investment

It is also important to ask whether the design of the financial system provides incentives to invest in or alternatively to consume the assets provided by multilateral institutions. Over the past two decades members of the UN development system have focused on the delivery of aid. They secured business by charging relatively little, a practice made possible by a heavy subsidy from core budgets. This reality served as a considerable disincentive to provide core resources. It is not just that 75% of the business was being subsidised by 25% of the contributions (ie the core). The fact that the core had to provide that subsidy acted as a severe drain on the use and focus of those core resources.

Nonetheless, the model appeared to work. Overall, with respect to total contributions, the overhead ratio looked good, project costs were low, and donors complained about the hidden subsidy but lived with it. The thinning out of core resources from critical normative and policy work was given little serious attention. Member states, donors and recipients alike, were comfortable consuming the assets available rather than investing in them. It follows that the value of those assets depreciated accordingly.

A critical challenge for the future of multilateralism is to move from a consumption-based to an investment-oriented model. We have been accustomed to a period dominated by the logic of project delivery. The amounts implemented by the UN development system were large enough to warrant a focus on delivery rather than leverage. Efficiency was defined by the percentage of resources actually being programmed at the country level. We can expect that over the next decade aid implementation will become less important, except for a group of perhaps the 30–40 poorest countries, whereas policy support, coordination, advocacy, norm and standards promotion will gain in importance.

In this regard countries can choose to be either 'consumers' or 'investors' in the way that they relate to UN institutions. For investors the UN is a way to exercise leadership. They see the world organisation as the best way to achieve certain results after considering all options. Investors are looking for long-term value. For consumers, however, the United Nations is an alternative to leadership, a default option. They view the world organisation *à la carte*, as a menu with options to be selected according to desires. Consumers are looking for short-term returns.

The move from consumption to investment is part of the solution to the thorny issue of rebalancing core and non-core resources. A critical dimension to the problem of low levels of core contributions is the high percentage of core that is devoted to overheads for the administration of non-core projects and programmes. Investors see this as a subsidy to non-core project delivery. Far from being protected they are highly vulnerable politically. Formulating definitions fit for today's purposes would make a major contribution to relieving that pressure. Another way to tackle this problem is proposed below, which would be for the great bulk of investment costs to be paid through some form of assessed contributions. This change would neutralise the political vulnerability to which investors are subject.

Practical considerations

Finally, for practitioners, a completely different set of calculations might be in play because strengthening multilateralism might be more about concrete options than abstract principles. The actual choice faced by a multilateral agency might be to secure bilateral funds that have already been earmarked by a government and to have access to those resources by accepting those earmarks or forfeiting the opportunity to manage those resources out of an objection in principle to the earmarking. Often this choice is made because for many governments earmarking thematically or for a specific country is the only way politically to get resources appropriated. The practical consequences of the options taken are extremely important. Is it logical to take the position that accepting earmarked contributions that would otherwise have been channelled bilaterally somehow weakens multilateralism? Should genuine multilateralism not embrace practices that will serve to strengthen multilateral channels, even with earmarking as the instrument of choice?

In short, additional caution is in order in characterising different financial instruments as more or less 'multilateral'. Responding to today's challenges to multilateralism requires an array of approaches and instruments.

Emerging financing instruments and implications for multilateralism

A number of new financing instruments are emerging or on the horizon. Four are worth exploring here: integrated budgets; resources from emerging powers; other innovations; and system-wide financing.

Towards integrated budgets

Currently a major initiative to strengthen the multilateral character of the resources provided to the UNDS lies in the push to adopt 'integrated budgets'.[9] The underlying premise behind this initiative is that core resources are highly unlikely to increase significantly. The idea is to compensate for the lack of balance between core and non-core income by finding ways of increasing core-like qualities such as flexibility in the allocation of non-core resources. The starting point is to ensure that all available and projected core and non-core resources are consolidated within an integrated budgetary framework, based on the priorities established and agreed in each of the strategic plans adopted.[10] The adoption of the framework implies, on the one hand, that governments have approved its contents and, on the other hand, that an individual organisation must remain within the parameters of the approved framework and should not engage in resource mobilisation efforts outside it.

The lack of balance between core and non-core resources, when combined with the lack of flexibility in the allocation of non-core, exacerbates the probability of misalignments between supply and demand. Empirically there is a marked concentration of non-core funding in certain themes and countries. Increasing the quality of non-core contributions can be made either by increasing the level at which the earmarking is done, or simply by introducing more flexible provisions. The idea is that, within the assurances provided by an approved structure of an integrated budget, donors might be willing and able to introduce such flexibilities.

An important component of any progress in improving the quality of non-core funding is the need for far greater transparency in the allocation of non-core resources in all areas of an integrated budget. A completely transparent online reporting system that captures in real time both surpluses and shortfalls in the allocation of non-core income within the budgetary framework is critical to a specific donor's understanding of why flexibility can lead to increased effectiveness.

The introduction of an integrated budget is most advanced in the WHO. What lessons can be learned, however tentative, from the experience to date? The WHO was facing a situation in which only about 25% of its financing came from obligatory assessments. The likelihood of significant increases in such resources was unrealistic. So the WHO focused on the need for increased transparency, predictability, alignment, and flexibility of non-core resources so that these could be deployed in a way that better matched supply with demand. In turn a robust strategic framework established clear priorities and a genuine sense of focus. The key was greater discipline about the WHO's priorities that was the trigger for exploring better alignment and greater flexibility in the use of earmarked resources. A critical piece in the emerging jigsaw puzzle was transparency through online, real-time mechanisms. The WHO website under construction is thus viewed as an essential element for the system's viability.

The technique of integrated budgets is a fruitful and potentially widely applicable attempt to reconcile the loss of control over the allocation of resources implicit in non-core resources with the transparency and reassertion of control embedded in the construction of an overall framework that preserves the integrity of organisational priorities. This procedure could strengthen the multilateral character of the financial package by subjecting non-core allocation processes to an agreed overall framework, increasing transparency and articulating clear goals supported by the WHO's member states.

Two things remain unclear. First, will the core resource base of UN organisations be further eroded by making non-core resources more acceptable by embedding them in an overall framework and maintaining the strong subsidy provided by core to cover the costs incurred by non-core? Will this approach lead to a greater willingness by donors to invest in multilateralism?

Emerging powers

A significant source of new finance may be coming from the so-called emerging powers, the subject of this issue. It is important to note that, for a number of these countries, policy is determined by core principles related to South–South cooperation. Generally they provide their official development assistance (ODA) as part of integrated packages involving trade, investment, and other commercial ventures. Disentangling the ODA component from the rest of the package is often difficult, which leads to a number of definitional and reporting issues. Thus it is perhaps premature to reach a firm view of the long-term impact of new and potential flows from emerging powers on the overall architecture of development financing.

Nonetheless, the phenomenon raises some interesting issues in the context of finance and the future of multilateralism. The DAC paradigm has emphasised a set of principles that defined ODA; the purpose was to separate out and protect the integrity of ODA. If ODA was not clearly demarcated and distinguished from other types of financial relationships it would be eroded and subjected to much stronger and larger commercial interests.

The principles underlying South–South cooperation in some respects turn this logic on its head. These principles lead to a focus on a package of mutual interests that deliberately mixes and blurs many of the distinctions on which ODA is built. Does the logic of mutual interests lead to a 'bilateralisation' of multilateralism, or does it open up the possibility of a framework for a new multilateralism? This debate has just begun. Clearly a key issue for the future will be how to measure the results achieved by the implementation of the model embraced by South–South cooperation. How will the development results and impact be measured and captured? How will these measurements be compared with those monitored by DAC?

Innovative sources

Another approach to the challenge of securing multilateral funding has been alternative and innovative sources. A number of possible approaches were analysed by Bill Gates for the G20 in 2011.[11] The practical advantages and disadvantages of different means have been debated at some length both inside and outside various UN fora. Some remain highly contested but have already made headway for groups of countries. The levy applied to aeroplane tickets by a number of countries provides one example. Innovative financing is a long and winding path down which progress might be made but undoubtedly not at great speed.

Market mechanisms and private-sector contributions provide two important sources of finance. For the former the use of Advance Market Commitments and the experience of the International Finance Facility provide examples. Private sector contributions have already become highly significant in some parts of the UN system.[12] For example, UNICEF is projecting that some 50% of its resources will be from private sources by 2017 (estimated to be about $1.75 billion).[13] A significant component will come from individual donations to core resources. By contrast, today the WHO gets about $500 million from companies and foundations (including over $200 million from the Gates Foundation).[14] The World Intellectual Property Organization (WIPO) provides an altogether different model. Some 90% of its funding results from fees related to granting patents. In fact, the private sector is in this sense its client, which raises the broader question of whether production of global public goods should create the opportunity for charging for services.

There has always been something of an implicit assumption for many observers of the UNDS that non-state sources of income were provided in the form of specified contributions. In reality this impression is inaccurate and could seriously distort strategic thinking on future financing for the system. There are two sources of non-state income that constitute reliable and predictable sources of regular non-specified income. Private donations (as evidenced by UNICEF's extremely successful experience) and fees (as evidenced by WIPO's financial model) are arguably successful models to date for the UN system; they have more potential than the more extensively discussed innovative sources that rely on new governmental sources of income.

There is an interesting question as to the extent to which opportunities and constraints to pursue different financing models are heavily influenced by the characteristics of different sectors. The role of the Gates Foundation, for example in financing multi-stakeholder partnerships in the health sector, is noteworthy. The success of UNICEF in attracting contributions in the form of donations is unique in terms of its scale. But is such fundraising unique for children?

Much of the discussion around financing continues to assume that foreign assistance is a single pot of resources that gets allocated to that portion of a country's budget dedicated to foreign affairs.[15] The concept of global public goods suggests a very different approach. A horizontal internalisation of financing the international dimensions of producing public goods is required. In a globalised world national line ministries have to cope with both national and international dimensions in their areas of responsibility as a matter of effective national policymaking. In that sense, line ministries need to have both an internally and an externally oriented part of their budgets. The challenge is no longer funding external relations but the international dimension of dealing effectively with a national issue.

Table 2 identifies the source of finance within governments for a broad range of UN functions. In practice global budget lines are developing within national ministry budgets. In reality the greatest expansion of funding for development cooperation is likely to occur through the diffusion of the responsibility for funding across broad segments of national budgets. This presents a critical change and opportunity for the UNDS's approaches to funding. The opportunity exists because powerful line ministries become advocates across government for global expenditures.

For many defenders of traditional ODA this opportunity also presents a significant risk, because the dispersion of resources for international purposes across a wide range of ministries could easily lead to a significant weakening of the safeguards around the special characteristics of ODA. There is a strong parallel between the logic of this analysis and the tension between multilateralism as control over the allocation process versus multilateralism as the purposes for which financing is provided. The traditional approach focuses on the need to control allocations in foreign and development ministries so as to protect the integrity of the use of ODA. New cross-ministry approaches focus on the ability to leverage the power of sectoral interests to generate more effective ways of mobilising the resources required to achieve intended goals.

Back to the future: system-wide financing

One scenario that can probably be eliminated is the notion of reverting to central funding for the system. Most recently the High-level Panel on System-wide Coherence showed interest in resurrecting the concept of central funding to impose discipline on the system.[16] In the end the diversity of funding sources that characterises the flow of resources today and the strength of vertical funding make this option impractical.

Instead, the panel turned to 'One UN' funds at the country level to complement agency funding. Providing resources centrally at the country level to be managed by UN resident coordinators would drive greater country coherence. The rationale was to create a financing instrument that would provide some flexible financing to complement that already secured within the framework of the One UN Programme by each agency; it would provide incentives to support and work within the overall framework. It was also intended to strengthen the incentives of working as a team under the broad leadership of the UN resident coordinator. It was in essence residual funding to support those components of the One UN Programme that remained underfunded. The challenge with the concept of a residual fund is that it requires a very high level of confidence in the overall framework such that those pieces that have not been picked up will still strongly deserve to be funded. However, only a few years later this financing instrument is drying up.[17] In effect, three types of funding were running side by side – core agency funding, extra-budgetary funding, and the One UN Fund. As such the One UN Fund would never be more than a residual source, which made it politically unsustainable as a major alternative source.

By contrast, over the past five years or so two new financial instruments have been developed that have shown some promise. The Multi-Partner Trust Fund (MPTF) was established as a system-wide window so that donors could contribute to a UNDS-wide programme without having to decide with which specific organisation to partner.[18] Faced with a choice between the World Bank or some 30 UN entities, most donors preferred the World Bank. With a choice between a UN system-wide window and any other partner many donors were interested in working with the United Nations. This situation arose in immediate postwar Iraq; and from a financial point of view, the UN–Iraq Multi-Donor Trust Fund performed above expectations. Since its establishment in 2004, the Multi-Donor Trust Fund Office has become a broad-ranging facility with a portfolio of some $7 billion.

The rationale in setting up this facility was to make it possible for donors to contribute to the UN system as a whole and to rely on internal distribution mechanisms to allocate resources in alignment with programme priorities and needs. There was an interest in using the UN as a financial instrument, but it was conditioned on the UN's having a credible way of operating as a system. Within it there are different types of contributions, ranging from highly earmarked to flexible. The same characteristics emerge as with any system that allows for flexibility: the combination of the need for an overall framework with a high level of transparency, giving rise to scope for flexibility. A further dimension of flexibility is achieved because the contributions are not all earmarked to a specific organisation, thereby allowing for flexibility to allocations within the system to where the resources are most badly needed for programme effectiveness. This approach has proved especially useful in emergency situations and humanitarian crises. The multiplicity of MPTF-like instruments, from global-thematic to country-level transition funds, is both an opportunity and a source of greater fragmentation.

The MPTF experience suggests the potential for exercising leverage from system-wide approaches. At the same time whether the incentives exist in the system to ensure the sustainability of this model remains an open question.

A second instrument is the Spain–UNDP MDG Achievement Fund.[19] This instrument was established in 2006 as a result of a $720 million contribution from the Spanish government. Spain was seeking a partnership with the UN to make a significant impact on the achievement of the Millennium Development Goals (MDGs). The UNDP was confronted with the need to develop a new instrument that would meet the Spanish requirement of a single credible management partner while being acceptable to agency partners. The Spanish proposal revealed the vacuum that a system-wide vision would inevitably encounter. In this respect the dual structure created by the UNDP – a political strategic steering committee limited to Spain and the UNDP, along with a thematic agency-led steering committee to allocate resources – was a significant innovation. The MDG Achievement Fund broke some new ground, but it remained the initiative of a single donor made possible by a one-time source of revenue.

Financing for a new multilateralism

The secretary-general's 2014 report on the implementation of the Quadrennial Comprehensive Policy Review (QCPR) makes a number of assertions with respect to the value added of core resources.[20] They are the most efficient way of building relevant and effective partnerships with programme countries in the delivery of operational activities; provide the highest quality, flexibility, and efficiency; and are central to ensuring independence, neutrality, and trust.

These arguments represent long-established truths and command widespread acceptance. Nonetheless, each is questionable. A project-driven system does not provide a compelling case for core resources. The evidence for asserting that they lead to higher-quality programming is not obvious, and the aura of independence and neutrality derives from association with the UN as a whole and not from the source of financing. There are very compelling arguments for investing in core, but they are not captured in this account.

The heart of the case for the spectrum of regular financing that includes assessed, negotiated pledges, and voluntary core resources lies in the function that is to be performed. The argument here is that building the case for the components in this financing spectrum around function is the only plausible way forward to break through the current financing logjam.

The financing of multilateralism in the future requires going beyond the core/non-core conundrum. What is required in the future is to design financial instruments that are best suited to secure the relevance of multilateral institutions. As stated in the abstract, the principles underlying the call for rebalancing core and non-core sources represent wishful thinking. There is no credible rationale for core funding to grow in order to finance a project-driven system. Redressing the balance between core and non-core financing can only be done in the context of a much broader bargain around function. This is an approach that could also be of interest to the growth economies.

A broader bargain could be constructed around four types of function, each supported by a different financing model.[21] The first could be described as the 'platform function', and includes the core normative and standard-setting functions as well as securing presence and convening power. The cost of this function should be assessed as an integral cost of membership in the component parts of the UNDS. Normative and standard-setting work should not be financially dependent on groups of interested parties.

The second function relates to the UN's role in providing global public goods. By definition the core challenge in providing them is their under-provision and the need for a collective response. Negotiating a collective response and allocating responsibilities is a *sine qua non* for their provision. The agenda for global public goods will give birth to a variable geometry in the character of collective responses. Different groups of countries will have varying interests with respect to a specific public good. On the one hand, financing will have to be negotiated in line with the prevailing variable geometry for any specific good. On the other hand, financing cannot be purely voluntary, because it should reflect and be true to the allocation of responsibility agreed that made the collective response possible. Bringing these two points together suggests that negotiated pledges are the best way to proceed with respect to the financing of major global public goods.

The third function relates to financing humanitarian operations and programmes in crisis countries. In practice, one could envisage hybrid financing arrangements. On the one hand, some form of assessed budget or negotiated pledge would be important to give the UN a secure base enabling it to be responsive and effective. On the other hand, major financing of large-scale programmes will invariably be country-specific and often come from earmarked sources in national budgets for those target countries.

The fourth function relates to the 'classical' anti-poverty and capacity-building development programmes that have been such a large part of the UN development system's activities over several decades. A number of countries are committed to supporting these types of activities independently of burden-sharing considerations. They remain well suited to the types of core voluntary as well as earmarked contributions that have long characterised the funding of the UN's development programmes and funds.

Conclusion

Against this background an agenda with five building blocks results for funding the UNDS in the next decade. First, it is important to recognise that the values conveyed by the concept of multilateralism have evolved. At the height of the Cold War and the process of decolonisation it was entirely appropriate that the soul of multilateralism reside in control of the allocation system. Today demonstrating relevance to leveraging solutions is more important than control over the mechanisms. The historical focus on control over the allocation process risks defining multilateralism in a way that will only serve to marginalise it further.

Second, moving beyond the core/non-core stalemate requires a new variable geometry that brings into play assessed, negotiated pledges, and voluntary core and non-core instruments. Making use of assessed budgets and negotiated pledges for a very rigorously defined set of functions provides the key to unlocking a solution for the broader core/non-core impasse. Integrated budgets can be a useful element in this discussion, but ultimately a new variable geometry requires a more comprehensive bargain.

Third, it is necessary to introduce a package of new incentives. These are required to move beyond a narrow focus on delivering aid to leveraging solutions and working with partners.

Fourth, the UNDS requires an alternative set of definitions. These should be designed to reward and provide political protection to investors and not give consumers a free (or at least not overly subsidised) ride.

Fifth, central funding may well be dead as a practical financial option for the UN development system. At the same time, there is an urgent need to build on the foundations laid in recent years for system-wide instruments that enable the United Nations to respond as a system to specific needs.

Notes

1. Jenks and Jones, *United Nations Development at a Crossroads*, 22–27.
2. See, for example, Mitrany, *A Working Peace System*; and Mitrany, *The Functional Theory of Politics*.
3. Claude, Jr., *Swords into Ploughshares*, 17.
4. United Nations, *A Capacity Study*; Murphy, *The UN Development Programme*; and Browne, *The United Nations Development Programme*.
5. United Nations, *Report of the Expert Group*.
6. Jenks and Jones, *United Nations Development at a Crossroads*, 27.
7. OECD, *Reshaping the 21st Century*.
8. OECD, *Paris Declaration*.

9. This section draws on an informal paper produced by New York University's Center on International Cooperation in 2014 to support intergovernmental dialogue mandated by General Assembly resolution 67/226.
10. United Nations, *Quadrennial Comprehensive Policy Review*, para 41.
11. Gates, *Innovation with Impact*. See also Mohieldin, *Financing*.
12. This discussion draws from an informal paper on non-state sources of income submitted by Bruce Jenks to the Office of the Secretary-General in 2013.
13. UNICEF, *Private Fundraising*.
14. WHO, *Voluntary Contributions*.
15. Jenks and Jones, *United Nations Development at a Crossroads*, 116.
16. United Nations, *Delivering as One*.
17. United Nations, *Report of the Secretary-General on the Implementation*.
18. See UNDP, Multi-Partner Trust Fund Office, http://mptf.undp.org.
19. See World Bank and UNDP, Climate Finance Options, http://www.climatefinanceoptions.org/cfo/node/59.
20. United Nations, *Report of the Secretary-General on the Funding*.
21. Jenks and Jones, *United Nations Development at a Crossroads*, 118–119.

Bibliography

Browne, Stephen. *The United Nations Development Programme and System*. London: Routledge, 2011.

Claude, Jr., Inis. *Swords into Ploughshares: The Problems and Prospects of International Organization*. New York, NY: Random House, 1964.

Gates, Bill. *Innovation with Impact: Financing 21st-century Development*. Report to G20 Leaders at Cannes Summit, November 2011. http://www.gatesfoundation.org/What-We-Do/Global-Policy/G20-Report.

Jenks, Bruce, and Bruce Jones. *United Nations Development at a Crossroads*. New York: Center on International Cooperation, 2013.

Mitrany, David. *The Functional Theory of Politics*. London: lse/Robertson, 1975.

Mitrany, David. *A Working Peace System*. London: Broadwater Press, 1943.

Mohieldin, Mahmoud. *Financing a Post-2015 Development Framework*. High-level Panel Working Papers Series, prepared for Bali meeting, March 24–27, 2013. Washington, DC: World Bank, 2013.

Murphy, Craig N. *The UN Development Programme: A Better Way?* Cambridge: Cambridge University Press, 2006.

OECD. *Accra Agenda for Action*. Paris: OECD, 2008.

OECD. *Paris Declaration on Development Aid Effectiveness*. Paris: OECD, 2005.

OECD. *Reshaping the 21st Century: The Contribution of Development Cooperation*. Paris: OECD, 1996.

UNICEF. *Private Fundraising and Partnerships Plan 2014–17*. http://www.unicef.org/about/execboard/files/UNICEF_Private_Fundraising_and_Partnerships_Plan_2014-2017.pdf.

United Nations. *A Capacity Study of the United Nations Development System*. Geneva: UN, 1969.

United Nations. *Delivering as One: Report of the High-level Panel on UN System-wide Coherence*. New York: UN, 2006.

United Nations. *Quadrennial Comprehensive Policy Review*. General Assembly resolution 67/226.

United Nations. *Report of the Expert Group on Agency Support Costs*. New York: UN, 1990.

United Nations. *Report of the Secretary-General: Analysis of Funding of Operational Activities for Development of the UN System for 2011*. New York: UN Department of Economic and Social Affairs, 2013.

United Nations. *Report of the Secretary-General on the Funding of Operational Activities*. New York: UN Department of Economic and Social Affairs, 2014.

United Nations. *Report of the Secretary-General on the Implementation of General Assembly Resolution 67/226 on the QCPR of Operational Activities*. New York: UN Department of Economic and Social Affairs, 2014.

WHO. *Voluntary Contributions by Fund and by Donor for the Financial Period 2010–2011*. WHO document A/65/29 Add1, April 5, 2012. http://www.who.int/about/resources_planning/A65_29Add1-en.pdf.

Emerging powers at the UN: ducking for cover?

Silke Weinlich

Centre for Global Cooperation Research, University Duisburg-Essen, Germany

The economic rise of China, India, South Africa, and Brazil has turned these countries into important providers of development assistance. While they seem increasingly comfortable in their bilateral relations with other developing countries, they are struggling to adapt their position within global institutions such as the United Nations. Do they turn their increased weight into a greater influence at the UN, and if not, why not? This article analyses financial contributions and political positioning at the UN in the area of development. Despite small changes, the four countries mostly insist on keeping their traditional status as recipients and 'ordinary' developing countries. This reservation can be explained in two ways: first, a more explicit leadership creates political and material costs that outweigh the potential benefits. Second, their shared experiences as developing countries make it hard to break ranks at the UN.

Mostly thanks to a long phase of economic growth at rates significantly above those of industrialised countries, so-called emerging powers such as China, India, Brazil, and South Africa are now experiencing a rapid transformation of their geopolitical relevance, national interests and, possibly, identities.[1] Similar to the West coming hesitantly to terms with its decreased significance in the global economy, the Southern powers are grappling with their rise in the international system. They face decisions about how to position themselves in the global governance system. This includes their attitude towards traditional South–South alliances such as the Group of 77 (G77) or the Non-Aligned Movement (NAM), and their relations and coordination of interests bilaterally and in groupings such as IBSA (India, Brazil, and South Africa) or BRICS (Brazil, Russia, India, China, and South Africa). Last but not least, the four countries have to decide on how to behave towards multilateral organisations, which are commonly associated with the 'old' world order.[2]

Development is a policy field in which the rise of these four countries has been particularly visible. They have gradually shifted from being recipients to substantial providers of aid and other forms of development assistance. Their successful individual development experiences have put them in a position to offer a wide range of technical development expertise, goods, and services to other developing countries, although they still face significant development challenges within their own borders.[3] While South–South cooperation (SSC) has existed for more than half a century,[4] we are currently witnessing a massive expansion of financial and technical cooperation between emerging powers and other countries from the global South. To be sure, their individual development cooperation programmes differ in terms of size, geographic orientation and modalities.[5] However, Brazil, China, India, and South Africa all emphasise that their form of development cooperation is distinct from the traditional, asymmetric donor–recipient model, consisting instead of a mutually beneficial relationship among development partners. They claim that more similar social, cultural, and economic environments make such cooperation more effective and appropriate.[6] While South Africa and, to a lesser degree, India also use multilateral channels for their assistance, China and Brazil emphasise bilateral cooperation, which allows for direct influence and an instrumental use of aid for economic, geostrategic, and other interests.[7]

All four countries express support for reaching internationally agreed development goals such as the Millennium Development Goals (MDGS) and generally place their assistance within this context, yet they do not perceive the need for more concrete guidelines or commitments with regard to their development assistance.[8] This stance is mirrored in their attitude towards international aid and development coordination processes such as that on aid effectiveness, which originated in the Development Assistance Committee of the Organisation of Economic Co-operation and Development (OECD-DAC) and has continued through the Global Partnership for Effective Development Cooperation (Global Partnership). While all four countries endorsed the so-called Paris Principles on aid effectiveness, they only did so in their capacity as recipients of aid; they reject the application of those principles to their own cooperation with developing countries. Initially, when China, Brazil, India, and South Africa endorsed the creation of the Global Partnership in Busan in 2011, commentators interpreted it as a cautious willingness to engage with Western donors on a common framework, as well as an official acknowledgement of their status as donor countries.[9] However, when the Global Partnership met for the first time in Mexico in 2014, China and India did not attend the meeting, Brazil's diplomats emphasised that they were mere observers, and South Africa sent a delegation that commentators found lacking in weight.[10]

The starting point of this article is the empirical observation that the emerging powers show an interest in repositioning themselves in the policy field of development, where the asymmetries of power between the 'developed' and the developing world are strong. Just as they have sought a greater voice in international organisations such as the IMF or the World Bank, it seems that they could throw their weight behind an attempt to overcome the dominant system of postcolonial aid-giving. Already in 2003 India had begun to reject any tied aid and limited the number of bilateral donors from which it accepts aid. In 2011 China published its first white paper on foreign aid, in which it takes the position of an aid provider. Brazil has been an outspoken critic of the aid effectiveness process under the auspices of DAC, which it perceives as being unbalanced; it rejects efforts that aim to impose Western norms and values on its own development policies. Both in rhetoric as well as in their actual development cooperation the four countries present a challenge to the existing aid paradigm and its institutional structures and processes dominated by traditional donors.[11]

Given the generally high appreciation of the United Nations by China, Brazil, India, and South Africa,[12] we would expect the four countries to use the organisation for articulating their changed status, possibly even in the form of leadership aspirations. In fact, they do so in areas other than development, and the UN's membership (dominated by the global South's numbers) and consensus decision making favour the four. Three of them aspire to make the UN's bodies in other policy areas mirror their enhanced status in world politics. While China already is a Security Council member, the other three have voiced their aspirations to join the council on a permanent and equitable basis.[13] The sheer number of developing countries in the universal membership UN mean that the four countries are potentially able to influence decisions to a greater degree than in organisations in which votes are determined by economic power, and in organisations such as the OECD and the G20, which are strongly shaped by institutionalised cooperation among industrialised countries. Of course, favourable voting structures do not guarantee a policy outcome, as the failure to implement the New International Economic Order in the 1970s reminds us.

However, it is an open question whether industrialised countries could still thwart attempts for change, even more so where development is concerned, given that many industrialised countries have been very accommodating in order to secure participation by emerging powers in the aid/development coordination processes.[14] The articulation of demands in the General Assembly, the governing boards of UN organisations, and the Economic and Social Council (ECOSOC) would not even necessitate institutional reform. Finally, UN development activities stand somewhat apart from the traditional aid paradigm. Several UN organisations, often under the leadership of officials from the global South, have been recommending alternative concepts to challenge the dominant discourses.[15] In addition, developing countries take part in the funding, oversight, and governance of the UN development system, which should be particularly open to novel ideas.

Taken together, these structural parameters make it relatively easy – at first glance – for the emerging powers to influence the overall directions of UN development work to a greater degree, which provides the background for this article to investigate the behaviour of emerging powers. How does their changing status play out in the area of development policy? Have they altered their behaviour at the UN, and do they aspire to exercise more responsibility and leadership than previously? Three cases are analysed: financial contributions, the role of SSC, and global norms and standard setting on development policy in the UN Development Cooperation Forum (DCF). The article suggests that, so far, the four countries have behaved rather reluctantly and are instead sticking to their traditional attitude as 'ordinary' developing countries. The article's final section explores possible explanations and discusses some implications for multilateral development cooperation and the UN.

Emerging powers and UN development policy

The United Nations plays a dual role in global development. First, it provides a forum for debate and decision making on development questions. Even if in the areas of economy, trade, and finance industrial states have shifted many decision-making processes to organisations with more favourable majorities for themselves, the UN remains the formal arena in which norms and standards are set that apply worldwide. Prominent examples include internationally agreed development goals, such as the MDGs, or norms and standards in the areas of human rights, labour, and gender. Although such norms and standards are not legally binding and their implementation cannot be enforced, they stipulate benchmarks to measure the behaviour of states.

Second, the UN is a sizable development actor on its own. Roughly 30 UN agencies, funds, and programmes engage in operational activities (that is, development assistance and humanitarian aid) to assist developing countries. The UN's development policy is unique in the sense that it is universal and hence truly multilateral. Industrial and developing countries jointly oversee the operational UN activities; developing countries usually contribute financially or in kind to the assistance that they receive from the UN system. Many developing countries' governments not only contribute to UN activities in their own country but also make a symbolic contribution to the UN's development work in general. The various UN development actors enjoy a high reputation and a special kind of legitimacy among developing countries, and the UN is said to be more neutral than other bilateral or multilateral development actors.[16]

But has the actual behaviour of the four countries changed at the UN? The article now takes a closer look at (1) their financial contributions; (2) SSC at the UN; and (3) global norms and standard setting on development policy.

Financial contributions to the UN development system

UN development activities are mainly financed by voluntary contributions.[17] Contributions, a large share earmarked, are often a means to exert direct and indirect influence on the overall direction and work of UN organisations. Although the share of nongovernmental actors has been going up over the past decade, DAC members still contribute the majority of funds.[18] In 2012 roughly 64% of the total sum of $23.9 billion funding of the UN's development and humanitarian activities was paid by DAC members.[19] In addition, industrialised countries contribute substantial funds through other multilateral channels, such as the EU. In comparison, the contributions from developing countries, including emerging powers, carry little weight. Non-DAC members provided some 7% of the resources for UN operational activities in 1993; that figure had risen to 11% by 2012.[20] However, a large part of these funds is allocated to UN projects and services within these countries' own borders (so-called local resources). These figures show that currently, despite the multilateral veneer, the UN development system (including its humanitarian delivery) is almost exclusively funded by industrialised countries.

Table 1 compiles financial information on contributions to development-related UN activities between 2009 and 2012 by the four selected emerging powers and contrasts them with the top four DAC donor countries. The emerging powers only made modest contributions. Consequently, their positions rank in the 20s (China) to mid-30s (South Africa) when the absolute numbers are taken as a point of reference. Also, when the contributions are adjusted by considering gross national income, their rankings do not improve – on the contrary, they actually move to the bottom of the top 50. In 2012 all four emerging powers together contributed roughly 1% of the funding for the UN development system. The four have graduated from the ranks of the developing countries in terms of their net contributions to the UN development system. When compared with the USA's share of roughly 9%, or that of Norway (roughly 5%), however, their share seems marginal.

Of course, such a comparison is not fair in the sense that it neglects the poverty and inequalities that the emerging powers continue to face within their own borders. However, if we use as a frame of reference the burden that the four countries – after lengthy and fierce negotiations – were willing to shoulder with regard to the UN general budget, the picture does not change. Here, all four countries pay a significantly larger share than they do when it comes to financing the UN development system, a generalisation that also holds true for Japan and the USA.

All in all, it seems appropriate to say that the financial behaviour of the four countries does not reflect an aspiration towards leadership. Moreover, it also does not indicate any sign that they are beginning to use the UN to pursue their own South–South development agendas.

Outside of the UN, at minimum, China and Brazil provide more development assistance than they receive;[21] but at the UN, thus far, three out of the four countries prefer to remain net recipients. If we exclude contributions directed at UN services within their own borders, until 2010 none of the four countries made contributions to UN development and humanitarian activities that were larger than those they received. From 2011 on this reality changed only for Brazil. As of 2012 India, China, and South Africa remain net recipients of UN development assistance, which is especially striking for India. In 2011 the UN development system spent roughly $29 million in India, while India's overall contributions amounted to about $5 million.[22] Other countries, such as Saudi Arabia and Argentina, have long switched to being net-providers of UN development assistance.[23]

Table 1. Selected contributors to funding development-related UN activities (2009–12).

Contributors	Total contributions (excluding local resources) (millions of current US$)				Country share of UN total (%)				Country share of UN General Budget (%)
	09	10	11	12	09	10	11	12	2010–12
China	61	70	64	70	0.5	0.5	0.5	0.4	3.19
India	33	26	30	30	0.3	0.2	0.2	0.2	0.53
Brazil	29	45	52	29	0.2	0.3	0.4	0.2	1.61
South Africa	11	13	11	12	0.1	0.1	0.1	0.1	0.38
USA	1305	1787	1499	1519	10	12.3	10.6	9.4	22
Japan	802	1048	1039	964	6.1	7.2	7.4	6.0	12.53
UK	744	836	1025	1216	5.7	5.8	7.3	7.5	6.60
Norway	694	748	805	763	5.3	5.2	5.7	4.7	0.87

Source: Weinlich, *Funding the UN System*, 83.

Again the impression arises that at least three out of the four countries are not interested in using increased contributions to the UN development system to signal their changed status at the organisation, nor do they seem to want the greater clout that accompanies them. This attitude somewhat contradicts the self-assured demeanour of the four countries in other contexts relevant for international development – for instance, in the IBSA grouping or in their ambitions to establish a BRICS development bank. For the multilateral UN development system nearly exclusive funding by industrialised countries is likely to continue for some time. The emerging powers and other developing countries take part in the governance of the UN development system. However, in reality, industrialised states often seem to take a much keener interest in how their contributions should be spent.[24]

If we take a more detailed look across a longer time horizon and at individual UN organisations, there seems to be some movement that might foreshadow a change of strategy. The upward trend is more ambiguous for India and South Africa than for Brazil and China. Between 2003 and 2011 China has roughly tripled its contributions to development-related and humanitarian activities from $39 million to $117 million; in 2012, however, its contributions declined to $97 million. Both India and South Africa show less steady increases, but overall the trend is also upwards. Brazil is the outlier. It has consistently provided relatively large contributions to the UN development system. However, in the past Brazil stood out mostly because the government supplemented its contributions with substantial payments for the delivery of services within Brazil.[25] In 2012 Brazil's self-supporting contributions amounted to more than $170 million out of a total of roughly $92 million.

Humanitarian aid is an important field of activities for the emerging powers. For the first time in history China channelled part of its humanitarian aid for the victims of the Indian Ocean Tsunami and the Pakistan earthquake through the UN system. Brazil recently increased its contributions to the World Food Programme (WFP) from $1 million in 2009 to $76 million in 2012, including more than $28 million of non-earmarked contributions that are especially valuable for UN organisations. India nearly quadrupled its contribution to the successor of the UN Development Fund for Women, the UN's most recent new organisation, called 'UN Women'. In 2012 China and India were among the top 30 contributors to the UN Development Programme (UNDP) and, with their contributions of $5.2 and $2.1 million, respectively, ranked higher than Italy or Portugal.[26]

This more targeted support seems to be beneficial in terms of senior positions in the UN development system. For instance, Chinese officials now head three UN entities, including the World Health Organization, the UN Industrial Development Organization (UNIDO), and the UN Department of Economic and Social Affairs (UNDESA). In 2012 a Brazilian was elected to lead the Food and Agriculture Organization.[27]

Emerging powers and South–South cooperation at the UN

This brief analysis of the financial contributions did not give many indications that China, India, Brazil, or South Africa aspire to shape UN development policy to a greater degree than in the past. But financial contributions only tell one part of the story, and it is important therefore to examine whether and how the emerging powers promote ssc under UN auspices, and the extent to which they rely on the UN development system as a partner for transmitting their knowledge and expertise to other developing countries.

ssc and the United Nations have been intertwined for many years, most notably as a result of the work of India and later China. Advocated by developing countries in the G77 and NAM, the recognition and promotion of cooperation between countries of the global South have long been objectives articulated within the UN General Assembly. Already in 1974 a special unit had been set up within the UNDP with the aim of fostering technical cooperation among developing countries. Support for ssc has picked up over the past few years. In 2009 the UN hosted a well-attended high-level conference on ssc in Nairobi, to commemorate the 30th anniversary of the adoption of the *Buenos Aires Plan of Action for Promoting and Implementing Technical Cooperation among Developing Countries*. Previously the General Assembly addressed an agenda item on ssc every other year, but it is now annual. In 2012 the special unit was upgraded to the UN Office for South–South Cooperation. In response to a request by the High-level Committee on South–South Cooperation, the UN developed operational guidelines to inform and promote support by its funds, programmes, and agencies to South–South and triangular cooperation.[28] In 2014 the UN secretary-general appointed a special representative on the topic. Prompted by demands from the General Assembly and individual programme countries, but also increasingly driven by UN organisations that have begun to realise that middle-income countries will be crucial for the future of the UN system, nearly all UN entities now have small South–South units and offer support for countries to share their development experiences.[29]

India, South Africa, Brazil, and China are vocal supporters of further strengthening the ssc agenda at the UN. They do not set themselves apart from other developing countries in this regard; they always align themselves with the position of the roughly 130 developing countries represented in the G77.

Three distinct features in this position deserve a mention. First, the G77 argues that ssc, when supported by the UN, still fundamentally differs from other traditional development activities, including UN initiatives. ssc should therefore not be subjected to any rules other than those already specified in previous high-level conferences on ssc. This stance is identical to the position that emerging powers have articulated within the aid/development coordination processes outside the UN. Second, ssc should not be a replacement but rather a complement to North–South cooperation; the industrialised economies still need to fulfil their development commitments. This argument is often articulated by emerging powers inside and outside the UN to fend-off Western desires and hopes for burden sharing in times of austerity. As the Indian ambassador pointed out at the 2014 session of the High-level Commission on South–South Cooperation:

> The starting premise has to be therefore the single most important acknowledgement, which has been consistently established in every UN document and Resolution on South South Cooperation: that South–South cooperation can **supplement** North–South Cooperation but cannot substitute or dilute the obligation and quantum of North–South aid flows. **Mr President**, The other basic tenet that needs to

be observed is that, through the actual implementation of South South cooperation, the actual manner in which such cooperation takes place are clearly known,
defined and well established. Any attempt therefore by outside commentators and
bodies to shackle the agenda of South South cooperation through guidelines, mapping frameworks and imposing accountability in the name of 'aid effectiveness'
are **simply not** acceptable to the South.[30]

Third, all developing countries have argued that ssc within the UN should be
qualitatively and quantitatively intensified. South–South and triangular cooperation should be mainstreamed and expanded across the UN development system.
Thus, additional resources will be needed – proposals mention that UN organisations should apportion not less than 0.5% of core budget resources for this
purpose. In addition, the office for ssc should be strengthened and its status
enhanced.[31] For instance, as a Chinese delegate argued in 2013:

> The Chinese delegation believes that, as the High-level Committee on South–
> South Cooperation Secretariat and the United Nations system South–South cooper-
> ation coordinator, the Office's position, function and resources should be further
> strengthened to ensure that it has sufficient capability to track, analyze and
> research the South–South cooperation development dynamics, and to promote and
> implement South–South cooperation for development policies particularly in the
> LDCS.[32]

These ideas are a matter of heated debate between advanced economies and the
G77 because, as elaborated above, the industrialised countries pay most of the
bill. So far, the ssc office has not profited much from the renewed interest in
and boost to ssc, at least in terms of financial resources. While the unit produces
pertinent analysis and functions as the secretariat of the High-level Committee
on ssc, it can do little to overcome the persistent reluctance of Southern countries to move beyond bilateral relations, make use of the UN, and endow it with
funds. The IBSA trust fund presents a small exception. India, Brazil, and South
Africa chose the ssc office to administer the fund that was established in 2004.
Its objective is to identify replicable and scalable projects that can be
disseminated to interested developing countries as examples of best practices in
the fight against poverty and hunger. Each country committed to contribute $1
million per year. This sum, however, seems far too small to create a systemic
impact.[33]

On the practical side of ssc at the UN, there is less concern with principled
debates and more with action. The most visible mechanisms of engagement are
centres of excellence on various issues with relevance to development. Here,
UN organisations and emerging powers team up to make experience, knowledge, and technologies available to other developing countries. Examples
include the UNIDO centres on South–South Industrial Cooperation hosted by India
and China or the recently opened WFP Centre of Excellence against Hunger in
Brazil. The UNDP country programmes of China, Brazil, India, and South Africa
include the objective of having the UNDP assist them in strengthening their cooperation with other developing countries. More recently the UNDP has begun to
develop strategic partnerships with a selected group of emerging powers and has
concluded agreements with China, Brazil, South Africa, and India (as well as

with Turkey, Mexico, Indonesia, and others). Signed by the UNDP administrator and the minister of foreign affairs or another high-level official, the agreements mainly have three objectives: to lay the foundation for sharing knowledge and development experiences; to create space for strategic dialogue; and to build the basis for increased financial contributions. These strategic partnerships could very well become the mechanism by which the four emerging powers gain more influence and take over more responsibility with regard to the policies of the UNDP, the lead agency in the UN system, in which it also plays a coordinating role.

On the ground in the operational work of the UN, there is little fear of contact between the UN's 'regular' development work, trilateral cooperation, and SSC; but at the rhetorical level the emerging powers emphasise the uniqueness of their development cooperation. They underline their commonalities with poorer developing countries and continue to be members of the G77. Any similarities to Western donors or the traditional aid paradigm are denied. By setting themselves so starkly apart, the four countries do not fully acknowledge that they are also involved in the governance and oversight of the rest of the UN's development operations on a formally equitable basis. Instead of reaching out to influence and shape the larger part of the UN's $23.9 billion operational activities, they seem to confine themselves to an SSC niche which, however, they want to expand. At the same time their own contributions to financing such an expansion are marginal; the four emerging powers want industrialised countries to pay – while opposing any form of Western infringement as well as any attempts to discuss multilateral norms and rules beyond the to date rather vague SSC principles.[34]

Global norms and standard setting at the UN

The United Nations is the primary forum for norms and standard setting on development – as for many other issues. Not least because the majority of member states emphasise questions of development that involve not only aid but also trade, economy, and finance, policy processes on these very issues play a major role, notably in the General Assembly. Over almost seven decades the international community has adopted an extensive body of normative principles and objectives for poverty eradication and universal development.[35] To the great frustration of the global South, many of these resolutions have not been implemented.[36]

So far – and regardless of whether these negotiating processes are related to high-level events or form part of the regular sessions of the General Assembly's second committee or ECOSOC – the four countries have aligned themselves with the G77. While it seems to take more time to come up with a joint G77 position, given the increasingly divergent interests among so many countries, the alliance still holds.[37] The four countries are active to differing degrees in the various negotiation processes. However, they share an unwillingness to abandon the alliance and leave it in the way they did it as the BASIC (BRICS minus Russia) group did during the Copenhagen climate talks.[38] In the ubiquitous North–South conflict that is especially prominent at the UN, the four remain firmly on the side of the global South and do not use their dual role as recipients and providers of development assistance to define a new perspective.[39]

This stance is also applied with regard to a relatively new UN forum for international dialogue on questions of development. The DCF was created after the 2005 World Summit as part of a reform package to revitalise ECOSOC. The forum was established to bridge the institutional gap in the international aid architecture by providing an inclusive platform for dialogue and joint learning that is open to all development actors.[40] DCF's purpose is to review trends in international development cooperation, promote greater coherence among the development activities of different development partners, and strengthen the normative and operational link in the UN's work. Its inclusive nature gives the DCF a major advantage vis-à-vis the OECD and the Global Partnership. So far, however, the DCF has struggled to establish itself as a serious forum whose deliberations matter for discussing global development. It plays this weak role not only because its modest structures are no match for the concentrated powers of the OECD secretariat but also because most DAC members hesitate to fully support the DCF. They do not want to duplicate DAC's work and remain wary of what they perceive as cumbersome UN processes.

The emerging powers, notably the selected four, are also rather cautious in their engagement with the DCF, although all of them have participated in the programme of one or more of the DCF's three sessions held so far. China is the most active, sending representatives to many of the global preparatory meetings and participating three times at ministerial level in the DCF. At the same time China sees the DCF's role foremost as a forum for dialogue and exchange. Brazil has championed the DCF for its universality and multilateralism and has shown some openness towards having a stronger DCF with decision-making powers. South Africa has not been overly visible, nor has India, although both are represented on the DCF advisory panel, as is Brazil. Although generally supportive, the emerging powers have not seized the opportunity to make the DCF more relevant and to use it for their own purposes. However, in the preparations for the 2014 DCF, a group of Southern providers of development cooperation formed and met repeatedly to exchange and identify ways and means to strengthen SSC. This group included government representatives as well as members of the research communities of the four countries; it might herald a change towards making more purposeful use of the forum. Now that three out of four of the emerging powers have officially distanced themselves from the Global Partnership, the DCF might also benefit. Indeed, it still has the potential to become the principal forum for global dialogue and policy review on the effectiveness and coherence of international development cooperation.

Some elements of explanation

What are the possible explanations for the observed pattern that none of the four countries, despite their growing power and new donor roles, openly aspires to a leadership role in the policy field of development at the UN? Of course, the domestic qualities of each of the four countries provide a partial explanation. For instance, Amitav Acharya has argued that, thanks to a similar cultural background based on Asian philosophy and principles, China and India are more concerned with developing and legitimising their national power aspirations than with contributing to and taking a leadership role in global

governance.[41] However, and despite nuanced differences among the four countries, they all share the same tendency of rather ducking away from instead of
attempting to challenge the dominant paradigm at the UN in the area of development and shape it to a greater extent. Therefore it seems plausible to assume
that there must be more systemic factors explaining their common behaviour. In
principle, we can broadly distinguish a rationalist explanation that emphasises
cost–benefit calculations from a constructivist explanation that underlines the
importance of culture and history.

All four countries have made the assessment that changing their behaviour
and seizing power in the area of development at the UN is more costly than
maintaining the status quo. By acting up, showcasing their own development
model to a greater degree, and demanding greater influence at the UN, they
could lose more than they would gain. Indeed, there are several indications of
the plausibility of this explanation. In several interviews with diplomats, delegates from China, India, and Brazil indicated financial concerns. They expected
advanced economies to pressure them to contribute ever more to funding the
world organisation. A case in point is the scale of assessments for obligatory
contributions to the regular UN budget, which is revised every three years. For
several years the advanced economies have been successfully trying to make the
emerging economies pay more.[42] Although the emerging powers have accepted
to pay a greater share, they still profit from a system of discounts.[43] Similarly,
when famine hit the Horn of Africa, there were many voices publicly calling for
the emerging powers to make more generous contributions. Accordingly the
cost–benefit calculation could be that, once emerging powers take over more
responsibility, they will have less ground to reject calls for higher contributions
for humanitarian and development assistance. In times of financial austerity in
the industrialised economies, even domestic inequalities and poverty challenges
are not enough of an argument to fend off demands for greater financial
contributions.

Another cost might occur in the form of a possible break-up or diminished
salience of the G77. So far membership (or 'association' in the case of China)
brings political benefits that would be lost if one of the four countries were to
leave the alliance, either formally or informally (as they did in the climate talks).
At the UN political negotiations are very much dominated by the North–South
divide. The G77 comprises two-thirds of UN member states. The calculation for
South Africa, Brazil, and perhaps India might be that, individually, they would
wield less influence on the global scene and within multilateral organisations
without the backing of other developing countries. Brazil and South Africa were
recently counted among the 10 most active players in the G77. Their leadership
in the group enables them to translate their priorities into UN politics, backed
up by a group that represents two-thirds of UN membership.[44] This argument
might be less pertinent for China, which is already a political heavyweight.
However, China's status as an associate of the G77 and as a NAM observer provides it not only with greater legitimacy but also with the opportunity to shape
the position of a powerful group at the UN.

While the costs of breaking ranks with the G77 in terms of money and
political influence seem potentially high, the likely benefits appear rather low. In
the field of development, forging an alliance with Western powers might not be

a very attractive option, because they have elaborate aid structures and modalities that are not easily challenged. Furthermore, the Western aid paradigm, despite micro-successes, does not have a proven track record of macro-successes. In addition, stepping up and participating in or even leading norm setting on international development might be rather detrimental to increased reputation and influence among other developing countries that can be reached more readily through bilateral ssc.

Alternative explanations build on ideas growing from the assumption that states are guided by rules of appropriate behaviour. It seems plausible to assume for India and South Africa, but also to some extent for Brazil and China, that their national identity has been profoundly shaped by being ex-colonies, developing countries, and belonging to such alliances as the G77 and nam.[45] Indeed, they even played important roles in the founding and evolution of these organisations. The essential purpose of these groupings has been to boost the role of developing countries and gain influence in setting the global agenda, and to display a countervailing power within multilateral institutions vis-à-vis the well-organised and coordinated countries of the North. Following this line of explanation, the behaviour of the four countries would be guided by a strong resentment towards the sense of superiority and arrogance that is displayed by many of the richest countries in the UN, and a profound feeling of not belonging. Many of the issues that gave rise to the founding of the G77 and nam persist, such as asymmetries in trade and finance and immense development gaps between richer and poorer countries. Moreover, for many years the four countries have been at the receiving end of development assistance. From this perspective issues of aid and development effectiveness are considered the wrong priority; they allow many industrialised countries to avoid talking about their lack of commitment in respecting targets for official development assistance and making the international trade and finance systems more equitable.

Especially in New York and Geneva, the stages for many UN debates and decisions on development, the conflict between North and South is continuously re-enacted and fuelled. This 'theatre' has become possible since politics trumps substantial policy in many UN arenas, not least because the diplomatic corps mostly consists of foreign ministry officials.[46] It seems plausible that the experiences of being disadvantaged are engrained in the political cultures of the foreign offices of the four selected countries, which makes it difficult to find an alternative role at the UN outside the North–South dichotomy.

Conclusion

This article set out to determine whether China, India, Brazil, and South Africa have changed their behaviour at the UN in the field of development, given that they have experienced a period of economic growth; shown greater resilience against the impacts of the recent economic and social crises; have aspired to a greater voice in other institutions; and have become substantial providers of ssc. Analysing financial contributions along with patterns of engagement and political behaviour in various UN arenas, the four countries consistently continue to insist on being 'ordinary' developing countries. In general their financial contributions, though increasing, reflect more a lack of interest in the UN development system than leadership aspirations. Even in light of the substantial development challenges they face, these small amounts are a political choice not a necessity.

The strong insistence on the distinctiveness of ssc by all four countries reinforces the North–South dichotomy, although there was hope that the emerging powers, in their dual capacities as recipients and providers of development assistance, might help to bridge that divide. There exist many plausible motives why individual emerging powers continue a form of behaviour that Western observers perceive as ducking away at the UN. In the West there is an evident desire for new players not to block or spoil international negotiations but rather to constructively develop ideas for a new multilateral order. Perspectives and partners are sought that do not stick to what is perceived as an outdated agenda of the global South but are instead willing to take on greater responsibility. With particular pertinence for this special issue, new allies for the reform of the UN development system are wanted.[47]

The articulation of these expectations, however, is rarely accompanied by critical self-reflection about the role of the West at the United Nations and in the broader world order. It would surely be valid to examine the extent to which the behaviour of emerging powers reflects a reaction to the West as much as the former's own abilities, interests, and limitations – and vice versa. From a normative standpoint leadership by the governments of both the global South and the global North is desperately required if global public goods are to become a serious orientation for international public policy. The establishment of a rule-based world order – however imperfect – has been a considerable achievement, and the UN still stands for the idea of confronting the rule of the powerful with the power of the rule. The demands for a fairer world are getting louder, for instance in these 2014 words from an Indian ambassador:

> If the UN Development System still chooses to continue to ask what the South will do for it, rather than the other way around, it will only contribute to making the UN system irrelevant at a time when we are supposed to be discussing the outlines of the post-2015 Development Agenda...The rise in cooperation among developing countries is not a transient phenomenon. It is here to stay and its paradigms need to be accepted and acted upon.[48]

While these sentences can be interpreted narrowly as part of a persistent fight over the allocation of resources at the United Nations, they also stand for a demand for a world organisation that is less dominated by the industrialised economies and more aligned with what developing countries require. The UN's role would in this case provide the rules and norms for protecting the poorest against the power of the providers of development assistance, regardless of their geographical location.

Notes

1. A version of parts of this article was published in German as Weinlich and Fues, "Aufstrebende Schwellenmächte bei den Vereinten Nationen."
2. Stephen, "Rising Regional Powers."
3. UNDP, *Human Development Report 2013*.
4. SSC is usually conceptualised to encompass all forms of political and economic cooperation between developing countries. It is much broader than the OECD-DAC definition of aid, which excludes, for instance, support for peace operations or measures to promote production and trade from least developed countries. See Chaturvedi, "Development Cooperation."
5. Chaturvedi et al., *Development Cooperation*.
6. Quadir, "Rising Donors."
7. United Nations, *Development Cooperation*, 74.
8. Chaturvedi, "Development Cooperation," 24–25.
9. Birdsall, *Aid Alert*; and Kharas, *Coming Together*.
10. Fues and Klingebiel, *Unrequited Love*; and Glennie, *Development Partnership Conference*.
11. Quadir, "Rising Donors."
12. Ferdinand, "Rising Powers at the UN," 378–379.
13. Stephen, "Rising Regional Powers," 307–308.
14. Eyben and Savage, "Emerging and Submerging Powers," 460–461; and Bergamaschi, "New Faces in the Aid Crowd."
15. Weiss et al., *UN Voices*.
16. Browne and Weiss, *Post-2015 UN Development*; and Stokke, *The UN and Development*.
17. UN member states only have an obligation to pay for the UN's general budget, which finances mostly the infrastructure and staff of the UN Secretariat, as well as for the costs for peace operations and political missions. The respective contributions are assessed on the basis of a state's relative ability to pay, based on gross domestic product and other factors, such as foreign debt and per capita income, and negotiated among member states every three years. Hüfner, "Die Finanzierung des UN-Systems in der Dauerkrise."
18. Weinlich, "Funding the UN Development System."
19. UN Department of Economic and Social Affairs (UNDESA). *Implementation of General Assembly Resolution 67/226*, 10.
20. Ibid.
21. Walz and Ramachandran, *Brave New World*, 7.
22. UNDESA, *Statistical Annex*, Tables A-3, B-3.
23. Author's calculations on the basis of United Nations, *Statistical Annex to Funding Report 2009; 2010; 2011; 2012*, Tables A-3, A-5, B-3.
24. Weinlich, *Reforming Development Cooperation*.
25. In the mid-1980s the Brazilian government began to channel funds (often loans from the World Bank or regional development banks) through the UN. It was thereby able to work around its own administrative structures, which were slow to reform. Self-supporting contributions have gained prominence among middle- and high-income countries. Thanks to their economic growth, they tend to receive less money from the UN system and have to pay for development services from the UN system by themselves. Self-supporting contributions are not uncontroversial. On the one hand, they correspond very much with the principle of national ownership. On the other hand, there are signs that UN agencies cannot properly be advocates of global norms, coordinators, or capacity builders, if they act as a development contractor. See Galvani and Morse, "Institutional Sustainability."
26. UNDP, *Annual Report 2012/13*, 40.
27. Browne and Weiss, *Emerging Economies*.
28. United Nations, *Framework of Operational Guidelines*.
29. For a brief overview, see United Nations, *The State of South–South Cooperation*, 13–16.
30. Statement of Ambassador Asoke K Mukerji, Permanent Representative of India to the United Nations, at the 18th Session of the High-level Committee on South–South Cooperation, New York, May 19, 2014. https://www.pminewyork.org/pages.php?id=1928.
31. United Nations, *Measures to Further Strengthen*.
32. Statement of the Chinese Delegation at the High-level Committee on South–South Cooperation, Closing Segment, New York, June 4, 2013. http://ssc.undp.org/content/dam/ssc/documents/HLC%20IS/statements/13%20China%20Statement_Intersessional%20HLC.pdf.
33. Stuenkel, *Institutionalizing South–South Cooperation*, 17.

34. For a different interpretation, see Abdenur and Da Fonseca, "The North's Growing Role."
35. Jolly et al., *UN Ideas*.
36. The commitment by advanced economies to spend 0.7% of their gross national product on aid was first made in 1970 and was repeatedly reaffirmed in international agreements, including the Conference on Financing for Development in Monterrey 2002. To date, only five countries fulfil this commitment. The implementation of MDG 8, which set the goal of developing a global partnership (eg a fairer trading and financial system, debt relief, access to essential drugs) is very much lagging behind.
37. Swart, "Organizational Framework."
38. Qi, "The Rise of BASIC."
39. See also Ferdinand, "Rising Powers at the UN," 387.
40. South Centre, *Reshaping the International Development Cooperation Architecture*.
41. Acharya, "Can Asia Lead?"
42. China, as the world's second largest economy, currently still pays less than 3% of the UN's general budget (2010–12), but has had to accept a 0.5% increase compared to the previous period (2007–09). Brazil's share nearly doubled from 0.9% to 1.6%. India's share went up from 0.45% to 0.54%, while South Africa's share increased from 0.29% to 0.83%. Browne and Weiss, *Emerging Economies*. In parallel, the share of some Western countries went down. For instance, Japan's contribution decreased from 16.6% to 15.5%; Germany's share went down from 8.6% to 8%. See Weinlich, *Reforming Development Cooperation*, Table 2.
43. Swart, "Organizational Framework," 11–13.
44. Ibid., 21–22.
45. Brazil has never been a NAM member.
46. Weiss, "Moving Beyond North–South Theatre."
47. Weinlich, *Reform of the UN Development System*.
48. Statement of Ambassador Asoke K Mukerji, Permanent Mission of India to the UN.

Bibliography

Abdenur, Adriana Erthal, and João Moura Estevão Marques Da Fonseca. "The North's Growing Role in South–South Cooperation: Keeping the Foothold." *Third World Quarterly* 34, no. 8 (2013): 1475–1491.

Acharya, Amitav. "Can Asia Lead? Power Ambitions and Global Governance in the Twenty-first Century." *International Affairs* 4, no. 87 (2011): 851–869.

Bergamaschi, Isaline. "New Faces in the Aid Crowd: Strategies and Patterns of Association and Participation of Non-member Countries from the Global South at the OECD/DAC in the 2000s." Paper presented at the groupe de recherche seminar on "Organisations Internationales", Centre d'Etudes et de Recherches Internationales, Paris, May 5, 2014. On file with the author.

Birdsall, Nancy. *Aid Alert: China Officially Joins the Donor Club*. CGD Blog, Global Development: Views from the Centre, May 12, 2011. http://www.cgdev.org/blog/aid-alert-china-officially-joins-donor-club.

Browne Stephen, and Thomas G. Weiss. *Emerging Economies and the UN Development System*. Briefing 10. New York: Future United Nations Development System, September 2013.

Browne, Stephen, and Thomas G. Weiss. *Post-2015 UN Development: Making Change Happen?* New York: Routledge, 2014.

Chaturvedi, Sachin. "Development Cooperation: Contours, Evolution and Scope." In *Development Cooperation and Emerging Powers: New Partners or Old Patterns?*, edited by Sachin Chaturvedi, Thomas Fues, and Elizabeth Sidiropoulos, 13–36. London: Zed Books, 2012.

Chaturvedi, Sachin, Thomas Fues, and Elizabeth Sidiropoulos eds. *Development Cooperation and Emerging Powers: New Partners or Old Patterns?* London: Zed Books, 2012.

Eyben, Rosalind, and Laura Savage. "Emerging and Submerging Powers: Imagined Geographies in the New Development Partnership at the Busan Fourth High Level Forum." *Journal of Development Studies* 49, no. 4 (2013): 457–469.

Ferdinand, Peter. "Rising Powers at the UN: An Analysis of the Voting Behaviour of BRICS in the General Assembly." *Third World Quarterly* 35, no. 3 (2014): 378–379.

Fues, Thomas, and Stephan Klingebiel. *Unrequited Love: What is the Legacy of the First Global Partnership Summit?* The Current Column, April 17, 2014. Bonn: German Development Institute, 2014.

Galvani, Flavia, and Stephen Morse. "Institutional Sustainability: At What Price? UNDP and the New Cost-sharing Model in Brazil." *Development in Practice* 14, no. 3 (2004): 311–327.

Glennie, Jonathan. *Development Partnership Conference: What did We Learn? Guardian* Poverty Matters Blog, April 22, 2014. http://www.theguardian.com/global-development/poverty-matters/2014/apr/22/development-partnership-co-operation-conference.

Hüfner, Klaus. "Die Finanzierung des UN-Systems in der Dauerkrise." In *Praxishandbuch UNO: Die Vereinten Nationen im Lichte globaler Herausforderungen*, edited by Sabine von Schorlemer, 615–641. Berlin: Springer Verlag, 2003.

Kharas, Homi. *Coming Together: How a New Global Partnership on Development Cooperation was forged at the Busan High Level Forum on Aid Effectiveness.* Analyses of the Elcano Royal Institute 164/2011. Madrid: Real Instituto Elcano, 2011.

Jolly, Richard, Louis Emmerij, and Thomas G. Weiss. *UN Ideas that Changed the World.* Bloomington: Indiana University Press, 2009.

Qi, Xinran. "The Rise of BASIC in UN Climate Change Negotiations." *South African Journal of International Affairs* 18, no. 3 (2011): 295–318.

Quadir, Fahimul. "Rising Donors and the New Narrative of 'South–South' Cooperation: What Prospects for Changing the Landscape of Development Assistance Programmes?" *Third World Quarterly* 34, no. 3 (2013): 324–328.

South Centre. *Reshaping the International Development Cooperation Architecture: Perspectives on a Strategic Development Role for the Development Cooperation Forum (DCF).* Analytical Note SC/GGDP/AN/GEG/9. Geneva: South Centre, 2008.

Stephen, Matthew. "Rising Regional Powers and International Institutions: The Foreign Policy Orientations of India, Brazil and South Africa." *Global Society* 26, no. 3 (2012): 289–309.

Stokke, Olav. *The UN and Development: From Aid to Cooperation.* Bloomington: Indiana University Press, 2009.

Stuenkel, Oliver. *Institutionalizing South–South Cooperation: Towards a New Paradigm?* UN High-level Panel on the Post 2015 Development Agenda, 2013.

Swart, Lydia. "Organizational Framework of the Group of 77." In *The Group of 77: Perspectives on its Role in the UN General Assembly New York,* edited by Swart, Lydia, and Lund, Jacob. New York: Center for UN Reform Education, 2011.

UN Department of Economic and Social Affairs (UNDESA). *Implementation of General Assembly Resolution 67/ 226 of the Quadrennial Comprehensive Policy Review of Operational Activities for Development of the United Nations System (QCPR).* Report of the Secretary-General. UN document A/69/63–E/2014/10, 06.02.2014.

UNDESA. Statistical Annex to Funding Report (2012). New York, 2014.

UNDP. *Annual Report 2012/13: Supporting Global Progress.* New York: UNDP, 2014.

UNDP. *Human Development Report 2013: The Rise of the South – Human Progress in a Diverse World.* New York: UNDP, 2013.

United Nations. *Development Cooperation for the MDGs: Maximizing Results.* New York: UN, 2010.

United Nations. *Framework of Operational Guidelines on United Nations Support to South–South and Triangular Cooperation.* Note by the Secretary-General. UN document SSC/18/2, April 12, 2012.

United Nations. *Measures to Further Strengthen the United Nations Office for South–South Cooperation.* Report of the Secretary-General. UN document SSC/18/3, April 23, 2014.

United Nations. *The State of South–South Cooperation.* Report of the Secretary-General. UN document A/68/ 212, July 29, 2013.

United Nations. *Statistical Annex to Funding Report 2009; 2010; 2011; 2012.* http://www.un.org/esa/coordination/dcpb_stat.htm.

Walz, Julie, and Vijaya Ramachandran. *Brave New World: A Literature Review of Emerging Donors and the Changing Nature of Foreign Assistance.* Working Paper 273. London: Center for Global Development, 2011.

Weinlich, Silke. "Funding the UN Development System." In *Post-2015 UN Development: Making Change Happen?* edited by Stephen Brown and Thomas G. Weiss, 75–94. New York: Routledge, 2014.

Weinlich, Silke. *Reform of the UN Development System: New Multilateralist Reform Coalition Needed.* Briefing Paper 1/2011. Bonn: German Development Institute, 2011.

Weinlich, Silke. *Reforming Development Cooperation at the United Nations: An Analysis of Policy Positions and Actions of Key States on Reform Options.* DIE Studies 59. Bonn: German Development Institute, 2011.

Weinlich, Silke, and Thomas Fues. "Aufstrebende Schwellenmächte bei den Vereinten Nationen." In *Die großen Schwellenländer: Ursachen und Folgen ihres Aufstiegs in der Weltwirtschaft,* edited by Andreas Nölke, Christian May, and Simone Claar, 299–316. Wiesbaden: Springer Verlag, 2013.

Weiss, Thomas G. "Moving Beyond North-South Theatre." *Third World Quarterly* 30, no. 2 (2009): 271–284.

Weiss, Thomas G., Tatiana Carayannis, Louis Emmerij, and Richard Jolly. *UN Voices: The Struggle for Development and Social Justice.* Bloomington: Indiana University Press, 2005.

A changing world: is the UN development system ready?

Stephen Browne

Ralph Bunche Institute for International Studies, The City University of New York Graduate Center, USA

This article examines five contemporary areas of development concern that have become major drivers of global transformation since the turn of the millennium: the plight of fragile states; the emergence of new powers and new development funds in a changing aid landscape; the need for developing countries to manage the growing resources at their disposal; encroachments on the political sovereignty of states; and new global challenges that demand global action, including climate change, migration, and food security. These drivers of change call for responses from the UN – and in particular its development system of some 30 organisations. The ongoing protracted debate on the future UN development agenda should take cognisance of these changes if the system is to remain relevant after 2015. But the signs are not promising that either the agenda or the UN development system are up to the task.

The United Nations development system (UNDS) comprises more than 30 separately governed organisations and a similar number of research and training institutions. Although a disparate family, it is a source of ideas (including research, information, and advocacy), a value-based source of norms and standards and, operationally, a purveyor of technical assistance. This article is about the search by the UN for a new agenda to guide all of its development activities, but especially its technical assistance operations, in a world of change.

The article first outlines how the world is changing with reference to five clusters of development challenges of growing importance. These challenges are not just to future development progress, but to the UN itself; they require a response by the global body. They present new tests of the UN's readiness for its next development decade-and-a-half, which it has designated as 2016–30.

Next the article describes how the UN has been going about its search for a new development agenda. As a forum for airing contemporary concerns, the UN is indispensable and unrivalled, and it has had a comprehensive development framework in place since 2000. Its actions, however, have not measured up to the aspirations of this framework, and have centred around the achievement of the Millennium Development Goals (MDGS), which have been a partial and imperfect agenda for its operations. The challenge for the UN now is not just to indulge in more protracted deliberations in order to discover a new agenda, but more especially to determine how best to fulfil that agenda and frontally address the major development concerns analysed below. The article concludes with an answer to the question posed in the title.

The world is changing

Five areas of development concern have deep temporal roots that have become major drivers of global transformation, particularly since the turn of the millennium. In September 2000 the UN General Assembly approved its Millennium Declaration in resolution 55/2 as a basis for a new development agenda. The changes described here – or more exactly the rapidly emerging development challenges – have accompanied that agenda, have become more pronounced, and can be expected to continue to be significant drivers of change beyond 2015 when the development UN expects to reset its priorities. These challenges, therefore, may be considered 'five tests' of the future readiness of the UN in its development role. They concern the role of the UN in conflict-prone states; the UN as strategic international partner; the UN as mobiliser and monitor of resources; the UN as an active custodian of human development, security, and rights; and the UN as an effective global forum to govern critical emerging issues.

Rising inequalities and conflict-prone states

Since 1980, but especially over the past 15 years, economic growth has ensured a process of convergence between richer and poorer countries.[1] After 2008, when capitalism in the developed world faced its worst crisis since the Great Depression, the developing countries continued to catch-up, helping to maintain global economic momentum. Even in sub-Saharan Africa, where average gross national product per capita stagnated between 1990 and 2000, it then rose by some 30% up to 2012.[2] Comparing 2008 with 1990, the size of the middle class (people living on US$2–$20 per day) is estimated to have roughly doubled in Africa and increased by much larger numbers in China and Latin America.[3]

Over the same period the human development index (HDI) – composed of income, education, and life expectancy – of most countries has continued to show improvement. These indicators have shown some convergence, with accelerated increases in the countries with lower HDI rankings, which are now closer to achieving full enrolment in primary education and 50% enrolment at the secondary level.

These are average numbers, however, and they fail to reveal the full picture of deprivation. Life expectancy and child mortality rates are still far worse in low HDI countries than in those with high a HDI. For hundreds of millions of people the development crusade has passed them by. Their lives are still Hobbesian: poor, nasty and brutish, as well as short for those susceptible to HIV/AIDS and other infectious diseases. Appearances can be deceptive. There are more public services but access is inhibited by cost, distance, and quality. Schools may be 'free' but the expense of uniforms, meals, transport, and teacher truancy keeps children at home or in fields or workshops. Many children enrol but fewer complete their education. Clinics and hospitals have new medicines, but poor storage and few staff to administer them.[4] Modern transport infrastructure has never reached many of the poorest regions, perpetuating their isolation.

Also within countries at different HDI levels there are continuing and in some cases worsening inequalities of income. Economic growth has been hailed as an indispensable goal but the plight of the income-poor is not determined by the aggregate income levels of their countries. Moving to middle-income status does not guarantee poverty eradication and often leads to growing inequality. There are more impoverished people in the dynamic economies of India and China than in the whole of Africa.[5] And in some fast-growing African countries – for example Tanzania and Uganda – poverty also is not decreasing.[6]

Development has opened up wide disparities within countries, the poorest as well as those at middle-income levels. But it is the plight of the poor in the still large number of fragile economies, where people are least able to help themselves and where violence and instability are endemic, which should preoccupy the UNDS. Its operations on the ground will become increasingly superfluous in middle-income countries, which have the resources and increasingly the know-how to tackle their own development challenges. The UN will need to concentrate on those countries where external intervention is required to restore stability and promote reconstruction. The UN's record in stopping conflicts has been mixed. But when hostilities cease, there is the even harder task of establishing normality and bringing states back to a development path. This peacebuilding role – formally initiated with the creation of the Peacebuilding Commission in the middle of the past decade but a reality for much longer – also has a chequered record in the UN, for two reasons. One concerns the nature of the response: there is not always an adequate understanding of the causes of conflict and the necessity of carefully sequencing the transition through peace to development. The other is organisational. Peacebuilding has at least four dimensions: security, political, social, and economic.[7] Taking the system as a whole, the UN encompasses all four dimensions, to which should be added humanitarian assistance. But its effectiveness is hampered by poor communication – and worse, turf battles – within the system, which undermine attempts at integration.

New powers, new funds, new partners

The development assistance landscape is undergoing fundamental change. The number of countries providing assistance or cooperation has grown rapidly; there are large new vertical funding mechanisms; and more private sector and philanthropic entities are involved in development. The UNDS needs to adjust to these changing realities as its role as a donor becomes marginalised.

The four countries known as BASIC (Brazil, China, India, and South Africa) account for nearly three billion people; three of those countries are among the top seven economies in terms of GDP. They and other emerging powers (including Argentina, Chile, Indonesia, Malaysia, Mexico, Peru, South Korea, Thailand, Turkey, and several Arab states) account for half the world's population and a growing proportion of the global economy (Table 1). Almost all have active development cooperation programmes, which display some of the characteristics

Table 1. Thirteen emerging powers: key indicators.

	Human Development Index	Gross domestic product (millions of current US$)	GDP per capita (current US$)	Population (millions)
Argentina	0.811	446,044	10,952	40.7
Brazil	0.730	2,476,652	12,576	197.0
Chile	0.819	251,191	14,513	17.3
China	0.699	7,321,935	5447	1,344.1
India	0.554	1,872,845	1534	1,221.1
Indonesia	0.629	846,341	3471	243.8
Malaysia	0.769	287,934	10,012	28.8
Mexico	0.775	1,158,147	9703	119.3
Peru	0.741	176,925	5974	29.6
South Africa	0.629	401,802	7943	50.6
South Korea	0.909	1,114,472	22,388	49.8
Thailand	0.690	345,672	5192	66.6
Turkey	0.722	774,775	10,605	73.1
Total 13		17,474,735		3,481.8
Total world		72,440,000	10,138	7,046.0
% global		24.1		49.4

Sources: World Bank, *World Development Indicators*; and United Nations, *Human Development Reports*.

of those of the traditional donors as vehicles of commercial, political, and other forms of influence.

Their stance towards multilateralism generally, and towards UN organisations in particular, is more difficult to gauge, although it is notable that Brazil, China, and India are more actively seeking influence here through the sponsorship of candidates for senior posts and the hosting of global and regional UN institutions in domains that accord with their domestic interests. UN organisations have openly encouraged closer collaboration with emerging countries, often motivated by increased funding for their operations. Individual countries like Brazil and Argentina have channelled substantial funds of their own (called local resources) through the UN Development Programme (UNDP), which is used as a procurement mechanism for their own national programmes.

Besides the emerging bilateral donors, other established multilateral sources – notably the European Commission, World Bank, and regional development banks – have grown substantially and now fund development assistance activities similar to those of the UN. There are also new funding mechanisms, particularly in the domains of health and the environment, which have attracted donors from the private sector and from philanthropic organisations. Some of these alternative sources of development assistance are a direct response to the perception of UN organisations as excessively bureaucratic and cumbersome, as well as to the belief that the UN is hesitant about involving new partners in its activities. (A Future United Nations Development System (FUNDS) global survey of 2012 put the simplification of business procedures and the need for more partnership at the top of the list of 14 UN priorities in the next five years.[8])

As their donor role has diminished, UN organisations have turned themselves into implementing agencies for these other major aid sources in order to maintain the scope of their operational activities. The two largest sources of funding for the UNDP are now the EU and the Global Fund, which appoints the UNDP as its 'principal recipient' in some 40 countries.

More important than seeking by any means to continue to attract funding to implement the agendas of other donors, the UN needs to adapt to new partnership roles. It should facilitate, not duplicate, the involvement of other actors besides governments in development cooperation. The UN played an important role in assisting in the creation of new global funds (the Global Fund itself, GAVI Vaccine Alliance, and the Global Environmental Facility among others) and its organisations are members of their governing bodies. It should continue to encourage new stakeholders, including emerging economic powers and the global private sector, to take up development roles. Resources are needed for the provision of global public goods, including the development and deployment of the kind of technologies which individual countries could not afford on their own. In the fields of health, energy, and the environment the UN should continue to facilitate the mobilisation of resources to these ends.

Partnership goes beyond funding. Nongovernmental organisations (NGOs) and other stakeholders are engaging with the UN in other ways. In the process leading to the 1992 Earth Summit, there was the beginning of a huge expansion in the number of NGOs listed by the UN Economic and Social Council 'in consultative status'. Agenda 21, an outcome of the Rio conference, recognised nine sectors as the principal channels through which citizens could organise and participate in international efforts to achieve sustainable development through the UN.[9] These 'major groups' include business and industry, children and youth, farmers, indigenous peoples, local authorities, NGOs, the scientific and technological community, women, workers and trade unions. Major groups have been involved in subsequent consultations. While preserving its exclusively intergovernmental character in matters of security, the UN should draw up new rules to allow more systematic participation of nongovernmental interests in all its deliberations on development issues.

Changing role of states: managing economic sovereignty

The Westphalian foundation of states has been progressively eroded over several decades. While postwar national independence movements gave renewed impetus to the concept of sovereignty among the UN's member states, the monopoly that individual states enjoyed in power and policy has yielded to external pressures that are both conscious and inadvertent. Through long-term aid relations many states have consciously given up some part of their sovereignty to foreign influence. Consequently, it is outsiders who have played a part in steering their development paths. Notwithstanding appeals for more country ownership, it can be argued that 'donorship' has become stronger. The new sources of aid and cooperation are driving highly focused agendas with substantial and targeted resources.

Rampant globalisation, especially since the turn of the millennium, has rapidly opened up global private markets in capital and products. These markets are harsh censors of economic performance and have constrained domestic policy space. Capital has the freedom to move to or from countries according to the perceptions that distant external investors hold about an economy's health and prospects – amply illustrated by the advance and retreat of funds into and out of the emerging economies since 2010. Capital also flees from countries where resources are poorly managed and where corruption is rife.

Trade penalises weaker economies that have limited productive capacity in, and quality of, exportable goods. Small, poorer economies are still heavily dependent on fickle trends in international commodity prices. They find themselves at the un-remunerative starting points of increasingly long global value-chains, where they are subject to the actions of powerful international companies.

Access to more resources is an opportunity as well as a challenge. External influences can be tamed. Overall the flows of official development assistance (ODA) to developing countries are of diminishing significance as other sources have grown in importance. Besides capital and the proceeds from trade, overseas remittances are three times as large as ODA,[10] foreign direct investment between five and six times,[11] to which may be added oil and mineral royalties that stand to benefit many sub-Saharan African countries. Managing resources has assumed primary importance. Some countries have turned globalisation to their advantage, channelling growing external resources to the cause of development. As in all instances of privatised markets, responsible regulation is needed. The role of individual governments will be to focus on the qualities of their domestic governance, institutions and policies in attracting, retaining, and managing the growing resources available from external sources.[12] There will still be constraints, the most critical being the external trade regime, which continues to remain hostile to the development interests of poorer countries.[13]

The future value of the UNDS will lie in its capacity to help ensure that developing countries can gain maximum development advantage from these external resources. Part of this effort at the global level will be to continue to press for a fairer international trade regime, particularly for the smaller weaker economies; to urge for more robust foreign investment guarantees; and to assist countries to negotiate advantageous terms with multinational companies. In these roles, the UN is considered by many developing countries to be their most trusted partner. Another aspect of this role is more controversial, however; it concerns the prevention of resource diversion within countries and to havens abroad. There are several mechanisms already in place to track and monitor abuse, including Transparency International and its Corruption Perceptions Index, and the Extractive Industries Transparency Initiative. The UN should encourage countries to cooperate with these initiatives. Its own Convention on Corruption, administered by the UN Office for Drugs and Crime, has been in force since 2004.[14] As is the case with many conventions, however, the UN has been more vigorous in getting agreement than in ensuring compliance. This task should be applied in all countries and aimed at all enterprises and institutions wherever they are located.

Changing role of states: towards development democracy

The UN has been instrumental in assisting countries to accede to self-determination, which has also been the rationale for supporting regime-change in countries like South Africa and East Timor. For long it has operated on the assumption of non-intervention and the view that member states were governed by regimes that were sovereign, legitimate, and committed to development.

These assumptions have now begun to change, with pressure coming from above and below.

The outcome document of the UN's 2005 summit spelled out in paragraph 138 of General Assembly resolution 60/1 the notion of sovereignty encompassing a 'responsibility to protect (R2P)': 'each individual state has the responsibility to protect its populations from genocide, war crimes, ethnic cleansing and crimes against humanity'. A 2009 report from the UN secretary-general on the implementation of R2P outlined how it might be put into practice, including the circumstances under which the international community could engage. Subsequent UN-endorsed efforts in Kenya (2007–08), Côte d'Ivoire (2011), Libya (2011), and Central African Republic (2013) have been cited as examples. R2P has been described as 'the most important shift in our conception of sovereignty since the Treaty of Westphalia in 1648'.[15]

From below the legitimacy of regimes and their actions is being increasingly challenged by civil society, in democracies as well as autocratic states. In another manifestation of globalisation new information and communication technologies (ICTs) have played a large role in giving vent to civil society concerns. While ICTs have been used by governments for their own causes (as in the egregious example of *Radio Mille Collines* in the Rwandan genocide), the spread of social networks empowers large numbers to broadcast evidence of government actions that regimes might have preferred to keep hidden. They raise mutual awareness and can rapidly crowd-source issues and grievances. They can encourage people onto the street at short notice. These technologies have also opened windows to the world outside, where conditions in other countries raise popular aspirations.

These challenges to state sovereignty have mixed consequences. Our purpose, however, is not to pronounce judgement on the advantages and costs of these new contestations of government legitimacy, but to note that a combination of information and activism can be a potent and beneficial force for change. The UN already undertakes universal periodic reviews (UPRS) of the human rights records of all member states. In the future it needs to consider broadening its monitoring tasks from a focus on human rights to include the performance of member states in matters of personal security. In development the UN has been an effective monitor of MDG achievement, even if it has not provided sufficient analysis of why and where countries are either achieving the goals or falling short. Its development organisations cover a wide range of domains, and they are the custodians of many norms and conventions that govern different kinds of development standards. From child protection to labour safety, environmental pollution, land rights, and many other domains, the UN's operations should devote more resources to universal compliance in all countries, accompanied by full records of compliance status and analysis of the reasons for success and failure. The UN could and should facilitate the greater involvement of citizen groups (the 'third UN') in dialogues at country level,[16] including the monitoring of development outcomes. As with the UPRS, all such monitoring should be objective and universal.

New global development challenges: migration, climate change

Several other major development-related issues have highlighted the absence of effective global governance mechanisms to address them. Two are mentioned here which will each demand the growing attention of the UN beyond 2015: international migration and climate change.

Another concern related to globalisation is the movement of people. In countries with high inequalities and limited opportunities for advancement outward migration is an escape route for the poor and unemployed as well as for the wealthy and educated, with costs and benefits in development terms. Out-migration reduces skills available at home but also boosts remittances to poor countries; a few countries have promoted the training and 'export' of skilled people as a foreign-exchange earner. However, the costs of financial transfers have risen and new barriers are being set up (often for fear of aiding money laundering).[17] On the more positive side, some countries of emigration have become more attractive to their diasporas and have succeeded in persuading them to return in growing numbers.

Migration invokes far-reaching economic, social, and political concerns. The movement of people follows global market trends, as opportunities open up in dynamic economies with labour shortages. Many people move voluntarily but substantial numbers are refugees from conflict or are illegally trafficked. In receiving countries large-scale immigration provokes problems of assimilation and holds governments hostage to xenophobia. Virtually every country is affected by migration and the phenomenon raises issues of human rights, protection, labour standards, and a multitude of other concerns that are not yet being adequately addressed. It has been said that 'the lack of a comprehensive approach to migration is the most important challenge for developing truly global governance'.[18] Many UN development organisations are already engaging with separate aspects of international migration. The UN's Global Migration Group, established in 2006, now has 16 entities on board with an annually rotating chair. The purpose of the group is 'to encourage the adoption of more coherent, comprehensive and better coordinated approaches to the issue of international migration'. While migration is expected to be another critical item on the post-2015 development agenda, it will demand greater cohesion and not just better coordination from the UN.[19]

In the future more people will also be moving as a result of environmental stresses. Climate change, if not tackled effectively, will begin to alter physical landscapes irreversibly and affect resource balances. Some regions, particularly in developing countries, could become less productive in the cultivation of key crops. There will be consequences for the availability of water and for human health. Rising sea-levels could force the displacement of large numbers of people from islands and coastal areas. The remedial costs of compensating for and reversing the consequences of climate change could range from $70 to $100 billion per year, according to the Intergovernmental Panel on Climate Change.[20]

Through this joint initiative of the UN Environment Programme and the World Meteorological Organization, the UN is already the principal source of scientific information on climate change via its seven-year assessments. But an effective international convention to succeed the Kyoto Protocol of 1997 is still elusive, even after many attempts to negotiate through conferences of the parties (COPS). International agreements may be long in coming through the cumbersome COP process. More important will be the necessity of urgent action supported by sufficient resources.

These are just two of the global development challenges that the UN is uniquely placed to tackle if the solutions are to have universal validity. Others include food security and governing cyberspace. The UN's governance problem is that it relies to an excessive degree on time-honoured but cumbersome processes of intergovernmental consultation in the quest for solutions. The search for a successor to the Kyoto Protocol is a good case in point. While the UN has generated the scientific evidence for an impending calamity, the essential destination of a global agreement has so far eluded multiple intergovernmental conferences. The all-or-nothing consensual approach, in which 193 countries can effectively wield a veto, is not working. Instead of a universal top-down approach, the UN should be instrumental in fostering what the Oxford Martin Commission calls 'creative coalitions', which it describes alliteratively as 'A Coalition of the Working between countries, companies and cities to counteract climate change'.[21] These coalitions would report to the UN Framework Convention on Climate Change, which runs the negotiations, in the expectation that successful 'minilaterism' could lead more rapidly to a multilateral solution.

Another aspect of the problem lies within the UN's own organisational complexity. With respect to food security, UN organisations formed a 'high-level task force' in 2008 after the alarming rise in food prices, in spite of the fact that, since 1974, there has been a Committee on World Food Security comprising the UN's three agricultural agencies in Rome. Because it took several months to set up the task force, which eventually included no fewer than 20 UN entities, the UN was slow in arriving at a plan of action, which all members were expected to help implement.

Thus, even if the first UN can reach agreement on global norms and conventions, the second UN's actions are often mired in time-consuming coordination procedures.

The UN has not changed (yet)

Will the UN be ready by 2016? This section outlines the process by which the UN is searching for a new agenda for its development operations. It argues that it is likely to be more of the same, but that it will be important if the UN builds on the agenda that it has approved in the past, while factoring in the new development changes and challenges outlined above. That may be the easy part. The hard graft that needs to follow – involving all three UNs (governments, agencies, civil society) – will be the process of adapting the UNDS to be effective in responding to these challenges.

A new agenda: plus ça change

Summitry has long been a feature of the development UN. Several high-profile meetings were convened from the 1970s. Since the 1990s there has been a long series of global development conferences, sponsored by one or more of the 30-some UN development organisations. In 2000 the largest-ever development summit (to that date) of heads of state and government was convened in New York. Almost 150 state leaders signed the Millennium Declaration in September 2000, a striking blueprint for progress over the following 15 years. One year later international terrorism struck the USA and spread to other locations, in which UN country offices also became targets. These incidents helped to tilt the balance towards security for the next summit on the UN's 60th anniversary in 2005. Another large gathering of heads reaffirmed the Millennium Declaration's principles and elaborated an even more detailed blueprint for UN action, including counterterrorism, R2P, and peacebuilding. The 2005 statement in particular encompassed the full range of UN responsibilities, across peacekeeping, humanitarian relief, justice and human rights, in addition to development.

An agenda of needs, however, is not an agenda for action. Following the Millennium Declaration the UN applied a much narrower lens to extract from it the MDGS as the basis for its development operations. This was the easiest option because the MDGS were little different from the 'international development targets' that had been derived, at donor urging, from the earlier global conferences. The MDGS were therefore a convenient blueprint for the UNDS and were associated with measurable benchmarks. However, the MDGS did not encompass other chapters of the Millenium Declaration with such essential priorities as human rights, security, and good governance.

The more elaborate 2005 declaration included almost 180 paragraphs. A decade later there is nothing which could have rendered any part of it obsolete. Nonetheless, the UN set about the task of seeking a new 'post-2015' agenda, a confusing journey with multiple layers of consultation. Reverting to summitry, the UN convened the Rio+20 gathering in 2012 on sustainable development, which resulted in another outcome document in General Assembly resolution 66/288 called 'The Future We Want'. UN member states called for a 'sustainable development agenda'. While the statement reaffirmed many of the principles of good governance, respect for human rights and inclusion, it defined sustainable development in three dimensions – economic, social, and environmental – and called for their integration. This was misleading because of its imposition of a sectoral approach on a set of more comprehensive normative standards, which had been explicitly outlined in the summit declarations.

Also in 2012 the UN came up with the idea of asking 'we, the peoples' for their objectives for a better world. The campaign was intended as a contribution to the debate on the post-2015 agenda for the UN. It was much less sophisticated than the 'Voices of the Poor', an analysis of 60,000 people in 60 countries conducted by the World Bank in 2000,[22] and it amassed over 5 million responses from all countries. The exercise was a positive one in terms of communication. The UN was asking the supposed beneficiaries of development for their views – something it has done rather infrequently in the past – and more detailed consultations were held in over 80 countries.

The poll was conducted online and asked respondents to pick their six most important goals from a choice of 16 options. Not surprisingly the two principal public services, education and healthcare, were ranked at the top. The next highest were 'an honest and responsive government' and 'better job opportunities'. These four priorities remained the highest, even when filtered by gender, age, and income level of the country. But, as a guide to the future UN agenda, the exercise was a false scent. Phone and internet access were ranked rather low, but that was presumably because all online respondents were already connected. Consistently at the very bottom of the rankings was 'action taken on climate change', an area in which the world organisation might be expected to make a crucial contribution.

In the same year, the UN secretary-general appointed a high-level panel to advise him on the content of a new set of development goals as the core of a future agenda. Not surprisingly the panel recalled past declarations. Its May 2013 report proposed to build on the MDGS, while stating that:

> they did not focus enough on reaching the very poorest and most excluded people. They were silent on the devastating effects of conflict and violence on development. The importance to development of good governance and institutions that guarantee the rule of law, free speech and open and accountable government was not included, nor the need for inclusive growth to provide jobs. Most seriously, the MDGS fell short by not integrating the economic, social, and environmental aspects of sustainable development as envisaged in the Millennium Declaration.[23]

The panel report might have added that the Millennium Declaration was already the basis for a much broader and meaningful agenda than the MDGS extracted from it.

Again the panel called for integrating the three sectors of sustainable development as a top priority, without showing how this approach might be meshed with other critical aspects of development. However, it put forward a set of 12 suggested goals (and 54 targets), which are intended to be universal, rather than setting up a grand bargain between an increasingly artificial North and South.

Following a series of consultations, the discussions on the agenda went into an intergovernmental body, the Open Working Group (OWG) on Sustainable Development Goals, which in turn held more consultations with many stakeholders, including UN development organisations, keen to push their own mandates. The OWG underlined several important principles for the new development goals. As recommended by the panel (and the Rio+20 declaration), they are to be applicable to all countries. Also in common with the panel, the OWG broadened the potential agenda outwards from the original narrower ambit of the MDGS. Its initial list of concerns – grouped into 19 'focus areas' – ran to over a hundred. Most of these would have been recognisable from the earlier declarations of 2000 and 2005, and indeed they have mostly built on past UN resolutions and declarations. Thus the UN's decision to embark on a highly elaborate process of further consultation has been a largely circular process designed to result in another declaration, likely to be no better or worse than those of 2000 and 2005. What has been lacking is a fuller analysis of how the world is changing. And not just of what needs to be done, but how, and by whom.

From agenda to operations: the MDGS

The UN has made its summit declarations – its 'needs' agendas – the basis of its 'doing' agenda for development. As noted, in 2000 the MDG agenda was drawn from the Millennium Declaration. The eight MDGS amounted to a grand bargain: the North facilitates, the global South advances. The most important outcome of the MDGs was in the importance it gave to monitoring progress, a process that the UN pursued assiduously.

But while all the organisations of the UNDS eventually signed up to the MDGs, the goals were an imperfect basis for a UN agenda – besides it being only partial. There are at least two important reasons for this. First, the MDGs are aggregates and, as noted above, are insufficient measures of deprivation. Globally aggregated statistics have shown significant improvements in the human condition over several decades and the MDGs, which measure some of the symptoms of development progress, have advanced further than anticipated in many emerging and poor countries. But these indices mask evidence of the numbers of the poor left behind and the reasons for their marginalisation. There is no better demonstration than the fact that Egypt, Syria, and Tunisia were among the best performers in the Arab region in terms of MDGs, but their long-standing grievances among the poor led to violent uprisings.[24]

Second, and perhaps more surprising, UN development assistance has little impact on the MDGs. In part, this is a result of the UN's relative ineffectiveness overall.[25] More fundamentally aid from any source is not critical to achieving the MDGs. If it were, there would be a clear causal relationship between aid flows and MDG achievement. Public services and infrastructure in developing countries have been supported by decades of development assistance. But in many countries they are still failing the poor. Many of those countries that have received substantial amounts of aid over long periods are still among the poorest MDG performers. There is certainly no automatic 'hydraulic' approach of aid in, development out.[26] It has even been claimed that aid, and technical assistance in particular, have made things worse in many countries.[27] Rather than aid itself – particularly the many thousands of small aid projects implemented by the UNDS – it is other, country-specific factors that are more important in tackling poverty and marginalisation. These include the robustness and inclusiveness of institutions and the responsible management of resources, as noted above. Development is crucially dependent on the policies and practices of the ruling powers in each country. In fact, politics is often the most important factor in reducing poverty.[28] Success or failure has been equated with 'inclusive' and 'extractive' approaches to development, respectively.[29] And if a new Manichean axis is still instructive in development terms, this distinction is more meaningful than divisions by North–South or other measures of income levels.

So, while the United Nations has been an effective monitor of MDG progress, it has drawn the wrong conclusions from the exercise. The more successful countries have been applauded, and the less successful have been excused on the invalid grounds of insufficient development assistance. Believing in the aid–development connection, the UN has used MDG achievement as a rationale for its operational role and as a justification to seek more resources for its technical assistance.

However, it would be wrong to conclude that, because the pursuit of the MDGs by the UN has been ineffectual, it has no valid future operational role. Quite the contrary. The successive declarations cited earlier and the one that will follow the 2015 summit of the General Assembly should still be the basis of a comprehensive new agenda. It should acknowledge, and give adequate priority to, the new realities. Beyond a statement of needs, it will require a full implementation plan, a scaled-up version of the ones that accompanied human rights and peacebuilding.

That is the harder but essential task. The plan should reflect how some of the assumptions on which past declarations were based have changed. And it will need to apportion responsibilities for the achievement of the new goals among the three UNs: the first UN of member states the second UN of organisations, and the third UN of civil society. The process should go beyond governments choosing a limited number of goals and asking international civil servants to help in implementation.

Conclusion

Comparing the UN development system's current roles and capacities with the changing global context brings up a poor balance sheet: in fragile and conflict-prone states there is a lack of coherence across its various pillars that undermines its effectiveness in peacebuilding. As a declining source of development assistance, the UNDS has not adequately adjusted to a role of strategic partnering with growing numbers of increasingly influential stakeholders. Relatedly it must not only concentrate on helping to mobilise development resources but also help ensure that these are responsibly managed. In every country UN organisations should concentrate more on their normative roles and pursue monitoring and compliance more assiduously along the lines of universal periodic reviews. In the search for solutions to major new global challenges the UN is too cumbersome; it should examine new consultation processes and find ways to streamline its operational responses.

While the UN is getting prepared, it has not yet adequately adapted to a changing development environment. Therefore, as important as the negotiation of a new post-2015 agenda will be a practical implementation plan that acknowledges the current shortcomings, builds on the UN's strengths, and eschews it weaknesses. Without adaptation, the UN risks becoming increasingly marginalised in its development role.

Notes

1. Nayyar, *Catch Up*; and Mahbubani, *The Great Convergence.*
2. UNDP, *Human Development Report 2013*, Fig. 1.2.
3. Charbonnier and Sumner, "Reframing Aid."
4. World Bank, *World Development Report 2014.*
5. Sumner, *Where do the World's Poor Live?*
6. Economic Commission for Africa and African Union, *Economic Report on Africa 2013.*

7. del Castillo, *Rebuilding War-torn States.*
8. FUNDS Project, *2012 Survey on the Future of the UN.*
9. Adams and Pingeot, "Strengthening Public Participation."
10. World Bank, "Developing Countries."
11. UNCTAD, *World Investment Report 2013.*
12. Acemoglu and Robinson, *Why Nations Fail.*
13. Wilkinson, *The WTO, the UN, and the Future of Global Development.*
14. UNODC, United Nations Convention against Corruption.
15. Slaughter, "Endorsement."
16. Weiss et al., "The 'Third' United Nations."
17. World Bank, *Migration and Development.*
18. Chetail, "Migration and Global Governance," 16–17.
19. United Nations, *Making Migration Work.*
20. Intergovernmental Panel on Climate Change, *Climate Change 2014.*
21. Oxford Martin School, *Now for the Long Term,* 57.
22. Narajan et al., *Voices of the Poor.*
23. United Nations, *A New Global Partnership,* Executive Summary.
24. United Nations, *A Regional Perspective.*
25. Picciotto, *The UN has lost the Aid-effectiveness Race.*
26. Deaton, *The Great Escape.*
27. Easterly, *The Tyranny of Experts.*
28. Banerjee and Duflo, *Poor Economics.*
29. Acemoglu and Robinson, *Why Nations Fail.*

Bibliography

Acemoglu, Daron, and James A. Robinson. *Why Nations Fail: The Origins of Power, Prosperity and Poverty.* London: Profile Books, 2012.

Adams, Barbara, and Lou Pingeot. "Strengthening Public Participation at the United Nations for Sustainable Development: Dialogue, Debate, Dissent, Deliberation." Study for the UN DESA/DSD Major Groups Programme, June 2013.

Banerjee, Abhijit V., and Esther Duflo. *Poor Economics: A Radical Rethinking of the Way to Fight Global Poverty.* New York: Public Affairs, 2011.

Charbonnier, Gilles, and Andy Sumner. "Reframing Aid in a World where the Poor live in Emerging Economies." *International Development Policy Journal* 13 (2012): Table 1.3.

Chetail, Vincent. "Migration and Global Governance: Time to Act." *Globe* 13 (Spring 2014): 16–17.

Deaton, Angus. *The Great Escape: Health, Wealth, and the Origins of Inequality.* Princeton, NJ: Princeton University Press, 2013.

del Castillo, Graciana. *Rebuilding War-torn States: Is the UN System up to the Challenges?* FUNDS Briefing 8. New York, July 2013. http://www.futureun.org/media/archive1/briefings/FUNDS_Brief8_July2013_Final. pdf.

Easterly, William. *The Tyranny of Experts: Economists, Dictators, and the Forgotten Rights of the Poor.* New York: Basic Books, 2014.

Economic Commission for Africa and African Union. *Economic Report on Africa 2013.* Addis Ababa: UN, 2013.

FUNDS Project. 2012 *Survey on the Future of the UN.* http://www.futureun.org/media/archive1/surveys/Summary-Results-of-2012-Survey2.pdf.

Intergovernmental Panel on Climate Change. *Climate Change 2014: Impacts, Adaptation, and Vulnerability.* Report of Working Group II. Geneva: UN, 2014.

Mahbubani, Kishore. *The Great Convergence: Asia, the West, and the Logic of One World.* New York: Public Affairs, 2013.

Narajan, Deepak, Raj Patel, Kai Schafft, Anne Rademacher, and Sarah Koch-Schulte. *Voices of the Poor: Can Anyone Hear Us?* Washington, DC: World Bank, 2000.

Nayyar, Deepak. *Catch Up: Developing Countries in the World Economy.* Oxford: Oxford University Press, 2013.

Oxford Martin School. *Now for the Long Term.* Report of the Oxford Martin Commission for Future Generations. Oxford: Oxford University Press, 2014. http://www.oxfordmartin.ox.ac.uk/downloads/commission/ Oxford_Martin_Now_for_the_Long_Term.pdf.

Picciotto, Robert. *The UN has lost the Aid-effectiveness Race: What is to be Done?* FUNDS Briefing 14. New York, February 2014.

Slaughter, Anne-Marie. "Endorsement." In *Responsibility to Protect: The Global Moral Compact for the 21st Century,* edited by Richard H. Cooper and Juliette Voïnov Kohler. New York: Palgrave Macmillan, 2008.

Sumner, Andy. *Where do the World's Poor Live? A New Update.* IDS Working Paper 393. Brighton, UK: Institute of Development Studies, 2012.

UNCTAD. *World Investment Report 2013*. Geneva: UNCTAD, 2013.

UNDP. *Human Development Report 2013: The Rise of the South*, 2013. New York: UN, 2013.

United Nations. *Making Migration Work: An Eight Point Agenda for Action*. UN High-level Dialogue on Migration and Development, Report from the Secretary-General. New York: UN, October 2013.

United Nations. *A New Global Partnership: Eradicate Poverty and Transform Economies through Sustainable Development – The Report of the High-Level Panel of Eminent Persons on the Post-2015 Development Agenda*. New York: UN, 2013.

United Nations. *A Regional Perspective on the Post-2015 UN Development Agenda*. New York: UN, 2013.

UN Office for Drugs and Crime (UNODC). United Nations Convention against Corruption. New York: UN, 2004. https://www.unodc.org/documents/treaties/UNCAC/Publications/Convention/08-50026_E.pdf.

Weiss, Thomas G., Tatiana Carayannis, and Richard Jolly. "The 'Third' United Nations." *Global Governance* 15, no. 1 (2009): 123–142.

Wilkinson, Rorden. *The WTO, the UN, and the Future of Global Development: What Matters and Why*. FUNDS Briefing 15. New York, March 2014. http://futureun.org/media/archive1/briefings/FUNDSBriefing15-Wilkinson.pdf.

World Bank. "Developing Countries receive over $410 billion in Remittances in 2013, says World Bank." October 2, 2013. http://www.worldbank.org/en/news/press-release/2013/10/02/developing-countries-remittances-2013-world-bank.

World Bank. *Migration and Development*. Brief no. 20. Washington, DC: World Bank, 2013.

World Bank. *World Development Report 2014: Making Services Work for Poor People*. Washington, DC: World Bank, 2004.

South–South cooperation and the future of development assistance: mapping actors and options

Paolo de Renzio and Jurek Seifert

Institute of International Relations, Pontifical Catholic University, Rio de Janeiro, Brazil

International development cooperation is undergoing fundamental changes. New – or often re-emerging – actors have gained importance during the past two decades, and are increasingly challenging the traditional approach to development cooperation associated with the members of the Development Assistance Committee of the OECD. Their supposedly alternative paradigm, 'South–South cooperation' (SSC), has been recognised as an important cooperation modality, but faces contradictions that are not too different from those of its North–South counterpart. SSC providers are highly heterogeneous in terms of policies, institutional arrangements, and engagement with international forums and initiatives. This article contributes to current debates on SSC by mapping the diversity of its actors – based on illustrative case studies from the first and second 'wave' of providers – and by presenting and discussing some possible scenarios for the future of SSC within the international aid system.

The landscape of international development cooperation is in a state of flux. What had been termed a 'silent revolution' only a few years ago has turned into a noisy (and somewhat confused) process of evolution and change.[1] This mirrors a series of fundamental shifts in global power relations since the end of the Cold War, with new players gaining ground and old ones having to accommodate them and negotiate new rules of the game. In the field of development cooperation these new – or re-emerging – players have gained ever more importance during the past decade.[2] They have significantly increased their engagement in development assistance and technical cooperation, and questioned the predominance and legitimacy of more traditional forms of development cooperation. But who are these new actors? And how are they going about changing the face of development cooperation?

For decades, since the onset of development assistance efforts beginning in the late 1940s, countries belonging to the Organisation for Economic Co-operation and Development (OECD) and to its Development Assistance Committee (DAC) formed a club that provided a forum for coordination of all matters related to development cooperation. DAC defined what could count as development assistance and what could not, kept accurate records of members' foreign aid flows, and developed principles, standards, and procedures that members were invited to follow. Over most of this long period, DAC members provided the lion's share of global development assistance resources to developing countries, and DAC's leadership remained intact until a few years ago. While some of the countries now calling DAC's role into question are hardly new to development cooperation – for instance, Russia and China offered development cooperation during the Cold War, and Arab states provided assistance during the oil bonanza of the 1970s and 1980s – their role and weight, alongside that of other emerging powers, has now increased substantially and deserves more intense scrutiny and assessment.

These countries are often grouped under different labels, ranging from 'new development partners'[3] to 'non-traditional donors',[4] to 'emerging (or re-emerging) donors'[5] to 'Southern providers'.[6] They have in common an at least partial rejection of DAC-related principles and practices and a rhetoric promoting a different kind of engagement with the countries to which they provide assistance. South–South cooperation (SSC), as it is commonly known, is supposedly based on solidarity, horizontality – as opposed to the perceived vertical nature of traditional DAC aid – non-interference in domestic affairs, and mutual benefit. Apart from these similarities, however, SSC actors are very diverse in just about all other aspects of development cooperation, from strategic priorities to regional and sectoral focus to institutional arrangements.

This article aims to contribute to current debates on the role of SSC actors in the reform of international development cooperation institutions and practices in two ways. First, it asks how the diversity of SSC actors and practices can be usefully mapped. Second, it presents and comments on some of the possible scenarios for the future of SSC within the international aid system.

In the next section we provide a brief historical sketch of how SSC emerged and developed, including how it came to affect recent debates around the shape of global institutions aimed at coordinating and improving the effectiveness of development cooperation interventions. We then attempt to build a comprehensive map of SSC actors and their related practices. We discuss in more detail the cases of China and Brazil, two of the larger and more influential SSC actors, and we contrast them with Indonesia, Turkey, and Mexico, which belong to a newer group of SSC actors that are becoming more active and vocal. Before concluding, we discuss some of the different options that SSC actors have to engage in reforming global development cooperation arrangements – eg within DAC itself, the UN, or other groupings and institutions – and assess their advantages and problems.

From Bandung to Busan: a brief history of South–South cooperation

Historically SSC gained political relevance in the developing world after World War II, and more specifically during the Cold War, when the notion of solidarity among developing countries became increasingly popular. A first milestone in this context is the Bandung conference that took place in Indonesia in April 1955, when 25 countries from Asia and Africa met in order to increase cooperation among themselves and with other developing countries, with the intention of coordinating their interests and therefore strengthening their position vis-à-vis industrialised countries.[7]

In order to avoid having to choose sides in the Cold War, and to further fortify the notion of Southern solidarity, the Non-Aligned Movement (NAM) was founded at the Belgrade conference in 1961. In many cases NAM membership was associated with a struggle for greater economic and political independence by former colonies. In 1962, in Cairo, developing countries held another conference to develop a joint position, and in 1964 the United Nations Conference on Trade and Development (UNCTAD) was founded. UNCTAD is seen as a further step towards the institutionalisation of SSC that gave birth to the Group of 77 developing countries (G77). The conference, which was to be held every four years, became the major platform for developing countries to coordinate their interests when negotiating with developed countries during the 1960s and 1970s – with varying degrees of success.

UNCTAD and the G77 were instrumental in launching the idea of a New International Economic Order (NIEO) in 1974, another important milestone for SSC. As Philip Golup explains, 'the aim of [the NIEO] programme, which grew out of the 1955 Bandung conference of non-aligned states, but was far more ambitious and intellectually coherent than earlier non-aligned efforts, was to create and institutionalise a global redistributive order founded on new binding rules'.[8]

In 1978 the Buenos Aires Plan of Action was endorsed by the UN's Special Unit for Technical Cooperation among Developing Countries. Its aim was to 'promote, coordinate and support South–South and triangular cooperation globally and within the United Nations system'.[9] The plan can be considered the first real attempt to recognise and formalise in a multilateral context the importance of technical cooperation and development assistance ties among Southern countries.[10] Despite these various initiatives, however, SSC has suffered a series of obstacles since its early days.[11] Its various manifestations often involved a limited number of countries, governments with heterogeneous interests and weak economies with limited complementarities. This stood in the way of strong ties of economic and political cooperation, limiting SSC's potential for change.

The 1980s and 1990s showed little multilateral action in the SSC sphere, as many developing countries were mired in economic and fiscal crises. This situation started to change at the beginning of the new millennium, when a Goldman Sachs economist in 2001 branded a small group of large developing countries BRICS (initially Brazil, Russia, India, and China; then with the addition of South Africa in 2010). This grouping grew rapidly, both in economic terms and in political importance on the global stage. Its members started an impressive expansion of their development cooperation programmes as part of their foreign policy strategies. Although in previous decades SSC volumes had been marginal, they have since grown in importance and influence; they were estimated to be about 10% of global development assistance flows in 2010 and are expected to reach up to 15%–20% in the coming years.[12]

The growing importance of ssc is also reflected in the global discussions and agreements on development cooperation that have taken place over the past decade. The 2005 *Paris Declaration on Aid Effectiveness* was promoted by DAC and seen as a major reference for traditional North–South development cooperation, yet it made no reference to ssc actors and modalities; in contrast, the *Accra Agenda for Action*, approved in 2008 as a follow-up to the *Paris Declaration*, recognised ssc as a 'valuable complement to North–South co-operation' and encouraged ssc providers to endorse the Paris principles.[13] The major shift, however, happened in the years leading up to the Fourth High-level Forum on Aid Effectiveness, held in the South Korean city of Busan in 2011. With DAC countries increasingly preoccupied with bringing ssc into the fold of existing development cooperation principles and institutions, a special task force was set up and frantic negotiations took place up until the last minute at the forum to ensure that important actors like China, India, and Brazil could be convinced to sign the final declaration. The Busan Partnership Document, as the final declaration is called, marks a turning point and gives full legitimacy to ssc as a development cooperation modality. The key paragraph reads:

> Today's complex architecture for development cooperation has evolved from the North–South paradigm. Distinct from the traditional relationship between aid providers and recipients, developing nations and a number of emerging economies have become important providers of South–South development cooperation [...] The Paris Declaration did not address the complexity of these new actors, while the Accra Agenda for Action recognized their importance and specificities. While North–South cooperation remains the main form of development cooperation, South–South cooperation continues to evolve, providing additional diversity of resources for development. At Busan, *we now all form an integral part of a new and more inclusive development agenda, in which these actors participate on the basis of common goals, shared principles and differential commitments.* On this same basis, we welcome the inclusion of civil society, the private sector and other actors.[14]

The apparent unity of intent that was meant to be the key achievement of the Busan process, and the driving force behind efforts to follow, is undermined by the 'differential commitments' referred to in the text above. China and Brazil in particular made it clear that they would not sign the declaration without explicit language that recognised the voluntary nature of South–South partners' compliance with the specific commitments, actions, and targets.[15] As we show in following sections, this contradiction became evident in the follow-up to the Busan meeting and with the creation of the Global Partnership for Effective Development Cooperation, the new coordination body aimed at enlarging membership to include ssc actors.

Mapping diversity in South–South cooperation: actors and practices

The emergence – or re-emergence – of ssc confronts the paradox of investigating a phenomenon that has gained increasing international attention while at the same time no consensus has been reached by scholars or practitioners on its exact definition or reach. As recognised by a speaker at a conference of Southern development cooperation providers in New Delhi in 2013:

the rapid growth in South–South cooperation requires greater efforts by Southern partners at arriving at a common and acceptable definition of the term 'South–South development cooperation'. This is essential, in my view, if we want to make both policy dialogue and norm-setting in this area more productive.[16]

The term is clearly not understood as a geographical category because a number of key SSC actors (eg China) are located in the Northern hemisphere. Rather, as the Busan declaration quote in the previous section suggests, the term seems to refer to technical cooperation, knowledge exchange, and financial assistance between pairs of developing countries. The recipient is a low-income country already receiving other types of foreign aid, the provider an emerging power with a recent history of economic growth and development success, along with an interest in expanding its international reach and influence, even if in some cases it still partly relies on external assistance to address poverty issues at home. As noted, the SSC 'brand' also serves as a distinguishing mark vis-à-vis the perceived shortcomings of North–South cooperation and the principles and practices it promotes through DAC.

In order to shed further light on what SSC is and how it works, it might be helpful to build a map of the relevant actors involved. In a previous similar attempt, former DAC chair, Richard Manning, takes as his starting point countries that are not DAC members but which have an active development cooperation programme.[17] He divides them into four groups: countries that belong to the OECD but are not DAC members (ie Turkey, South Korea, Mexico, and some Eastern European countries like Hungary and Poland); new EU members that are not members of the OECD (ie Bulgaria, Romania, and Croatia); Middle Eastern Arab countries and the development cooperation funds that they have set up – in some cases decades ago; and other countries that do not fall into the previous groups. This categorisation encompasses a wide array of countries, from Chile, Brazil, and Venezuela in Latin America to China, India, Malaysia, and Thailand in Asia, passing through Russia and South Africa. Another classification of 'emerging donors' proposed by the Center for Global Development simplifies things a bit, proposing a three-way categorisation: new donor countries that broadly follow the DAC model, basically bringing together the first two grouping indicated by Manning, plus Russia and minus Mexico; Arab countries and funds; and other 'Southern donors', including the rest of BRICS and some other smaller countries.[18]

While both these 'maps' are useful, the breadth of countries they cover goes beyond some of the key characteristics of SSC defined above. For example, Arab donors seem to form a separate, somewhat independent bloc, with a long history, specific geographic concentration and a model of development cooperation that does not coincide with the DAC model but that also does not question it, either in rhetoric or in practice. Similarly, new EU members and former Soviet states that have gone on to join the OECD cannot be seen as proposing a new and different way of structuring the relationship between providers and recipients of development cooperation and, if anything, are more likely to join DAC rather than try to reform it.[19]

For the purposes of our analysis it makes sense to exclude these two groups of actors and focus instead on countries which, besides having a newly established – or re-emerging – development cooperation programme, share a common discourse of at least partial opposition to the DAC model, present themselves as representatives of the global South, and claim to pursue the interests of developing countries in the international arena. These countries position themselves as providers of a different model of development assistance, a model based on more equal partnerships that encompass not only technical and financial assistance, but also strengthened trade and investment, and on the sharing of knowledge and experiences that are closer to, and more relevant for, the low-income countries to which they provide assistance.

Following these criteria two groups of countries can be considered as composing the broad set of SSC actors. The first includes a small group of large players, both in size and influence, which have been active in SSC for a longer period and share a stronger rejection of DAC-related principles and practices, including in the post-Busan process. These are China, India, and Brazil. The second group is larger and more varied; it includes a set of smaller middle-income countries whose aid programmes are more recent and have increased substantially in recent years, although they remain more limited in size and scope when compared with those of the first group. While these countries often use SSC discourse and language, they have engaged with DAC in more varied and complex ways, especially after Busan. This group would include at least Chile, Colombia, Indonesia, Malaysia, Mexico, South Africa, Thailand, Turkey and Venezuela. They can be said to represent the 'second wave' of SSC actors.

In the next two sub-sections we provide some details about the policies, institutional arrangements, and engagement with international forums and initiatives of a few of these actors. These are meant to be simple illustrative depictions and serve the purpose of highlighting the variety and diversity that characterise South–South cooperation.

China and Brazil: SSC leaders

China has turned from being a recipient of Western aid into a 'net donor' during the past decade, like many other countries falling under the 'emerging donor' label.[20] Thanks to its rapid economic rise and growing international weight, China has been able to mobilise impressive resources for its development cooperation programme, pursuing a very active expansion of its activities in many developing countries and mixing development cooperation with the pursuit of trade and investment opportunities, as well as access to natural resources. Chinese development assistance has been the subject of much controversy since the early days of its re-emergence in the past couple of decades. Some have termed it 'rogue' and accused it of blindly pursuing self-interested motives, undermining DAC donors' insistence on respect for human rights, good governance, and environmental sustainability.[21] Others have emphasised the broad and long-term nature of Chinese engagement in Africa, for example highlighting its potential developmental impact.[22]

The controversy has been fed by the fact that neither overall volumes of Chinese development cooperation nor its allocation criteria are transparent. Existing estimates vary substantially: the Center for Global Development estimated Chinese aid in 2009 to amount to between $1.5 billion to $25 billion, a staggering range.[23] As Gregory Chin points out, by using a 'broader definition of foreign aid', it is possible to arrive at estimated volumes of around $20–30 billion for

2010 as well.[24] As Deborah Bräutigam points out, only a small part of these flows falls under the DAC definition of development assistance, making comparison difficult. In general, the Chinese seem to have little interest in a clear separation between development cooperation and economic expansion.[25]

China's development assistance has mostly focused on infrastructure, energy, and agriculture, attending to sectors that have often received less attention from 'traditional' donors – especially the first two areas. With regard to geographic focus, China is a heavyweight in its own region – where it often competes with India for regional influence – but has also put a focus on Africa as well as on Latin America.[26] Broadly speaking Chinese activities have often been seen as a largely successful attempt to establish itself as an internationally relevant player, able to compete with Northern countries as well as with the other countries in the BRICS grouping.[27]

With regard to its engagement with the established system of international cooperation, China has maintained its distance from DAC and its members, endorsing neither the Paris nor the Accra declarations. China did, however, sign the Busan Partnership Document,[28] opening the possibility of voluntarily adhering to the principles established in the document and of supporting the Global Partnership for Effective Development Cooperation (GPEDC).[29] Yet it has had very limited engagement with the development of the GPEDC since Busan. In fact, there is little necessity for China to cooperate more closely with DAC donors, as it has all the necessary means to manage its development cooperation programme, and so far has been received rather positively by recipient countries.[30] Therefore, any further engagement in established development institutions by China should probably be attributed to political goodwill and the potential to improve the country's standing in international cooperation rather than to any urgency to adapt its model of development cooperation to existing DAC principles and standards.

Brazil's technical cooperation activities date back to before the creation of its development cooperation agency, the Agência Brasileira de Cooperação (ABC) in 1987. But SSC started to become increasingly dynamic as part of former president Luiz Inácio da Silva's (2003–10) foreign policy strategy. Similarly to other SSC actors Brazil has a comparatively small official budget for development cooperation activities (roughly $30 million in 2010).[31] However, this figure does not take into account the financial contributions of other government agencies involved in the development cooperation programme, which is why other estimates put Brazil's total development assistance at between $0.4 billion and $1.2 billion in 2010.[32]

Brazil divides its cooperation almost equally between Latin America and Africa, where the focus is mostly on Portuguese-speaking countries, based on cultural proximity and a common colonial past. Sectorally Brazilian development cooperation has focused mostly on agriculture and health, humanitarian assistance, and capacity building. Especially in the former two areas Brazilian institutions such as the Agricultural Research Corporation and the Ministry of Health's Oswaldo Cruz Foundation have achieved international reputation. Brazil emphasises its own experience as a developing country – and, more recently, as an emerging economy that still faces domestic development challenges – to sell its expertise in tackling local problems in partner countries,[33] highlighting the success of its domestic programmes to reduce poverty and increase food security.

Technical cooperation has been accompanied by significant debt cancellations ($897.7 million for 12 African countries in 2013)[34] – an important mechanism for creating the conditions for the expansion of Brazilian companies abroad, given that the country's development bank can only support operations in countries that do not owe money to the Brazilian government. Differently from China Brazil has made an effort to keep the country's economic interests separate from cooperation activities. Nevertheless, this approach might be changing, as Lula's successor, President Dilma Rousseff, announced plans for an agency that will handle both economic and technical cooperation with Africa in 2013.[35]

Internationally, despite Brazil's repeatedly emphasised commitment to multilateralism, in the field of development cooperation the government has taken a different stance, firmly emphasising its position as a Southern country and maintaining its distance from DAC positions. The Lula administration made use of an explicit rhetoric of solidarity and 'brotherhood' with other developing countries;[36] the Rousseff administration has continued to use a similar South–South discourse. Brazil presents its technical cooperation as an instrument with which to practise this solidarity and simultaneously strengthen its claim to represent its less developed partners in the international arena.[37] This stance has not prevented some important criticisms from being levelled against the country over the way it approaches some of its cooperation activities. The ProSavana project in Mozambique, one of the Brazil's largest, has been the focus of intense controversy, given the lack of consultation with local populations and its focus on replicating the agribusiness-oriented model of the Brazilian Cerrado regions.[38]

At a political level Brazil has acted similarly to China, not endorsing DAC declarations until they have explicitly recognised the different nature of SSC, and taking a limited interest in the formation of the GPEDC after Busan. At a more operational level, however, Brazil has shown interest in directly cooperating with traditional donors by engaging in triangular cooperation projects – namely with Japan, Spain, and Germany.

'Second wave' SSC actors: Indonesia, Turkey, and Mexico

Indonesia is seen as one of the most important emerging powers. It is a member of the G20 and was included in the OECD's Enhanced Engagement Initiative in 2007.[39] The country started its development cooperation activities as early as 1981 but was still taking steps towards institutionalisation at the beginning of 2013.[40] Its Bureau for Technical Cooperation responds to the State Secretariat of the Republic and the National Development Planning Agency, although the Ministry of Foreign Affairs and the Ministry of Finance are also involved in technical cooperation activities. The government has created a National Coordination Team on South–South and Triangular Cooperation that serves as a coordinating entity for these and other institutions involved in development cooperation.[41] Indonesia has been implementing development projects, for instance focusing on agriculture, small and medium enterprises, and health in Palestine; on community development in Afghanistan; and on infrastructure in Timor-Leste.[42]

The country presents itself explicitly as a member of the 'global South'. The Bureau for Technical Cooperation labels its activities either 'South–South cooperation' or 'Technical Cooperation among Developing Countries', and refers to the Buenos Aires Plan of Action from 1978 and NAM when presenting the origins of its cooperation initiative. In 2005 Indonesia – together with South Africa – was one of the driving forces for the establishment of the New African–Asian Strategic Partnership – an initiative that was presented as part of the global increase in SSC. Nevertheless, Indonesia's rhetoric and position with regard to the North–South divide in development cooperation appear to be softer than those of other actors like Brazil. It has endorsed the Paris and the Accra Declarations and is a co-chair of the GPEDC, representing other SSC actors.

Turkey launched its development cooperation programme in 1985 and founded the Turkish International Cooperation Agency (TIKA) as part of the Ministry of Foreign Affairs in 1992. TIKA disposed of a budged of close to $1.3 billion in 2011,[43] with around 93% being disbursed bilaterally.[44] The agency has increased its institutional capacities significantly in recent years and now counts 33 country offices. Turkey emphasises its cultural links to its immediate 'sister countries' (Kazakhstan, Tajikistan, Uzbekistan, Azerbaijan, and Kyrgyzstan), which are the main beneficiaries of its development assistance, but has extended its activities beyond its direct sphere of influence to other countries in Central Asia and Africa. TIKA has offices in Ethiopia, Senegal, and Sudan and has observer status in the African Union as well as a strategic partnership with the most important multilateral organisation in the region. TIKA's main cooperation areas are education – especially where a common language facilitates cooperation – institutional capacity building and infrastructure. Additionally Turkey has focused on humanitarian assistance and has made a name for itself thanks to its strong engagement in Somalia in recent years. Prime Minister Recep Tayyip Erdogan visited the country in 2011 and highlighted Muslim solidarity as a basis for Turkey's engagement – a recurring trend in Turkey's development cooperation.[45]

Turkey is a member of the OECD but not of DAC, in which it holds observer status. TIKA reports to DAC and adheres to its standards, which is why Turkish cooperation is also accounted for in official aid statistics. In fact, DAC offered Turkey full membership in 2012 but so far it has not accepted.[46] In spite of its proximity to DAC, the country uses the 'South–South cooperation' label for its development assistance activities, although its rhetoric resorts far less to 'North vs South' categories. Turkey has voluntarily endorsed DAC's aid effectiveness declarations and has participated in the Busan forum, as well as in the foundation of the GPEDC. Turkish development cooperation, therefore, seems to be aimed at fulfilling the function of a mediator between Northern and Southern positions and players by placing itself in neither camp.

Mexico established its first cooperation agency in the 1990s, subsequently replacing it with another one, Amexcid, in 2011.[47] Additionally, in 2009, Mexico established the Mexican International Development Cooperation Data System, which promotes improved coordination and access to data among ministries and institutions involved in cooperation. Mexico's aid programme focuses mostly on technical cooperation projects with other Latin American countries, with a concentration on public management, education, agriculture, and environmental protection.[48] While the country labels its own development cooperation activities SSC, since 1994 it has been a member of the OECD, though not of DAC. As an observer Mexico has therefore not signed the declarations from Paris and Accra, but it does endorse their principles on a voluntary basis. This has made it more difficult for Mexico to claim the position of a representative of the 'global South', because recipients see it as more closely linked to the DAC model of development cooperation. Again like Turkey, Mexico prefers to see itself as a mediator fostering dialogue between industrialised and developing countries.[49] It views the GPEDC favourably in maintaining its 'bridging' function, and it hosted its first high-level meeting in April 2014.

These brief sketches serve as a reminder that the term 'South–South cooperation' refers in fact to a widely varied set of actors and practices. SSC actors have differing priorities, sectoral and geographic foci, and institutional arrangements. More importantly for the purposes of this paper, they also do not seem to share a common vision of whether and how they should act jointly to ensure that SSC as an emerging development cooperation modality is recognised and develops as an alternative to more traditional forms of development assistance. For example, while no SSC actors are DAC members – though Turkey might soon join – their level of engagement with DAC-related forums and institutions, and their recognition of DAC principles and practices, vary substantially, with smaller and newer SSC actors like Mexico and Indonesia more willing to keep a foot in the GPEDC than bigger players like Brazil and China. Similarly, all SSC actors use a similar discourse when describing their development cooperation programmes and activities, but this rhetoric in fact hides very different ways of approaching relationships with recipients, and the pursuit of economic and political interests.

These differences in fact lead to an underlying question in the discussion about the re-emergence of SSC: is this modality really so different from its North–South counterpart? First, the heterogeneity of actors and approaches – at least so far – seems to trump genuine solidarity between emerging powers and other developing countries; it represents an obstacle to stronger coordination (or even institutionalisation) of this form of cooperation. Second, SSC providers often face contradictions similar to those experienced by traditional Northern donors. Because of their political and economic weight – and their economic and political interests beyond solidarity – their relations with SSC recipient countries are highly asymmetrical and *de facto* not as horizontal as they claim. They are often seen as gaining more than their receiving counterparts and as promoting foreign models that might not be effective in the contexts where they are being implemented.

In the following section we assess some of the options and opportunities that SSC actors face in influencing the future shape of the international development cooperation system, and how the evident diversity might affect their prospects.

South–South cooperation and the international aid system

Despite the contradictions, SSC has come a long way in gaining international recognition and legitimacy as an important modality in development cooperation. The shift from no mention whatsoever in the Paris Declaration to full recognition in the Busan Partnership Document is a testimony to the growing perceived importance and influence of SSC actors and practices. What is less clear is what the next step might be, especially in light of the diversity of SSC actors. A common agenda does seem to be evolving: at a conference of Southern providers supported by India in New Delhi in April 2013, a number of issues of common concern were discussed and interest in coordinated action gauged. These included some practical elements, such as the lack of systematic data collection and evidence-based analysis of SSC, which is partly responsible for some of the misperceptions about the work of Southern providers; and the need to strengthen the evaluation of SSC programmes and projects, in order to foster peer learning and inform institution building, to exchange experiences on the strengthening of national development cooperation agencies, to enhance mutual learning and communication among SSC providers, and to create a credible and inclusive platform for SSC actors to coordinate on strategy, policy, and operations, possibly through the United Nations.[50] The following sections elaborate some possible options and scenarios mostly linked to this last possibility.

Option 1: building and strengthening the Global Partnership

Recognising the large amount of negotiating time and political capital that went into striking the agreement that resulted in the Busan Partnership Document, SSC actors might want to give the GPEDC a chance to succeed as a 'post-DAC' forum for global standard setting in the field of international development cooperation. The issue of 'differential commitments' could be negotiated among various actors without excessive arm-twisting, by having separate targets and monitoring of indicators for traditional donors and SSC actors. The inclusive nature of the GPEDC's Steering Committee – which houses not only DAC members and SSC providers but also recipient countries and civil society representatives – could guarantee that the views and interests of different stakeholders are taken into account and reconciled.

While this option seems attractive on paper, it certainly did not get off to a good start. As noted, Brazil and China did not actively engage in the post-Busan process of establishing the GPEDC; they questioned its relevance for their development cooperation practices and left it to Indonesia and Peru to represent SSC providers on the Steering Committee. The GPEDC secretariat is now shared between DAC and the UN Development Programme (UNDP), but many SSC actors still believe that they have weak bargaining power vis-à-vis DAC members, and that DAC principles and practices are still being imposed on them. While they recognise the need for a coherent and cohesive SSC response to the post-Busan process and the GPEDC, so far no clear consensus exists. The first high-level meeting of the GPEDC in Mexico did little to dispel these doubts, leaving each SSC provider to decide by itself how to engage in the process.

Option 2: increased UN role

Several SSC actors have already expressed a preference for shifting debates and decisions on global development cooperation principles and standards away from DAC – or the GPEDC – to a more inclusive and representative UN forum. The obvious candidate is the UN Development Cooperation Forum (UNDCF), which is part of the UN's Economic and Social Council (ECOSOC). The UNDCF was created at the 2005 UN World Summit with the objective, among others, to

(1) review trends in international development cooperation, including strategies, policies and financing; and (2) to promote greater coherence among the development activities of different development partners.[51] Forums have been held every two years since 2008, providing a useful opportunity to discuss a number of different issues in development cooperation.

Clearly, for the UNDCF to take the place of the GPEDC as the main platform for global standard setting on development cooperation, many things would have to change. SSC providers would need to develop a joint position in its favour, the DAC should all but close shop, and additional resources would have to be found to support the UNDCF's expanded role. None of the above is easy or likely in the near future. Many fear the well-known inefficiencies of UN bureaucracies, while the inclusive nature of UN membership often means that decision-making processes are very slow and fraught with difficulties.[52]

Option 3: strengthened ssc coordination

If international mechanisms – of the GPEDC or UN– are difficult to navigate, the obvious alternative for SSC actors is to find ways to strengthen coordination among themselves. This alternative, of course, is already partly happening. The Delhi conference was an example, though very much ad hoc and isolated, like previous similar conferences. Other examples come to mind. The leaders of BRICS, which include the largest SSC providers, meet on an annual basis. Although development cooperation can be seen as a tiny issue in their broad agenda, some interesting ideas have developed, including the creation of a BRICS development bank that could eventually come to counter-balance the power of the World Bank in influencing the development decisions of poor countries. The India, Brazil, South Africa (IBSA) Dialogue Forum established a fund in 2004 to support SSC projects, although it is unclear how active it will be and IBSA summits themselves have been discontinued since 2011. The UN Office for South–South Cooperation was set up within the UNDP to support the kind of SSC coordination and knowledge exchange that many SSC actors say they want and need. It could be further strengthened and better utilised. Clearly, these examples fall far short of a comprehensive mechanism for coordinating SSC actors and activities, which would require strong leadership by one or more of the large players, along with adequate resources to support its operations.

Other options

The three options and scenarios above are not exhaustive. Other forums exist in which SSC actors could develop joint positions and further their agenda. The G20, for example, set up a Development Working Group in 2010 with 'global development partnership' as one of its key principles. And a zero option also needs to be considered, for which the current status quo of limited and fragmented coordination of SSC actors, resulting from inertia and diversity in priorities and interests, remains unchanged. These options are not particularly attractive, neither for the future and the potential of SSC nor for development cooperation more generally.

Conclusion

This article has provided an overall picture and assessment of South–South cooperation, its actors and practices, and its influence on ongoing changes in the international architecture for development cooperation. We have documented how, despite its long history, ssc has become increasingly prominent over the past decade or so, gaining space and coverage in international forums and declarations on development cooperation, most evidently in the Busan Partnership Document and its follow-up process. Despite this interest, it is not easy to come to a common understanding about what ssc actually means, or to a useful mapping of its actors and practices.

ssc actors share at least a partial rejection of the principles and practices supported by the OECD-DAC – the traditional donors' club – and a discourse based on solidarity, horizontality, and mutual benefit with countries receiving development assistance. They are also defined by their having recently gone through development challenges similar to the ones faced by low-income countries today and are therefore able to provide relevant knowledge and expertise. Broadly speaking they can be divided into two groups. The first is comprised of large countries with a long involvement in development cooperation, like China, India, and Brazil. The second aggregates a broader range of smaller, 'second wave' countries with a more recent engagement in development cooperation activities. Indonesia, Turkey, and Mexico belong to this group. A brief review of their ssc programmes, however, reveals a great diversity in policies, institutional arrangements, and positioning vis-à-vis international processes, development cooperation, and standard setting.

At this critical juncture ssc actors could greatly benefit from increased coordination and from developing a joint position in relation to the ongoing changes in the international aid architecture, mirrored in the post-Busan process and the creation of the GPEDC. For example, they could push for a transfer of the norm-setting function historically played by ssc to a more representative UN body. Or they could strengthen intra-ssc coordination mechanisms aimed at developing consensus and promoting knowledge exchange, institutional strengthening, and sharing of good practices. Yet their diversity and divergence of interests, evident in their differential engagement with DAC-led processes, might prevent such coordination and in turn hamper the reform objectives that South–South cooperation was originally set up to achieve.

Notes

1. Woods, "Whose Aid?"; Mawdsley, *From Recipients to Donors*; Chaturvedi et al., *Development Cooperation*; and Park, "New Development Partners."
2. Chin and Quadir, "Introduction."
3. Park, "New Development Partners."
4. Kragelund, "Back to BASICS?"
5. Mawdsley et al., "A 'Post-aid World'?"
6. UNDCF, "South–South Cooperation."
7. These were the early years of South–South Cooperation, strongly shaped by the ideas of anticolonial movements in colonial states or countries that during those times had recently gained independence. See de Sá e Silva, "South–South Cooperation."
8. Golub, "From the New International Economic Order."
9. For background on the United Nations Office for South–South Cooperation, see http://ssc.undp.org/content/ssc/about/Background.html.
10. United Nations Special Unit for Technical Cooperation among Developing Countries (TCDC), *Buenos Aires Plan of Action (1978)*.
11. Leite, "Cooperação Sul–Sul."
12. Quadir, "Rising Donors"; and Park, "New Development Partners."
13. OECD, *The Paris Declaration*.
14. OECD-DAC, "Busan Partnership." (emphasis added)
15. Mawdsley et al., "A 'Post-aid World'?"
16. See "Closing Remarks by Navid Hanif, Director of Office of ECOSOC Support and Coordination, Department of Economic and Social Affairs, United Nations." Conference of South–South Cooperation Partners, New Delhi, April 16, 2013. http://www.un.org/en/ecosoc/newfunct/pdf13/dcf_delhi_closing_statement_hanif.pdf.
17. Manning, "Will Emerging Donors?"
18. Walz and Ramachandran, *Brave New World*. See also Zimmermann and Smith, "More Actors, More Money."
19. Walz and Ramachandran, *Brave New World*; and Manning, "Will Emerging Donors?"
20. Chin, "China as a 'Net Donor'."
21. Naím, "Rogue Aid."
22. Bräutigam, *The Dragon's Gift*.
23. Walz and Ramachandran, *Brave New World*.
24. Chin, "China as a 'Net Donor'," 581. The question of how to estimate Chinese volumes has stirred up a lively discussion in, for example, Project Aid Data, *Does the Giver Matter?*; and Bräutigam, "Rubbery Numbers."
25. Bräutigam, "Aid 'with Chinese Characteristics'."
26. Fonseca and Da, "A China na África"; and Abdenur and Marcondes de Souza Neto, "Cooperación China en América Latina."
27. Stolte, *Brazil in Africa*.
28. OECD-DAC, "Fourth High-level Forum."
29. GPEDC, "Who Supports the Global Partnership?"
30. Woods, "Whose Aid?" More recently, however, some important critical voices have started raising concerns. See, for example, Sanusi, "Africa must Get Real."
31. Abreu, "Brazil and South–South Cooperation."
32. Cabral and Shankland, *Narratives of Brazil–Africa Cooperation*; and Inoue and Vaz, "Brazil as 'Southern Donor'."
33. Dauvergne and Farias, "The Rise of Brazil," 908–909.
34. Jordan, "Brazil to Cancel US$900M in African Debt."
35. Federal Government of the Republic of Brazil, "Entrevista concedida pela Presidenta da República."
36. Jordan, "Brazil to Cancel US$900M in African Debt."
37. Dauvergne and Farias, "The Rise of Brazil," 908.
38. Schlesinger, *Cooperação e Investimentos*.
39. OECD, "Indonesia and the OECD."
40. Bantug-Herrera, *A Platform for Asian Emerging Donors*.

41. More information is available on the Teams homepage: www.ssc-indonesia.org/index.php.
42. Japan International Cooperation Agency Research Institute (JICARI), *Scaling Up.*
43. Turkish Ministry of Foreign Affairs, "Turkey's Development Cooperation."
44. "Turkey."
45. Aynte, *Turkey's Increasing Role.*
46. UNDP Turkey, "Turkey is on the Way."
47. Amexcid is the Agencia Mexicana de Cooperación Internacional para el Desarrollo. More information on it is available at www.amexcid.gob.mx.
48. Amexcid, *Annual Report*, 2012.
49. Ibid., 4.
50. See Conference of Southern Providers, *South–South Cooperation.*
51. See ECOSOC," Mandate of the DCF."
52. Besharati, *Common Goals and Differential Commitments.*

Bibliography

Abdenur, Adriana, and Danilo Marcondes de Souza Neto. "Cooperación China en América Latina: Las Implicaciones de la Asistencia para el Desarrollo." *Íconos – Revista de Ciencias Sociales* 47 (2013): 69–85.

Abreu, Fernando D. "Brazil and South–South Cooperation." Presentation at the BRICS Policy Center, 2013. http://bricspolicycenter.org/homolog/arquivos/e.pdf.

Amexcid. *Annual Report*, 2012. www.amexcid.gob.mx/images/pdf/Informe-Anual-2011-CTC-AMEXCID.pdf.

Aynte, Abdihakim. *Turkey's Increasing Role in Somalia: An Emerging Donor?* Aljazeera Center for Studies Report. 2012. http://studies.aljazeera.net/ResourceGallery/media/Documents/2012/3/22/201232213350836734 Turkeys%20Increasing%20Role%20in%20Somalia.pdf.

Bantug-Herrera, Anna. *A Platform for Asian Emerging Donors.* Asia Foundation. 2013. http://asiafoundation. org/in-asia/2013/04/24/a-platform-for-asian-emerging-donors.

Besharati, Neissan A. *Common Goals and Differential Commitments: The Role of Emerging Economies in Global Development.* Discussion Paper 26/2013. Bonn: German Development Institute, 2013.

Bräutigam, Deborah. "Aid 'with Chinese Characteristics': Chinese Foreign Aid and Development Finance meet the OECD-DAC Aid Regime." *Journal of International Development* 23, no. 5 (2011): 752–764.

Bräutigam, Deborah, ed. *The Dragon's Gift: The Real Story of China in Africa.* Oxford: Oxford University Press, 2009.

Bräutigam, Deborah. "Rubbery Numbers for Chinese Aid to Africa." Accessed April 30, 2013. http://www.chi naafricarealstory.com/2013/04/rubbery-numbers-on-chinese-aid.html.

Cabral, Lidia, and Alex Shankland. *Narratives of Brazil–Africa Cooperation for Agricultural Development: New Paradigms?* Working Paper 51, 2013. Brighton: Institute of Development Studies.

Chaturvedi, Sachin, Thomas Fues, and Elizabeth Sidiropoulos. *Development Cooperation and Emerging Powers: New Partners or Old Patterns?* London: Zed Books, 2012.

Chin, Gregory T. "China as a 'Net Donor': Tracking Dollars and Sense." *Cambridge Review of International Affairs* 25, no. 4 (2012): 579–603.

Chin, Gregory, and Fahimul Quadir. "Introduction: Rising States, Rising Donors and the Global Aid Regime." *Cambridge Review of International Affairs* 25, no. 4 (2012): 493–506.

Conference of Southern Providers. *South–South Cooperation: Issues and Emerging Challenges.* Conference Report. Accessed June 5, 2014. http://www.un.org/en/ecosoc/newfunct/pdf13/dcf_delhi_conference_report.pdf.

Dauvergne, Peter, and Déborah Farias. "The Rise of Brazil as a Global Development Power." *Third World Quarterly* 33, no. 5 (2012): 903–917.

de Sá e Silva, Michelle M. "South–South Cooperation: Past and Present Conceptualization and Practice." In *South–South Cooperation in Education and Development*, edited by Linda Chisholm and Gita Steiner-Khamsi, 39–59. New York, NY: Teachers College Press.

ECOSOC. "Mandate of the DCF." http://www.un.org/en/ecosoc/newfunct/mandate.shtml.

Federal Government of the Republic of Brazil. "Entrevista concedida pela Presidenta da República, Dilma Rousseff, durante visita a Adis Abeba para o Cinquentenário da Unidade Africana (OUA) – União Africana." Accessed June 5, 2014. http://www2.planalto.gov.br/acompanhe-o-planalto/entrevistas/entre vistas/entrevista-concedida-pela-presidenta-da-republica-dilma-rousseff-durante-visita-a-adis-adeba-para-o-cinquentenario-da-unidade-africana-oua-uniao-africana.

Fonseca, João, and M. E. M. Da. "A China na África e o Campo da Cooperação Internacional para o Desenvolvimento." In *Os BRICS e a Cooperação Sul-Sul*, edited by Adriana Abdenur and Paulo Esteves, 167–194. Rio de Janeiro: Editora PUC-Rio, May 2013.

Golub, Philip S. "From the New International Economic Order to the G20: How the 'Global South' is restructuring World Capitalism from Within." *Third World Quarterly* 34, no. 6 (2013): 1000–1015.

GPEDC. "Who Supports the Global Partnership?" Accessed June 5, 2014. http://effectivecooperation.org/about-list.html.

Inoue, Cristina Y.A., and Alcides C. Vaz. "Brazil as 'Southern Donor': Beyond Hierarchy and National Interests in Development Cooperation?" *Cambridge Review of International Affairs* 25, no. 4 (2012): 507–534.

Hierarchy and National Interests in Development Cooperation?" *Cambridge Review of International Affairs* 25, no. 4 (2012): 507–534.

Japan International Cooperation Agency Research Institute (JICARI). Scaling up South–South and Triangular Cooperation: Conference Volume Prepared for the Global South–South Development Expo 2012. JICA Working Paper, 2012.

Jordan, Lucy. 2013. "Brazil to Cancel US\$900M in African Debt." *Rio Times*, May 28. http://riotimesonline.com/brazil-news/rio-politics/brazil-to-cancel-us900m-in-african-debt.

Kragelund, Peter. "Back to BASICS? The Rejuvenation of Nontraditional Donors' Development Cooperation with Africa." *Development and Change* 42, no. 2 (2011): 585–607.

Leite, Iara Costa. "Cooperação Sul–Sul: Conceito, História e Marcos Interpretativos." *Observador On-line*, no. 3 (2012).

Manning, Richard. "Will Emerging Donors Change the Face of International Co-operation Development?" *Development Policy Review* 24, no. 4 (2006): 371–385.

Mawdsley, Emma. *From Recipients to Donors: Emerging Powers and the Changing Development Landscape.* London: Zed Books, 2012.

Mawdsley, Emma, Laura Savage, and Sung-Mi Kim. "A 'Post-aid World'? Paradigm Shift in Foreign Aid and Development Cooperation at the 2011 Busan High Level Forum." *Geographical Journal* 180, no. 1 (2014): 27–38.

Naím, Moisés. "Rogue Aid: What's Wrong with the Foreign Aid Programs of China, Venezuela, and Saudi Arabia? They are Enormously Generous. And They are Toxic." *Foreign Policy* 159 (2007): 95–96.

OECD. "Indonesia and the OECD: Enhancing our Partnership." *OECD Global Relations*, 2010. http://www.oecd.org/globalrelations/46241909.pdf.

OECD. *The Paris Declaration on Aid Effectiveness and the Accra Agenda for Action.* 2005/2008. http://www.oecd.org/dac/effectiveness/34428351.pdf.

OECD-DAC. "Busan Partnership for Effective Development Co-operation." 2011. http://www.oecd.org/dac/effectiveness/49650173.pdf.

OECD-DAC. "Fourth High-level Forum on Aid Effectiveness." http://www.oecd.org/dac/effectiveness/busanadherents.htm.

Park, Kang-Ho. "New Development Partners and a Global Development Partnership." In *Catalyzing Development: A New Vision for Aid*, edited by Homi Kharas, Koji Makino, and Woojin Jung, 38–60. Washington, DC: Brookings Institution Press, 2011.

Project Aid Data. *Does the Giver Matter? The Human Development Impact of Chinese Aid.* 2013. http://aiddata.org/blog/does-the-giver-matter-the-human-development-impact-of-chinese-aid.

Quadir, Fahimul. "Rising Donors and the New Narrative of 'South–South' Cooperation: What Prospects for Changing the Landscape of Development Assistance Programmes?" *Third World Quarterly* 34, no. 2 (2013): 321–338.

Sanusi, Lamido. 2013. "Africa must Get Real about Chinese Ties." *Financial Times*, March 11.

Schlesinger, Sergio. *Cooperação e Investimentos do Brasil na África: O caso do ProSavana em Moçambique.* Rio de Janeiro: FASE, 2013.

Stolte, Christina. *Brazil in Africa: Just another BRICS Country Seeking Resources?* Briefing Paper. 2012. London: Chatham House.

"Turkey: A Problematic Emerging Donor." 2012. http://www.articlespolitics.com/2012/12/turkey-problematic-emerging-donor.html.

Turkish Ministry of Foreign Affairs. "Turkey's Development Cooperation." www.mfa.gov.tr/turkey_s-development-cooperation.en.mfa.

UNDCF. "South–South Cooperation: Issues and Emerging Challenges." Conference of the United Nations Development Forum, New Delhi, April 15–16, 2013.

UNDP Turkey. "Turkey is on the Way of OECD DAC Membership." 2013. www.tr.undp.org/content/turkey/en/home/presscenter/news-from-new-horizons/2012/05/turkey-is-on-the-way-of-OECD-DAC-membership.

UNECA, *Africa–BRICS Cooperation.* Addis Ababa: United Nations Economic Commission for Africa, 2013. http://www.uneca.org/sites/default/files/publications/africa-brics_cooperation_eng.pdf.

Walz, Julia, and Vijaya Ramachandran. *Brave New World: A Literature Review of Emerging Donors and the Changing Nature of Foreign Assistance.* Working Paper 2073. Washington, DC: Center for Global Development, 2010.

Woods, Ngaire. "Whose Aid? Whose Influence? China, Emerging Donors and the Silent Revolution in Development Assistance." *International Affairs* 84, no. 6 (2008): 1205–1221.

Zimmermann, Felix, and Kimberly Smith. "More Actors, More Money, More Ideas for International Development Co-operation." *Journal of International Development* 23, no. 5 (2011): 722–738.

Emerging powers as normative agents: Brazil and China within the UN development system

Adriana Erthal Abdenur

Institute of International Relations, Pontifical Catholic University, Rio de Janeiro, Brazil

Institutions are frequently thought of as 'socialising' member states into pre-established norms. However, this influence is not necessarily a one-way street; members can also affect institutions, whether individually or collectively. This article analyses the behaviour of two emerging powers – Brazil and China – within the field of international development. What roles have these two states played in shaping global development norms? The article examines the key motivations, positions, and initiatives taken by Brazil and China, with special reference to the UN development system (UNDS). Whereas Brazil and China's early behaviour within the UNDS diverged significantly, in the post-cold war period both have become increasingly interested in – and capable of – influencing UN norms. However, despite greater involvement in UN development negotiations, these countries' leverage in normative debates originates outside of the UNDS, through their South–South cooperation programmes. The current diversification of platforms through which the norms of international development are negotiated may enhance the influence of emerging powers, although their ability to channel this influence effectively will depend on their capacity for norm entrepreneurship, rather than mere norm blocking.

Institutions are frequently thought of as shaping the behaviour and strategies of member states by 'socialising' those states into pre-established norms. However, this influence is not necessarily a one-way street; states, either individually or collectively, can also shape traditional institutions. Examining these dynamics within the field of international development is particularly important because of the proliferation of arenas through which global development norms are being negotiated in the post-cold war era. There are traditional arenas, such as the United Nations development system (UNDS) and the Global Partnership, led by the Organisation for Economic Co-operation and Development (OECD); there are also new, loose coalitions such as that of Brazil, Russia, India, China, and South Africa (BRICS). This article analyses the behaviour of two emerging powers – Brazil and China – within the field of development, both within and outside the UN, with a focus on their normative roles: that is, their ability to influence debates about the principles and values governing development assistance. How and to what extent have Brazil's and China's individual and collective influence reshaped development debates at the UN?

Undertaking such a comparison helps to address the literature on global development norms in three key ways. First, while the existing social sciences scholarship has looked into the behaviour of emerging powers in relation to the UN's security mandate, there are few in-depth studies of their changing roles within its development system. Second, emerging powers have become important players within the field of development, especially after transitioning from net recipients to net providers of development cooperation. Brazil and China are increasingly relevant to the UNDS not only individually, but also through collaborations such as the BRICS and BASIC (ie BRICS without Russia) arrangements. Finally, if these emerging powers possess some degree of influence over the global development norm-setting process, they are bound to play a critical role in defining the post-2015 development agenda.

Through a combination of document analysis and interviews with government and UN officials, this article examines the positions taken by Brazil and China across time within the field of development, with special reference to the UNDS. Whereas these two countries' behaviour within the UNDS diverged significantly during the Cold War, over the past two decades they have become increasingly interested in – and capable of – shaping the UNDS. This two-way socialisation occurs through greater involvement in UN development negotiations and initiatives, but their greatest impact on the UNDS in fact arises out of their roles in development outside the UN altogether, through their respective South–South cooperation programmes. This finding suggests that the current diversification of platforms through which the norms of international development are negotiated may enhance the influence of emerging powers within the field of development. Their ability to exert this influence, however, will depend on their capacity for norm entrepreneurship, rather than mere norm blocking.

The analysis unfolds in the following manner. The next section of the article offers an overview of the literature on institutions and emerging powers, including the concept of two-way socialisation. The subsequent section analyse the changing roles of Brazil and China in international development, within and beyond the UNDS. The conclusion explores the implications of emerging powers' norm-blocking behaviour, as well as perspectives for more robust norm entrepreneurship.

Institutions and development norms

Institutions such as the UN are frequently viewed as socialising states into pre-set norms so that they can become 'functional members' of that cooperative architecture, adapting their behaviour to the principles and practices perceived as acceptable.[1] A. I. Johnston differentiates among three processes of socialisation in institutions: mimicking, social influence, and persuasion.[2] However, these processes are likely to be most effective with respect to 'novices' within the institution.[3] New arrivals do not have a full grasp of the rules of the game, and they may want to fit in and be accepted by more established members. In addition, the goals of new members within the institution may not yet be clearly defined. This framework has been applied to the way new member states are integrated into the EU, as well as to how individual states rely upon, and are affected by, international institutions.[4] However, the framework loses potency when applied to older members. Once a state is no longer a newcomer, it may prove less compliant with pre-existing rules, reflecting the limits of socialisation.[5] Socialisation theory as formulated thus far is therefore ill-equipped to explain the behaviour of non-novices within institutions. In addition, the socialisation framework tends to treat peripheral members individually, underestimating how alignments among such members may block, reshape, or even reverse the socialisation process by pooling leverage and articulating positions that do not necessarily support established norms.

The role of emerging powers within institutional socialisation processes needs further scrutiny precisely because states labelled as such are no longer 'newcomers' to established institutions – indeed, many were founding members. In addition, since the end of the Cold War, these states – countries that not only aspire to play a greater role in international affairs but which also call for reform of the current global governance architecture – have become increasingly important players within the international arena as US hegemony is cast into doubt. In response to this highly uncertain scenario, emerging powers increasingly coordinate their positions through loose coalitions such as BRICS, which – particularly since the 2008 onset of the global financial crisis – have amplified the call for a more representative and effective global governance architecture.[6] As a result, socialisation should be thought of more as a two-way process, with the normative preferences of emerging powers gaining ground in global rule-setting debates.[7]

Over the past decade the field of development has undergone deep change as emerging powers expand their South–South cooperation and increasingly contest the norms set through established institutions such as the UN and the Bretton Woods institutions. While challenges to UN development practices and norms date back to the Cold War – both the Group of 77 (G77) and the Non-Aligned Movement (NAM) helped developing countries criticise what they viewed as an unfair trade regime – the recent emergence of new economic growth nodes has given South–South cooperation providers new leverage in shaping development norms. In addition, the proliferation of norm-setting arenas has granted emerging powers new ways to contest norm-setting efforts that are perceived to be Northern-led – both those undertaken within the UN and those pursued outside it, such as the OECD-led aid effectiveness agenda. In contesting such initiatives, the emerging powers, including BRICS, also draw on their dual roles within the field of international development, since they have encountered development-related challenges both as recipients of assistance and as providers of development cooperation.

Because the literature on international institutions and norms views the socialisation process primarily as a one-way street – with institutions inculcating pre-established norms into member states – it tends to underestimate the degree to which non-newcomers such as emerging powers can influence the norm-setting process, however incrementally. This article helps to fill this gap by focusing on two rising states which, despite having experienced different trajectories within the field of development, have found considerable common ground over the past decade: Brazil and China. Individually these two countries have vastly expanded their respective development cooperation programmes, mostly on a bilateral basis. In addition, each emphasises that these initiatives are horizontal and unencumbered by the legacies of colonialism that they perceive as tainting Northern aid. Within the UN, even as Brazil and China have increased their contributions to its budget,[8] they remain wary of what they perceive to be donor countries' constant efforts to increase their own influence in the field. Outside the UN Brazil's and China's deepening ties, including via BRICS, have reinforced their common resistance to initiatives that they perceive to be skewed towards the interests of the advanced economies, including norms that they perceive as potentially infringing on the principle of national sovereignty.[9]

The next section looks at how Brazil's and China's respective engagements with international development across time, both through the UNDS and outside it, helped to shape their current roles and positions on international development. Rather than assume that they are passive actors within the system, they are treated as normative agents, capable (to varying degrees) of adopting strategies that range from blocking institutional norms to engaging in norm entrepreneurship: proposals for norms backed by political strategies meant to produce significant changes in terms of which principles and values are broadly viewed as acceptable.[10]

Brazil's frustrated norm entrepreneurship

Multilateralism, especially through the UN, has long been a cornerstone of Brazilian foreign policy, but its centrality is marked by both emerging power ambitions and a historic sense of injustice at being marginalised within the system. After World War II US president Franklin Roosevelt suggested that Brazil be included as a sixth member of the UN Security Council, but the idea was rejected by the USSR and the UK. Brazil's ensuing frustration helps to explain why, even as it seeks to 'fit in' at the UN, it has also actively pushed for systemic reform, including with respect to development. During the Cold War heavy emphasis on multilateralism became a way for Brazil – a large economy with a growing population, yet still beset by widespread poverty, sharp socio-economic inequalities, and other structural problems – to exercise influence beyond its immediate region. By 1964 Brazil was participating in 26 UN agencies, a participation level that trailed only those of the USA, the USSR, the UK, and France.[11] Thus, despite believing that the UN tended to reflect the interests and views of the Security Council's permanent five member (P5), Brazil was eager to become a 'good citizen' of the UN, actively engaging in multiple discussions and initiatives.

In the 1950s and 1960s, when global discussions about development focused heavily on trade, Brazil joined other developing countries in arguing that global commerce was asymmetrical and unjust, and that the UN tended to perpetuate these imbalances. Although Brazil was working to establish its industrial base, the export of commodities had been central to its economy since its days as a Portuguese colony. Although it did not join NAM, it expressed solidarity with the initiative and became an observer. By the mid-1970s Brazil had stopped supporting the positions of the colonial powers at the UN and recognised the independence of newly independent African states.

During this period Brazil's relevance within the UNDS increased primarily through its participation in normative debates, particularly political economy discussions in which developing countries sought to align themselves to gain pooled leverage. In 1964, for instance, Brazilian delegations to the UN Conference and Trade and Development (UNCTAD) defended the idea of 'collective economic security', which called upon the international community of states to implement reform of international trade so as to foster development in the 'backward' countries. In June 1964, in search of a more autonomous foreign policy vis-à-vis the USA, Brazil joined the G77, where it played a salient role in the coordination of Third World positions, particularly in defending the idea of the developmental state. In other words, rather than merely subjecting itself to socialisation into a set of pre-established norms, early on Brazil was already contesting (and helping to mobilise broader contestation of) certain norms, as well as proposing partial solutions. However, Brazil's normative entrepreneurship was constrained by its own scarce resources and by the rigidity of the era's bipolar configuration, which limited the concrete results produced by the G77. At the same time, by criticising the global trade system, Brazil was distancing itself from the East–West ideological divide and aligning itself more closely with other Third World countries, placing greater emphasis instead on the South–North dialogue.

Brazil's positions regarding trade and development, and in particular its opposition to protectionism by advanced countries, did not change significantly after the 1964 coup d'état that installed a military regime, and this was manifested inside and outside the UNDS. In 1965, for instance, Brazil refused to sign the Long-Term Arrangement Regarding International Trade in Cotton Textiles, negotiated through the General Agreement on Tariffs and Trade, because it considered that the deal promoted the doctrine of 'market disruption' through which Northern economies justified export restraints.[12]

As a normative actor Brazil also made intellectual contributions to development debates at the UN's Economic Commission for Latin America and the Caribbean (ECLAC or, in Spanish, CEPAL). Brazilian social scientists, including Fernando Henrique Cardoso and Anibal Pinto, were among the commission's original body of researchers and helped formulate dependency theory, both in terms of diagnosing underdevelopment and with respect to making policy prescriptions to foster development in the periphery.[13] Celso Furtado worked with Raúl Prebisch as part of the Keynes-inspired structuralist school of thought that emerged within CEPAL, and which argued for government intervention to stimulate economic development. Brazil's military regime drew on some of these ideas during the so-called Brazilian Miracle, a period during the late 1960s and early 1970s when the economy achieved double-digit growth, and import substitutions strengthened the country's industrial base. The growth spurt, however, was accompanied by deepening social inequalities and harsh political repression, and it gave way to prolonged economic stagnation and high inflation that lasted until the mid-1990s.

During this period Brazil and its allies at the UN managed to extract some concessions from the system, even if these concessions were expressed primarily outside the UNDS. For example, following UNCTAD debates regarding the Most Favoured Nation system's tendency to discourage rich countries from reducing tariffs and other trade restrictions, Brazil contributed towards the 1968 creation of the Generalized System of Preferences, through which developed economies grant improved market access to exports from developing countries. During the 1970s, at the peak of developing countries' coordinated participation within the UN, Brazil voiced its sharpest criticisms of the global asymmetries in trade and development. The country supported the New International Economic Order (NIEO), a set of proposals put forward by developing countries at a special session of the UN General Assembly, and through UNCTAD, to improve the terms of trade and to foment changes within the international economic system in favour of Third World countries.

Although the NIEO was meant essentially to replace the Bretton Woods system, over the next decade the proposal lost steam as the debt crisis of the 1970s and 1980s deepened in the Third World. The IMF and the World Bank began working closely together to implement structural adjustment packages, including in Brazil, and as a result the UNDS's role as a platform for coordinating the positions of developing countries was severely weakened. The idealism that the Third World had brought to UNCTAD had achieved modest results, and the organisation – once a forum for lively debate about development and a key platform for Brazil's positions – lost space to the Bretton Woods institutions, where Brazil had less clout. The efforts to boost South–South cooperation within the UN, which Brazil supported after the 1978 Buenos Aires Declaration, also lost steam, less as a result of the incapacity of countries such as Brazil to engage in norm entrepreneurship than to the structural changes in the global economy and the concomitant weakening of the UNDS relative to the Bretton Woods institutions.

Domestically, even as Brazil changed course politically, returning to democracy in the late 1980s after 21 years of military rule, its development remained closely tied to its financial and policy commitments to the IMF. The country continued to experience stagnant or negative economic growth, and its socioeconomic inequality increased sharply. In 1989, at the trough of this 'Lost Decade', Brazil defaulted on its IMF loans and had to renegotiate its debt. This prolonged crisis mode meant that Brazil's norm entrepreneurship within the UNDS lost momentum, and it also reinforced the sentiment among Brazilian policy elites that the global governance system was both unfair and inefficient. The experience also ingrained a degree of resentment at the country's lack of autonomy in implementing domestic policies, as well as producing widespread scepticism at the development norms promoted by the Bretton Woods institutions. For instance, Brazilian policy elites and analysts began to question the claim, frequently made by World Bank and IMF experts, that the Asian Tiger successes had been achieved through structural adjustment; instead, they argued that the deep articulation between state and market in those countries had generated positive results. This perception reinforced the belief among some Brazilian elites that, far from being an impediment, the state had an essential role to play in fostering growth and development – an idea that Brazil continued to champion via the weakened UNDS.

In the post-cold war era Brazil's domestic situation began to change, especially after macroeconomic stability was achieved through the 1994 Plano Real. After the 1995 establishment of the World Trade Organization, Brazil increased its activism within global commercial negotiations, with a focus on agricultural trade, but it also continued to push for innovations at UNCTAD, where it worked to rescue the UN's role of reflection on international development, including by encouraging the production of UNCTAD reports about the imbalances produced in developing countries by the increasing volatility of financial capital.

By the late 1990s the UN Development Programme – realising that the Bretton Woods structural adjustment packages were failing to foster growth – made poverty alleviation a more visible topic within the UN agenda. This shift helped to make the UNDS more relevant to development debates beyond the commercial arena, and it was a welcome change from Brazil's perspective, given its persistent problems with poverty. In 2000 Brazil signed on to the Millennium Development Goals (MDGS), and the government introduced national campaigns to raise public awareness and to reach the goals. However, Brazilian diplomats assert that, despite the organisation's consensus-building process, the MDGS were typical of the 'potential consensus' proposals that are pre-set by Northern countries and then presented to the broader UN membership as a done deal.

In the 2000s the Brazilian economy began to experience relatively high growth, fuelled in part by the rise in demand from China for Brazilian commodities such as iron ore and soy. The Workers Party-led government of Luiz Inácio Lula da Silva (president from 2003 to 2010) channelled some of this growth into redistributive policies, including the *Bolsa Família* conditional cash transfer programme. Millions of Brazilians rose above poverty levels, particularly in remote rural areas, and socioeconomic inequality began to decline. The country's balance of payments also changed dramatically – Brazil paid off its IMF debt in 2005, becoming a net contributor and accumulating foreign exchange reserves. In 2006 the state-owned oil company Petrobras announced the discovery of substantial oil reserves in the pre-salt layer off Brazil's South Atlantic coastline. Abroad Brazil's economic boom – combined with the leftist government's emphasis on diversifying its foreign relations beyond the USA and European countries – also helped to drive a major increase in Brazil's South–South development cooperation. These initiatives included not only technical cooperation in areas such as agriculture, public health and education, but also major investments in infrastructure, often with financing from the Brazilian National Development Bank. Brazil continued to receive development assistance, especially through international organisations, but it also became a major provider of South–South cooperation in Latin America and Africa. As a result, Brazil's influence in international development gained ground primarily via its bilateral development cooperation initiatives, rather than through its participation in the UNDS.

Emboldened by its experience of growth, at the UN Brazil not only stepped up its claim for a permanent seat in the Security Council, but it also defended the rebalancing of the UN's pillars, criticising what it perceived to be an excessive focus on security issues since the 9/11 attacks. At the intersection of security and development Brazilian diplomats have been particularly wary of categories such as 'terrorist group' and 'failed state', which they view as increasingly used by the North to justify self-interested interventionism, both through and outside the UN. As a result, Brazil has emphasised the principles of respect for national sovereignty, finding in other emerging powers common ground in objecting to norms that seem to infringe on government autonomy in policymaking. Brazil also deepened its involvement with the UN's broadening development agenda, for instance hosting the Rio+20 conference and subsequent efforts on sustainable development, participating actively in the post-Kyoto climate change negotiations, and continuing its work towards 'flexibilising' the international regime on intellectual property so as to facilitate the production of generic medications in case of public health emergencies.

During the past decade Brazil's normative potential within international development has been enhanced by its participation in informal coalitions that bring together emerging powers. Particularly through the BRICS grouping, Brazil has amplified its calls for reform of major development institutions, including the UNDS. Although the partial reform of IMF voting quotas has not yet translated into concrete change, the pressure for structural transformation in those institutions is maintained through BRICS's shared view that the global development governance architecture should be more representative of the current distribution of power.

With respect to broader development norms, Brazil has kept its distance from the OECD's efforts to codify norms of international cooperation through the Paris Declaration, the Accra Agenda, and the aid effectiveness agenda led by its Development Assistance Committee (DAC). Diplomats note that, although Brazilian South–South cooperation is actually compatible with some of the values and principles espoused by DAC, Brazil's emphasis on respect for national sovereignty and its refusal to impose political conditionalities as part of its South–South cooperation create points of tension with the OECD-proposed framework. Although Brazil signed the Paris Declaration, it asserts that it did so only as a recipient country, and not as a cooperation partner. Brazil's emphasis on the differences between aid and cooperation was also evident at the September 2008 Third High-level Forum of Aid Effectiveness in Accra: Brazil's initial reluctance to sign the declaration contributed towards the eventual inclusion within the text of a section addressing South–South cooperation, as well as to the softening of the language of commitment – the declaration 'recommends' rather than requires an orientation towards the norms established in Paris. Thus, despite Brazil's growing role as a provider of South–South cooperation, it has proven especially reluctant to engage in discussions it perceives as dominated by Northern interests, and as a result it was not part of the Steering Committee of the High-level Event on South–South Cooperation.[14] By maintaining this distance Brazil is primarily a norms blocker, contesting what it views as co-optation into a Northern-formulated normative framework.

Part of Brazil's discomfort with aligning with DAC members arises out of resistance to being pigeonholed into categories associated with Northern aid. Brazilian diplomats bristle at the suggestion that Brazil is an 'emerging donor' because they claim that the country is not a provider of aid but rather a solidarity partner in horizontal cooperation. In addition, Brazilian officials have maintained that DAC initiatives, undertaken outside the UN system and led by Northern donors, are inherently asymmetric and serve to weaken rather than bolster the UNDS – which Brazil views as the most legitimate venue for global development norm setting. Although Brazil proved amenable to the revised document of the Bali high-level panel on effectiveness, by the launch of the Global Partnership, Brazilian policymakers had returned to a sceptical stance, believing that Brazil had essentially been invited to a game whose rules had mostly already been set, rather than being part of an inclusive norm-setting process from the start.

To help boost the development pillar of the UN, Brazil has continued to push for increased relevance for the Economic and Social Council (ECOSOC) in economic norm setting. Within this arena Brazil has worked to dilute what it views as the disproportionate influence of Security Council members. For instance, when negotiations were underway for the creation of the Peacebuilding Commission (PBC), Brazil argued for a broader role for the mechanism, one that would encompass preventative diplomacy as well as post-conflict peacebuilding. Brazilian diplomats also fought to avoid making the new commission narrowly subordinate to the Security Council, fearing not only that the interests of the P5 would dominate the mechanism, but also that the PBC's mandate would be skewed towards security issues such as security sector reform at the expense of more traditional development efforts.[15] Broadly put, Brazil hoped that the PBC would strengthen the role of ECOSOC relative to the Security Council, helping to redress the overall imbalance between security and development at the UN by boosting the latter.

Formally Brazil has championed the UN Development Cooperation Forum (DCF) for being both universal and multi-stakeholder – even if, privately, some senior Brazilian diplomats acknowledge that DCF discussions have been sluggish, fragmented, and weighed down by lack of commitment from member states. Confronted with its limited capacity to relocate the global development discussions away from the Global Partnership to the UN, Brazil has increasingly turned to loose coalitions such as BRICS as a way of coordinating positions, boosting its calls for reform of the UN architecture, and contesting norms it perceives as emanating from the advanced economies. So far, however, these efforts have been more successful in blocking norms – as seen in these countries' common resistance to the aid effectiveness agenda – than in norm entrepreneurship in the sense of proposing and advancing alternative normative frameworks.

China's shifting development diplomacy

China has often been referred to as a mostly 'passive actor' or 'diligent apprentice' within the United Nations.[16] This is an oversimplification because China's behaviour and attitudes within the world organisation, including in its development system, have varied substantially over time and across topics, exhibiting a highly variable degree of normative engagement. Relative to Brazil, China was a 'late joiner' at the UN – it became a member state only in 1971 after UN General Assembly resolution 2758 recognised the People's Republic of China as the only lawful representative of China at the UN, allowing it to replace Taiwan within the organisation. Nonetheless, China's permanent membership within the Security Council granted it immediate heft. Although this weight was felt particularly within the realm of security, China's role in development – especially its early provision of financial and development support to newly independent states in Africa – played a key part in the country's ability to secure widespread support within the General Assembly for its UN membership. Even outside the UNDS this early Chinese cooperation strengthened Beijing's bonds of solidarity with other developing countries, a solidarity that still shapes China's role within the UNDS.

Once inducted officially into the UN, China at first maintained a low profile. At the Security Council Beijing cast only four vetoes between 1971 and 2002.[17] During its first decade of UN membership, China's aloofness reflected not only its government's preoccupation with attaining domestic stability after the turbulence of the Cultural Revolution, but also its deep distrust of initiatives by the international community of states that could be viewed as impinging on its national sovereignty – a serious concern for Chinese policy elites in light of the country's experience under Western imperialism. At the same time the UN offered China – a communist country with relatively few foreign ties – enhanced legitimacy and formal recognition in the international arena.

During this period China steadfastly declined to receive any development assistance from the UN.[18] This posture was a result not only of the inward-orientation of post-Mao China but also of lingering resentment among Communist Party elites regarding the UN: not only had UN peacekeeping forces fought China in the Korean War but also for two decades its rival Taiwan had been considered the legitimate representative of China at the UN. However, once at the UN China was quick to differentiate its identity as an actor in international development: Chinese representatives emphasised that China was a fellow developing country, and China became the only permanent seat holder to voice support for Third World demands for greater voice. In addition to supporting the positions that developing countries voiced through UNCTAD and ECOSOC debates, China backed the candidacies of developing country candidates to the post of secretary-general, including those of Peru's Javier Pérez de Cuellar and later Egypt's Boutros Boutros-Ghali. While this support allowed China to lend substance to its claim of 'championship without leadership' within the developing world, it also allowed Beijing to paper over China's conservative stance towards reform of the Security Council, where it has long resisted calls for greater inclusiveness.[19]

Outside the UN China expanded its bilateral cooperation in developing countries, including newly independent states in Africa and Asia, offering South–South development cooperation in areas including infrastructure and educational exchanges. The 'Eight Principles' that Premier Zhou Enlai had announced in 1963 – including mutual benefit, lack of conditionalities, avoidance of debt creation and dependence on China, and transfer of know-how – to this day serve as the normative foundation for the Chinese government's policy discourse on South–South cooperation.[20]

Starting in 1978, when Deng Xiaoping initiated the 'Open Door' reforms, participation in UN debates and initiatives became more important to Chinese foreign policy. In 1979 the General Assembly launched a new round of global economic negotiations in the hope that the North and South could reach a package solution on energy, raw materials, trade, development, money, and finance.[21] China sent a delegation to a small summit organised to advance negotiations across the North–South divide. At the event Chinese representatives emphasised that the unfair and unequal international economic order must be restructured so as to avoid further confrontation between North and South.[22] Just as significantly China abruptly ended its policy of self-reliance in development. It signed agreements to receive assistance from the UNDS covering a wide range of sectors, including agriculture, forestry, fishing, transportation, communications, energy, environmental protection, education and disaster prevention. In just three years China went from receiving zero assistance from the UNDS to receiving more multilateral technical aid projects (around 200) than any other UN member state.

Far from merely 'learning' the ways and rules of the UNDS, China began participating more actively in normative debates, for instance joining the G77 as a 'special invitee' starting with the Gabon meetings of 1981. Through its alignment with the G77, China strengthened three normative contributions. First, it called upon advanced economies to take on greater responsibility for fostering growth and social well-being in the least developed countries (LDCS) and heavily indebted poor countries (HIPCS). Second, Chinese representatives argued that South–South cooperation should remain a complement to, rather than a substitute for, official development assistance from Northern donors. And, third, Beijing insisted that the advanced economies should actively foster technology transfer, provide aid, and offer debt relief to developing countries. China has maintained these stances for the past three decades,[23] even as it began to experience double-digit economic growth.

As China's growth rate accelerated, Beijing looked for new ways to assume a more direct role in UN development debates. China diversified its involvement with the UNDS, hosting seminars, workshops, and training courses, especially for initiatives focusing on Asia, Africa and Latin America. By 1986 China was participating in all the agencies and divisions of the UNDS. China's Government Work Report of that year was the first ever in the series to mention multilateral diplomacy, with Premier Zhao Ziyang stating that China would abide by the UN Charter.[24] In the field of security China overcame its historic aversion to UN peacekeeping operations and began taking part in missions. With respect to the UNDS the country began working to boost South–South cooperation within the organisation. During a 1987 ECOSOC regular session, for example, the Chinese delegation proposed a draft resolution calling on the UN to reinforce incentives for technical cooperation among developing countries. The draft – approved by consensus before being adopted by the General Assembly – marked the first time that the assembly had adopted a resolution devoted to development.[25]

At the same time China's sudden engagement with international development multilateralism extended to the Bretton Woods institutions. China began to receive loans from both the World Bank and the IMF and by 1989 – only a decade after it reversed its position on development self-sufficiency – China had surpassed India as the world's biggest recipient of multilateral aid. In the 1990s China began sending some of its most qualified diplomats to the UN; these representatives became much more active participants in development debates. This shift reflected a broader change in attitude: from wanting to protect China from external influence to expanding China's role beyond its borders.[26] While China remained disengaged and often defensive within UN human rights discussions, resisting scrutiny of its own human rights record (especially after the 1989

Tiananmen crackdown), in the area of development the country intensified efforts to mobilise support for South–South cooperation within the UN. In 1997 China joined the G77 in appealing for a UN-convened South–South Conference on Trade Investment and Finance. The event, held in Costa Rica, yielded the San José Declaration and Programme of Action, which outlined concrete modalities of trade, finance, investment, and enterprise cooperation among developing countries.

These incremental increases in activism within the UNDS were underscored by China's remarkable transformation, as it changed its own development model through massive investment and urbanisation, internationalisation of state-owned enterprises, and the nurturing of trade relations. As productivity increased, new poles of prosperity and globalisation emerged, lifting more than 600 million people out of poverty between 1981 and 2004 alone.[27] As China grew both at home and abroad, the international community's expectations of China as an actor in international development institutions also changed, with calls for Beijing to assume greater responsibility through expanded contributions and more active participation in UNDS initiatives.

Chinese government officials tried to manage these expectations by emphasising that, despite the country's growth spurt, it still faced significant development challenges at home, including widespread rural poverty, a large 'floating' population of rural–urban migrants, worsening environmental problems, and increasing socioeconomic inequality. As a result, China has continued to self-identify as a 'developing country', both within and outside the UN. This discourse provides China with the legitimacy to mobilise (and often advocate on behalf of) a vast number of developing countries; and it boosts its discourse of peaceful development, which the Chinese government has been eager to promote in order to combat perceptions of the country as an aggressive, even exploitative, emerging power. At the same time China's insistence that it remains a developing country has also made it vulnerable to accusations of shirking responsibility within the international community.

China has drawn on its considerable resources to support, through bilateral means, the positions it promotes within the UNDS. In September 2005, for instance, President Hu Jintao announced at the UN World Summit that China had decided to grant zero tariff treatment to some imports from LDCs and to expand its bilateral cooperation programme with HIPCs.[28] Over the next two years China wrote off or forgave overdue debts by all HIPCs that maintained diplomatic relations with Beijing. It also began providing billions of dollars in concessional loans and preferential export buyers' credit to developing countries, and it increased its infrastructure projects in those countries. These efforts were particularly strong in Africa, where Chinese loans and investments are often accompanied by such 'soft power' elements as public-use buildings and health initiatives. The Forum on China–Africa Cooperation, launched in 2000 as an umbrella for China's bilateral cooperation with African states, deepened these ties considerably, while the discourse of win-win cooperation and non-conditionality was maintained (apart from the requirement that partners break off diplomatic ties with Taiwan). Through these initiatives China's accumulated concrete experiences in bilateral South–South cooperation, undertaken outside the UNDS, has helped Beijing to amass a great deal of goodwill among developing countries, whose governments are more likely than before to back Beijing's positions on development matters.

While most of China's South–South cooperation is mostly bilateral – a trend confirmed by the government's 2011 White Paper on Foreign Aid – the country has also ramped up its development multilateralism. In 2009, when the UN experienced a record $4.8 billion funding gap, emerging powers – and China in particular – were viewed as promising sources of funding.[29] Although Beijing stepped up its contributions to the UNDS (mostly membership dues to UNICEF, the, UN Population Fund, and material resources for humanitarian assistance and disaster efforts), its 2013 combined contributions reached a peak of $6 million.

The sum is modest compared to China's contributions to non-UN development institutions. China is now the third biggest shareholder in the World Bank, after the USA and Japan. Between 2006 and 2012 alone it contributed $80 million to the Bank. China is also a considerable source of funding for regional organisations. In 2012 it contributed $45 million to the Asian Development Bank, and it has pledged $486 million to the African Development Bank.[30] Thus, despite China's formal emphasis upon the legitimacy of the UN as the foremost platform for global development coordination, in practice it has boosted other institutions, especially those with weighted voting systems that give Beijing a greater say in fund allocation. The Chinese government may be concerned that more extensive use of UN agencies would enhance the perception (which Beijing wishes to avoid) of China as a donor state rather than a fellow developing country engaged in cooperation.[31]

In addition, the extent to which China views the UNDS as a set of resources for its own development strategies is fairly limited. Although China endorsed the MDGs, the goals were not central to the Chinese government's poverty alleviation strategy.[32] As a result, the MDGs have not been a particularly strong guiding force for China, either internally or in its South–South cooperation – as reflected in the scant attention paid to the MDGs within China's 2011 White Paper on Foreign Aid.

In normative debates China has resisted certain trends within the UNDS. Like Brazil, it has been reluctant to participate in country-level development dialogues because it views these activities as part of the Northern aid effectiveness agenda. Through its extensive bilateral cooperation, China already coordinates with state governments outside UN channels. An additional source of resistance is China's fear that country-level coordination may infringe on national sovereignty, especially since it views Northern-led efforts to include 'good governance' within the UN agenda as a potential venue for imposing political conditionalities, something it adamantly opposes. Instead, China has emphasised the need to 'flexibilise' cooperation in accordance with countries' specific needs, avoiding a cookie-cutter approach to development.

At the UN China has also resisted the formulation of certain quantifiable development goals, particularly when legally binding, and when Beijing considers the process to be unfair or rushed. During efforts to achieve an international agreement on climate change to replace the UN Kyoto Protocol, due to expire in 2012, China – currently the world's largest emitter of greenhouse gases – came under pressure to help put together a deal. Although Chinese resistance was far from the only factor behind the Copenhagen summit's weak results,

China's reluctance to endorse the quantification of climate goals has been cited as playing a role in the conference's outcome. Like many other high-emitting states, China opposes the principle of international verification, insisting instead upon consultations and analysis. To Northern governments China was shirking its responsibilities and undermining the summit,[33] while to many developing countries – including Brazil, India, and capacity-building support to developing and most of South America, all of which backed Beijing's position – China's stance was consistent with the principle of 'Common but Differentiated Responsibility'.

If anything, China's posture during the Copenhagen negotiations reflects its cautious approach to UN reform: it favours a gradual process, underlining the need for adequate consultation and coordination among all member states and eschewing moves it perceives to be either inadequately thought-through or skewed towards the interests of advanced countries. At the same time China demonstrated some clout in its capacity to mobilise emerging powers: it spear-headed the BASIC coalition in a commitment to act jointly during and after Copenhagen. The move is illustrative of Beijing's evolving strategy of using loose coalitions to boost support for its positions within the UNDS and to insist that advanced countries have a greater responsibility to boost the transfer of technologies, financing, and capacity-building support to developing countries.[34]

This coalition strategy includes efforts undertaken outside the UNDS. The emergence of BRICS as a political grouping has provided Beijing with an additional mechanism through which to enhance its multilateralism credentials. On reform of global development governance, China has been far more outspoken than on security issues, for which its permanent membership has made it more of a status quo power; and it is more willing to engage in concrete initiatives, as seen in its active advocacy of the creation of a BRICS development bank. At the same time, and much like Brazil, China remains deeply suspicious of OECD-led efforts to cod-ify principles of development assistance, and it considers the Global Partnership a donor-led process that detracts from the UNDS function of global coordination. Beijing has thus insisted that the DCF is the most appropriate arena for creating a truly global partnership for development. However, in contrast to Brazil and other South–South development cooperation providers, China has attained such scope and reach within its bilateral cooperation that it has far greater leverage in influ-encing discussions in international development, including blocking normative efforts by the OECD. At the Busan Partnership for Effective Development, for instance, key moments of the declaration negotiations were spent refining the lan-guage in accordance with China's insistence that the outcome document's adher-ence to the principles, commitments, and actions be voluntary for South–South partners. As a result of China's insistence on flexibility and reluctance to endorse binding commitments, the international community has become increasingly aware that any emerging development architecture undertaken without China's engagement will suffer in both legitimacy and efficacy.

Conclusion: emerging powers and normative agency

Far from being passively socialised into the UNDS, emerging powers have long engaged in normative debates and – especially over the past decade – have begun to influence those discussions. Brazil has a long history of directly challenging Northern-led development models and initiatives through the UN architecture, even if structural constraints and Northern opposition have limited the results of those initiatives. While China at first refused UN development assistance, once economic reforms were launched, it embraced UN assistance enthusiastically. After the turn of the millennium, as these countries experienced dramatic economic growth and expanded their South–South development cooperation, their relevance to international development grew primarily outside the UN channels.

The key change in these countries' roles within the field of development is that, despite their significantly divergent trajectories, the post-cold war scenario has offered both Brazil and China greater opportunities to find common ground, especially in resisting Northern-led norm setting and, increasingly, in coordinating some policy positions. This partial convergence does not come as a surprise. Both Brazil and China frequently claim to lobby on behalf of developing countries, which requires them to emphasise their identities as developing countries even as, in the field of security, they nurture great power ambitions. Preserving the label of 'developing country' allows both to maintain the bonds of solidarity established with other developing countries through bilateral South–South cooperation, while providing them with legitimacy when resisting what they perceive to be Northern-led initiatives.

Brazil and China have also found common ground (with normative implications) in the idea that the state should play a crucial role in fostering development. However differently the state may manifest itself in Brazil and China, this shared belief in the role of the state helps to explain the degree of distrust exhibited by their policy elites towards market-oriented models promoted abroad by advanced economies and established international organisations. Finally, despite their fundamental differences as plural democracy and single-party state, respectively, both Brazil and China decry the imposition of political conditionalities upon aid, doubling down on the discourse of respect for national sovereignty on behalf of themselves and other developing countries. In resisting the OECD's efforts to harmonise development norms, both have long argued that South–South cooperation activities are fundamentally different from Northern aid.

These common positions are likely to be strengthened as the political distances that once separated Brazil and China during the Cold War shrink – not only to deepening bilateral ties between the two countries but also to the appearance of new coalitions of emerging powers. The BASIC arrangement showed that China is capable of taking on a leadership role in promoting common but differentiated responsibility. The BRICS grouping, far more ambitious, has offered a common platform for the two countries – along with Russia, India, and South Africa – to push for institutional reform and to launch concrete initiatives. Efforts such as the BRICS development project serve not only to challenge the current architecture but also to launch new discussions about South–South cooperation and to attain a degree of policy coordination that can then be transposed into established institutions such as the UNDS. For both Brazil and China the BRICS grouping is more than the sum of its individual parts, allowing member states to collectively influence the field of development by contesting existing norms and blocking certain initiatives. Less certain is their capacity to propose alternative normative frameworks, which would require more mutual knowledge as well as a concerted effort to agree upon a 'lowest common denominator' of principles and norms derived from their South–South cooperation experiences.

Whether or not the BRICS and other loose groupings can become real platforms for norm setting within the field of development will depend not only on the success of pioneering initiatives like the BRICS development bank but also on the establishment of discussions, intellectual production, and the formulation of indicators necessary to boost coordination among these countries. Finally, these countries' ability to formulate new normative frameworks will also depend on how smoothly they handle the steep asymmetries between China, specifically, and the other member states, including Brazil. As the post-2015 development agenda appears on the BRICS's radar, the ongoing debates may offer a testing ground for the ability of emerging powers such as Brazil and China to engage in bolder norm entrepreneurship within the UNDS.

Notes

1. Finnemore, *National Interest*.
2. Johnston, *Social States*.
3. Wuthnow et al., "Diverse Multilateralism."
4. See Checkel, "International Institutions"; and Ikenberry, "The Rise of China."
5. Wang, "Multilateralism in Chinese Foreign Policy."
6. Hart and Jones. "How do Emerging powers Rise?"
7. Pu, "Socialisation."
8. Agence France-Presse, "Emerging China, Brazil and India."
9. Fues et al., "The Role of the UN."
10. Sunstein, "Social Norms and Social Roles."
11. Cervo and Bueno, *História da Política Exterior do Brasil*.
12. Ibid.
13. Cardoso and Faletto, *Dependency and Development*.
14. Cabral, "Brazil's Development Cooperation."
15. Fonseca, Jr., *O Brasil no Conselho de Segurança da ONU*.
16. Kim, *China*.
17. Global Policy Forum, "Changing Patterns."
18. Sen, "A New Stage."
19. Kim, "China and the UN"; and Shen, *In the Mood for Multilateralism?*
20. "China's Principles in Foreign Aid."
21. UN General Assembly, "General Assembly Resolution Global Negotiations related to International Economic Co-operation and Development." 34/138, December 14, 1979. http://www.un.org/documents/ga/res/34/a34res138.pdf.
22. Sen, "A New Stage."
23. See, for instance, Statement by Ambassador Wang Min at the 2014 Substantive Session of ECOSOC, February 26, 2014.

24. Zhao Ziyang, "Government Work Report to the Fourth Session."
25. Sen, "A New Stage."
26. Fullilove, *The Stakeholder Spectrum*.
27. World Bank, "Results Profile."
28. Statement by Hu Jintao at the UN Summit, New York, September 15, 2005. http://www.un.org/webcast/
    summit2005/statements15/china050915eng.pdf.
29. Stewart, "UN Short nearly $5bn"; and Agence France-Presse, "Emerging China, Brazil and India."
30. African Development Bank Group, "China."
31. Xu, "Speech."
32. Wheeler, "A Reluctant Leader?"
33. Fullilove, *The Stakeholder Spectrum*.
34. UNFCCC, "Statement by China."

Bibliography

African Development Bank Group. "China: Partnership Overview." http://www.afdb.org/en/topics-and-sectors/
topics/partnerships/non-regional-member-countries/china/(accessed November 10, 2014).
Agence France-Presse. "Emerging China, Brazil and India agree to increased United Nations Dues." December
26, 2012. http://www.rawstory.com/rs/2012/12/26/emerging-china-brazil-and-india-agree-to-increased-uni
ted-nations-dues/.
Cabral, L. "Brazil's Development Cooperation with the South: A Global Model in Waiting." Overseas Development Institute Op-ed. London, July 10, 2010. http://www.odi.org.uk/opinion/4952-brazils-development-
cooperation-south-global-model-waiting.
Cardoso Fernando Henrique, and E. Faletto. *Dependency and Development in Latin America*. Berkeley:
University of California Press, 1979.
Cervo, A., and C. Bueno. *História da Política Exterior do Brasil*. Brasilia: EdUnB, 2002.
Checkel Jeffrey. "International Institutions and Socialization in Europe." *International Organization* 59, no. 4
(2005): 801–826.
"China's Principles in Foreign Aid." China.org.cn, November 29, 2011. http://www.china.org.cn/opinion/2011-
11/29/content_24030234.htm.
Finnemore Martha. *National Interest and International Society*. Ithaca, NY: Cornell University Press, 2006.
Fonseca, Jr., G. *O Brasil no Conselho de Segurança da onu: 1998–1999*. Brasilia: IPRI/FUNAG, 2002.
Fues Thomas, D. Li, and M. Vatterodt. "The Role of the UN in the Global Development Architecture: Steps
towards Greater Coherence." Paper presented to the Annual Meeting of the Academic Council on the Uni-
ted Nations System, New York, June 6–8, 2007. http://www.die-gdi.de/uploads/media/Down
load_the_full_text__74_kb__01.pdf.
Fullilove, M. *The Stakeholder Spectrum: China and the UN*. Sydney: Lowy Institute, December 2010.
Global Policy Forum. "Changing Patterns in the Use of the Veto in the Security Council." http://www.global
policy.org/component/content/article/102/32810.html.
Hart, A., and B. D. Jones. "How do Emerging Powers Rise?" *Survival* 52, no. 6 (2010): 63–88.
Ikenberry, G. John. "The Rise of China and the Future of the West." *Foreign Affairs* 87, no. 1 (2008): 23–37.
Johnston, A. I. *Social States: China in International Institutions, 1980–2000*. Princeton, NJ: Princeton Univer-
sity Press, 2008.
Kim, K. *China, the United Nations and the World Order*. Princeton, NJ: Princeton University Press, 1979.
Kim, S. "China and the UN." In *China Joins the World: Progress and Prospects*, edited by E. Economy and
M. Oksenberg, 42–89. New York: Council on Foreign Relations, 1999.
Pu, Xiaoyu. "Socialisation as a Two-way Process: Emerging Powers and the Diffusion of International
Norms." *Chinese Journal of International Politics* 5 (2012): 341–367.
Sen, P. "A New Stage in the Development of China–UN Relations." In *Transformation of Foreign Affairs and
International Relations in China, 1978–2008*, edited by Y. Wang, 149–184. Leiden: Brill, 2011.
Shen, W. *In the Mood for Multilateralism? China's Evolving Global View*. IFRI Working Paper. Paris: Institut
Français de Relations Internationales, July 2008. http://www.ifri.org/files/centre_asie/Chinamultilateralism.
pdf.
Stewart, Heather. 2009. "UN Short nearly $5bn for Aid Projects as Global Recession hits Donations." *Guardian*,
July 21. http://www.theguardian.com/world/2009/jul/21/united-nations-budget-report-humanitarian.
Sunstein, Carl. "Social Norms and Social Roles." *Columbia Law Review* 96, no. 4 (1996): 903–968.
UNFCCC. "Statement by China on behalf of Brazil, India, South Africa and China at the Opening Plenary of the
Durban Platform." Warsaw, November 12, 2013. http://unfccc.int/files/documentation/submis
sions_from_parties/adp/application/pdf/adp2.3_basic_20131112.pdf.
Wang, H. "Multilateralism in Chinese Foreign Policy: The Limits of Socialization." *Asian Survey* 40, no. 3
(2003): 475–491.
Wheeler, T. "A Reluctant Leader? China and Post-2015." *Saferworld*, November 14, 2013. http://www.safer
world.org.uk/news-and-views/comment/117-a-reluctant-leader-china-and-post-2015.

World Bank. "Results Profile: China Poverty Reduction." March 19, 2010. http://www.worldbank.org/en/news/feature/2010/03/19/results-profile-china-poverty-reduction.

Wuthnow, Joel, X. Li, and L. Qi. "Diverse Multilateralism: Four Strategies in China's Multilateral Diplomacy." *Journal of Chinese Political Science* 17 (2012): 269–290.

Xu Haoliang. "Speech at the International Conference on Transforming Global Governance: China and the UN." *Shanghai*, January 13–14, 2014.

Zhao Ziyang. "Government Work Report to the Fourth Session of the Sixth National People's Congress." March 25, 1986.

Emerging powers and the UN development system: canvassing global views

Stephen Browne and Thomas G. Weiss

Ralph Bunche Institute for International Studies, The City University of New York Graduate Center, USA

The importance of emerging powers in the UN development system is undeniable, but their influence over the shape of the post-2015 agenda is less clear. This article examines recent survey data by the Future UN Development System (FUNDS) Project in order to better gauge the perceptions of the world organisation's problems and prospects.

The 'rise of the South', in particular the unprecedented growth of the large emerging economies, is one of the defining political changes of the past 15 years.[1] The implications have begun to be felt through the growing influence of the three largest emerging powers – Brazil, China, and India – in UN organisations. These countries are already forging closer institutional links with the UN development system, a loose family of over 30 separately governed organisations. But their influence over the UN's development agenda, currently a matter of protracted debate, is much less clear.

The role of emerging powers has been a feature of the surveys of the Future of the UN Development System (FUNDS) Project, which aims to gauge the nature of the UN system and its problems and prospects. These surveys are an original contribution and supplement a programme of research. Individual UN organisations conduct surveys of their own activities, and the Multilateral Organization Performance Assessment Network, comprised of 18 donor countries, also undertakes reviews. But there are no comprehensive surveys, besides those of FUNDS, which provide feedback on the development imprint of the UN as a whole and also compare the relevance, effectiveness, and other operational aspects of individual organisations. This feedback includes data from the main stakeholders of the system – member state governments and secretariats. They are included in all surveys, and their respective responses can be filtered. However, the largest numbers of respondents to FUNDS surveys are from the 'third UN' (civil society, private sector, and academia) who as 'we, the peoples' should arguably be the principal auditors of the system in addition to the 'first UN' of member states and the 'second UN' of secretariats.[2]

In 2013 and 2014 the project conducted surveys that have provided feedback on how the emerging powers are expected to influence the UN's agenda and its current and future performance and structure. In 2012–13 FUNDS carried out its second global perception survey.[3] More than 3,650 people from 156 countries across six occupational categories responded to the questionnaire, and the survey was extended to specifically garner more returns from Brazil, India, China, and South Africa (BICS).[4] Also in 2013 FUNDS conducted a survey of its informal global panel of some 200 persons, which aimed to gather opinions on the likely influence of the emerging powers on the UN and its agenda.[5] And in 2014 the third global perception survey, similar in scope to the second, was undertaken and the results filtered by three income categories: high income, emerging powers and developing countries.[6] The list of emerging powers comprised BICS, as well as 9 other middle and upper income countries: Argentina, Chile, Indonesia, Malaysia, Mexico, Peru, South Korea, Thailand, and Turkey. Participants in the surveys were drawn from lists of persons familiar with the UN's work; thus the surveys are not a random popular poll. Given the scant knowledge much of the public in various countries have of the organisation, the surveys have sought informed, critical views, although some results seem to coincide with public perceptions.

This article examines the evidence for the emerging powers' influence in the UN's development activities. It begins with a brief overview of recent developments before going into some depth on the findings of the three FUNDS surveys.

Organisational links and the new development agenda

The largest of the emerging powers have begun to actively seek influence in the UN development system (UNDS) through the appointment of senior officials, funding support, and other forms of partnership. In June 2013 China's candidate was easily elected as the new director-general of the UN Industrial Development Organization (UNIDO) against six other candidates. His acceptance speech acknowledged his government's support. He is the third Chinese national to head a UN entity (at under-secretary general level), with fellow nationals at the helms of the World Health Organization (WHO) and the UN Department of Economic and Social Affairs (UNDESA). China is putting forward other candidates to replace retiring UN agency heads. In 2012 a Brazilian was elected to lead the Food and Agriculture Organization (FAO). Outside the system proper there is also a new Brazilian head of the World Trade Organization (WTO).

Brazil, China, and India are also putting their mark on the world organisation through increased financial contributions. In 2012 their 'assessed contributions' to the core budget of the UN (a pattern followed by the specialised agencies) were raised significantly. Brazil nearly doubled its contribution to over $40 million (1.6% of the UN budget); China added $9.9 million (to 3.2%); and India raised its contribution by $1.6 million (to 0.5%). These three countries also provide growing amounts of non-core (earmarked) resources to many UN development organisations. Brazil contributes more than $100 million per year in 'local resources' to the UN Development Programme (UNDP), which uses the funds to provide a range of consultancy and other services to the country.[7]

The same three countries have also been establishing direct organisational partnerships. Both China and Brazil partner with the UNDS in sponsoring global and regional centres of excellence. Brazil established an 'international poverty centre' with the UNDP in Brasilia in 2004; in 2013 it set up the Rio+ Centre with the same body to undertake research on sustainable development goals (following its hosting of the 2012 Rio+20 Conference on Sustainable Development). China also established an international poverty centre with the UNDP in Beijing, a year after the centre in Rio de Janeiro opened. As an affirmation of its support for UNIDO, China also co-sponsors within its own territory no fewer than six out of 10 of that organisation's international technology centres, which are used in part to showcase Chinese technologies to the rest of the developing world. One of these China-based organisations is called the UNIDO Centre for South–South Industrial Cooperation; there is a similar one in New Delhi. India is also host to other global and regional centres in partnership with the UNDS. They include the Asia-Pacific Centre for the Transfer of Technologies, set up with the UN Economic and Social Commission for Asia and the Pacific, and the International Centre for Human Development, established with the UNDP. Other emerging powers, such as South Korea, Indonesia, Turkey, and Mexico also host international centres of excellence with organisations of the UNDS.

Partnerships with the UNDS are not new. Brazil's use of the UNDP as a local contractor, for example, dates back more than two decades. However, in recent years these partnerships have expanded steadily, manifesting two closely related features: a willingness to provide the major share of the resources in any joint venture with the UN; and the use of these partnerships as platforms for bilateral 'South–South' assistance. These growing relationships resemble those which the traditional donor governments have maintained for many years with UNDS organisations, using the system in part as a platform for their own development priorities.[8]

These organisational links are the most visible manifestations of the growing influence of emerging powers on the UN development system. But the system produces ideas, norms, and standards as well as practical operations. It is much less clear how these countries are likely to influence the global development agenda, particularly at a rather critical juncture when the three UNs are negotiating the post-2015 Sustainable Development Goals (SDGs), designed to supersede the Millennium Development Goals (MDGs) inspired by the Millennium Declaration of 2000. Traditionally, global negotiations through the United Nations in the domain of development have pitted the 'North' against the 'global South', the latter being represented by the Group of 77 (G77) and China. Despite heterogeneity, the G77 nevertheless manages to find common ground over issues such as financing. Most UN development summits culminate in wrangling about funding and the nature of norm setting between the two sides.

Two fundamental principles behind the SDGs have already been agreed: they are to be universal (as opposed to their predecessor MDGs, which were mainly aimed at performance in developing countries); and they are to encompass the three dimensions (economic, social, and environmental) of sustainable development, as well as very probably extending to peace, security, and human rights concerns. Negotiations on the composition of the SDGs are unprecedented in both their inclusivity and their thoroughness. While the MDGs were largely handed over to UN member states ready-formulated by the secretariat, based on previously agreed targets, the next generation of development goals is being hammered-out through an extensive process of meetings and consultations. The debate revolves around a 30-member open working group, which during 2013 and 2014 held many 'stock-taking' and 'decision-making' sessions with the participation of hundreds of experts and stakeholders. A separate intergovernmental committee of experts is charged with negotiating and mobilising the financial aspects of the goals. The outcomes of these negotiations are scheduled to be presented to the General Assembly for agreement by September 2015.

While the level of consensus and openness is being widely praised, so far the positive comments extend only to the broad principles; concrete agreements on the actual goals themselves, as well as how they are to be financed, have not yet been reached. Divisions are visible between the North and global South, not least on what the proposed universality of the SDGs actually means. The new goals are intended to create an alternative type of compact from which no country is exempt, with all members assuming some degree of responsibility to address global problems. This point of departure is being interpreted by many in the North as calling for greater contributions from other sources of development financing and support (including from emerging powers). Meanwhile, a dominant perspective from the global South is that universality requires the North to address its own unsustainable consumption, responsibility for climate change, and entrenched inequalities.

Any new global development agenda that does not take into account the expanding role of BICS and other emerging economies, with over 40% of the world's population and nearly half its wealth, will not live up to its global claims. However, it remains uncertain how emerging powers will ultimately position themselves in these negotiations, or whether they will engage more actively in the process as the parameters of the SDGs take shape. The current North vs global South battle-lines stubbornly remain and contribute to the polarisation of the post-2015 negotiations, as happened with previous UN development debates. The emerging powers have so far not engaged as new and distinct species of development partners but are positioning themselves firmly within the majority G77 and China bloc. They are thus resisting pressure from developed countries to take more global responsibility, particularly in areas such as mitigating climate change and financing other global public goods.

The discussions on the future agenda are being conducted under the auspices of an intergovernmental body, and the General Assembly of government representatives will approve the outcome. But what are the opinions of the global public, or the 'third UN', about the debate and about the future of the UN development system? The FUNDS global perception surveys are designed to ascertain opinions about the UN's role in development, as a contribution to a parallel, but only intermittently joined, discussion on the need to reform a system that requires urgent adaptation for the post-2015 realities. The first set of findings reflects the views of the 2013 expert panel about emerging powers. The second set of findings contains the views of a mix of respondents from the emerging powers, based mainly on the 2014 global survey, but with some insights from the 2012–13 global survey.

Views about the emerging powers from the expert panel

The three global surveys, with a total of 10,000 responses, as well as the most recent 'expert survey' (some 400 targeted individuals), obviously measure only perceptions. But such perceptions (respondents who are unfamiliar or have no opinions were excluded) are essential because they reflect back to the UN – its member states and organisations – images of performance and relevance that the world organisation itself too rarely seeks. Individual organisations conduct their own surveys, but they do not offer an overview of the system, or comparative perceptions across development domains and organisations within the United Nations.

Respondents to the 2013 expert survey were almost equally divided into those who had been previously employed within the UN system (48%) and those who had not (45%), with a small percentage (7%) still employed within the system. The majority (59%) described their occupational background as 'private sector'.

The survey reflected a strong sense of the crucial role that the emerging powers would play in the future UNDS (86% of respondents), with most seeing the growing role of these countries as more of an 'opportunity' for the UN (69%) than a 'challenge' (31%). These results are shown in Figure 1. While about one-quarter of respondents considered that emerging powers present a challenge for the world organisation, there are high expectations that they will influence the UNDS in a number of specific ways: 97% see an impact through a broader recruitment base with respect to senior positions; 94% see impact through a diversification of funding sources; and 85% expect a positive impact in relation to the development of international norms and conventions (Figure 2).

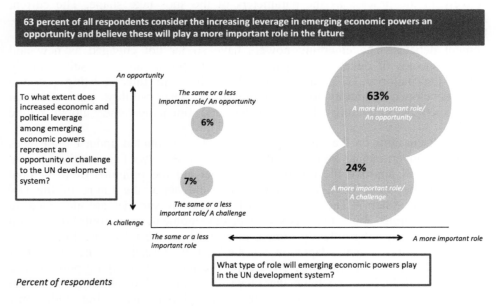

Figure 1. Prospects of emerging economic powers in the UN development system.
Source: FUNDS 2013, Expert Survey.

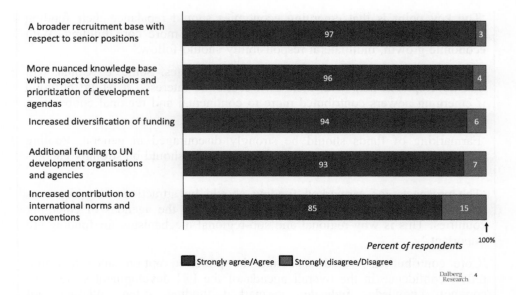

Figure 2. What could be some of the positive impacts of emerging economic powers on the UN development system when compared to developed economies?
Source: FUNDS 2013, Expert Survey.

A large majority of respondents (93%) predicted that the emerging powers would contribute additional funding to the UNDS. However, the sense of many of the respondents was that these countries should contribute core resources to UN development organisations rather than earmarking funds as do traditional donors (Box 1). This logical point of view, however, confronts the clear indications that emerging powers undoubtedly will patronise UN development organisations with their own priorities and agendas – just as other donors do – with the continued earmarking of funds and the establishment of more South–South centres and other initiatives through subcontracts with the UN.

The emerging powers thus are expected to play a significant role in influencing the evolution of the UN's development agenda, and a lesser but still significant role in implementation and monitoring (Figure 3). These expectations are linked to the perception that these countries' political and economic influence is expanding.

Box 1. Respondents' comments on funding from emerging powers for the UNDS

'As long as the criterion for contribution is based on ability to pay, then developed countries should continue to pay more than emerging economies to core and earmarked resources.'

'To prevent targeting specific policies that will have selective benefits, preference should be to fund overall UN system and not specific projects and/or areas.'

'The key point is that emerging economies should rebalance their funding mix from exclusively earmarked contributions to more core funding. With economic growth, multilateral responsibility should follow.'

'Different emerging powers will take different routes. Some, eg China, will link development help with their own economic interests. It would be good if emerging powers contributed more to continental and regional cooperation institutions.'

'Earmarking of funds should be strongly discouraged in general. Pooling funds mechanism and Delivering as One approach should be strongly encouraged.'

'The prospects for earmarked funding should be attractive. For this, UNDS must develop productive proposals which cater to the agendas of emerging countries. This is why regional and sub-regional mechanisms for funding are important.'

'Core contributions would constitute the preferred option since it would reflect confidence in the overall agenda of the UN development system; as common knowledge indicates, earmarked funding, often, although not always, hides political and strategic self-interest on the part of the donor and should be welcomed by the UN System only after thorough scrutiny.'

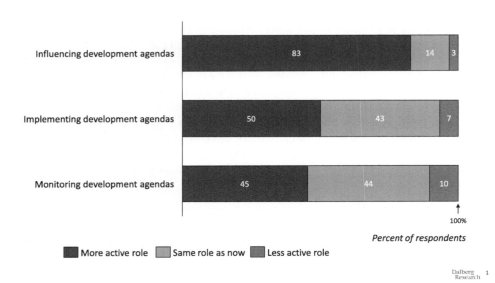

Figure 3. What will be the expected roles of emerging powers in the UN development system?
Source: FUNDS 2013, Expert Survey.

Box 2. FUNDS Global 2014 Survey: the demographics

In early 2014, the FUNDS Project sent out more than 25,000 email invitations to respond to a comprehensive questionnaire in six official UN languages. The list comprised people known to have worked with the UN, subscribed to its information services, or to be familiar with the development field. The questionnaire was also posted on several development-oriented websites around the world. There were 3,268 respondents, roughly the same number as in 2010 and 2012. They were drawn from more than 150 countries by origin and a similar number by location.

As in the previous global surveys, the largest cohort of respondents identified themselves as working in the private sector. Among those from emerging powers, almost one-third (32%) were from the private sector, followed by academia (26%), national governments and public sector (19%), NGOs (14%), UN organisations (8%), and other international public organisations (2%). Thus, the proportion of those from the 'third UN' was 73%, against 19% from the 'first UN' and 8% from the 'second UN'.

A majority (68%) of the 2013 expert survey respondents considered emerging powers to be more likely to align with one another in UN forums than with other developing or developed countries (Figure 4). These alignments are not mutually exclusive, of course, and could suggest that the emerging powers might form their own sub-bloc, broadly aligned with either developed or developing countries. The signs are that these countries are more likely to align with developing countries in global negotiations. The dominant politics of intergovernmental negotiations are likely to inhibit the emerging powers from any overt ruptures with developing countries, as evidenced in the Rio + 20 summit in 2012 and the ongoing debate about the post-2015 UN development agenda.

Views about emerging powers: 10,000 voices over four years

The 2014 global survey (Box 2) covered a range of issues pertaining to the present and future of the UNDS. The results were filtered by country income levels – developed, emerging, and developing – in order to ascertain how perceptions varied by origin. A quarter of respondents were from emerging powers, 38% from developing countries, and 37% from high-income countries. The survey sought to elicit the views of respondents from a representative sample of professional backgrounds.

Respondents across all categories agreed that humanitarian action was where the UN had the most positive impact, and by a significant margin (Figure 5). The next most positive impact in all cases was peacekeeping, while human rights also ranked high. Compared with these areas, virtually all the functions of the UN development system – including crisis recovery, setting global technical standards, research and analysis, global negotiation, advocacy, and technical assistance – were considered to have a lower impact. Among these development

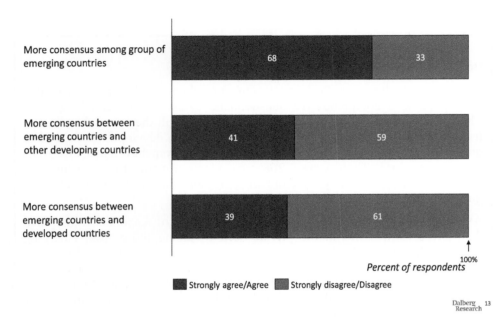

Figure 4. What will be the future impact of emerging countries on discussions in UN forums?
Source: FUNDS 2013, Expert Survey.

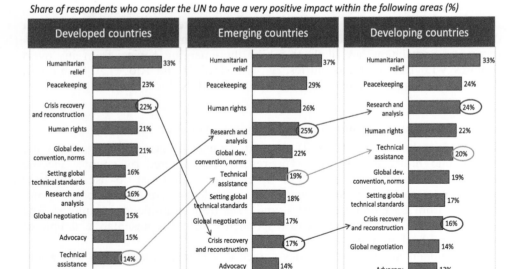

Figure 5. What impact does the UN have in the following functions?
Source: FUNDS 2014, Global Survey.

functions, however, there were only modest differences among the country categories. Those in emerging powers as well as in other developing countries considered the United Nations to have a lower impact in crisis recovery than those in developed countries. However, while the latter considered UN technical assistance to have the lowest impact (14%), emerging and developing countries rated it somewhat higher (19% and 20%). There was a similar pattern for research and analysis, which the emerging and developing countries considered to have the most positive impact of all the functions of the UN development system. At first glance, this surprising result reflects the fact that the written output of the UN is often its least visible activity. However, it would seem to indicate that the UN's ideas are still cherished at least as much as its operations.

Within the UN's principal development domains, respondents in all three categories agreed – and by a significant margin – that UN organisations were most effective in health, education, and human rights. In addition, respondents in emerging powers were more positive about the UN's effectiveness in regional cooperation, gender, and agriculture (Figure 6). Not surprisingly, these respondents ranked regional cooperation much higher than did those from developed and developing countries, reflecting a strong belief in the importance of regional South–South exchanges. Compared with respondents in developed countries, respondents from emerging powers also found the UN to be more effective in addressing the environment, international trade, science and technology, and social policy.

However, as might be expected, there are differences of perception of UN effectiveness within the emerging power category. In the 2012–13 global survey these were examined in depth for Brazil, China, India, and South Africa. Respondents from all four countries were in broad alignment with respect to the

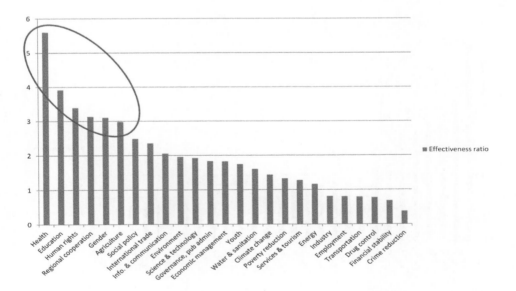

Figure 6. Emerging powers: effectiveness of UN development organisation by domain (Ratio of highly effective/effective to not effective).

higher effectiveness in health and human rights. But in other areas there were differences. China rated the UN's role in regional cooperation, poverty reduction, agriculture, and environment relatively higher. In several other domains, including drug control, economic management, industry, energy, services and tourism, and transportation, Brazil recorded lower ratings than the other countries. South Africa was the negative outlier in governance and in information and communications.

The 2014 global survey also asked respondents to rate individual UN organisations by effectiveness (Figure 7). The ratings by respondents from emerging countries could be expected to follow a similar pattern to perceptions of UN effectiveness by domain. Not surprisingly, therefore, the high rankings of the WHO, UNICEF, the United Nations Programme on HIV/AIDS (UNAIDS), and UNESCO reflect the perceptions of UN effectiveness in the health and education domains. The UNDP and FAO are also highly ranked by emerging powers. The UNDP is a close partner to those countries, playing the role of South–South facilitator as well as implementing agent for some upper-middle income countries (such as Brazil and Argentina) using their 'local resources'. The FAO's rating may be more surprising, however, given the plethora of agricultural development organisations that lie outside the UN and the critical views expressed worldwide about the institution. Respondents from the emerging powers rate the World Food Programme (WFP) lower (it is much less active in these countries) but share with those from other developing countries a higher appreciation of UN Women, the UN Environment Programme, UN Conference on Trade and Development, and the UN Framework Convention on Climate Change than developed countries. The emerging powers also differ from other respondents in their estimation of the five UN regional economic commissions: for Latin America and the Caribbean (ECLAC), Africa (ECA), Asia-Pacific (ESCAP), West Asia (ESCWA), and

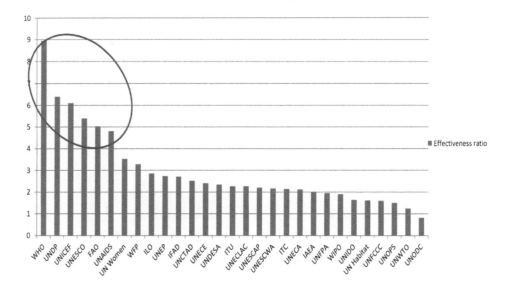

Figure 7. Emerging powers: effectiveness of UN organisations (Ratio of highly effective/effective to not effective).

Europe (ECE). Whereas in successive global surveys taken as a whole these commissions are ranked low in terms of both relevance and effectiveness,[9] the emerging powers view them in a slightly more favourable light, which probably reflects their stronger attachment to regional cooperation.

Impact of the emerging powers on the UNDS

From responses to all surveys conducted by the FUNDS Project since 2010, there has been a very strong sense of the need for dramatic reform if the UN's development efforts are not to become increasingly marginalised.[10] Respondents from all regions and income levels share this view, although there are varying degrees of optimism about the actual capacity of the system to change. From the 2014 survey, in fact, optimism was highest among respondents from emerging powers (85%). This is undoubtedly a glass more than half-full – one-third of respondents in developed countries felt that the UNDS was 'incapable' or 'strongly incapable' of significant reform (Figure 8).

The survey shows a high degree of agreement on the challenges facing the UNDS (Figure 9), with developed countries giving them generally far more emphasis and being more pessimistic about the possibilities for change. The perception is of a system that is under-resourced, in need of internal reorganisation, and ineffective. These problems are challenges for the first and second UNs, although the shape of funding is essentially for member states. The main difference of emphasis is in the lack of evidence for adaptation.

There is also a rather high level of agreement on the factors likely to improve UN effectiveness (Figure 10). Local knowledge figures prominently.

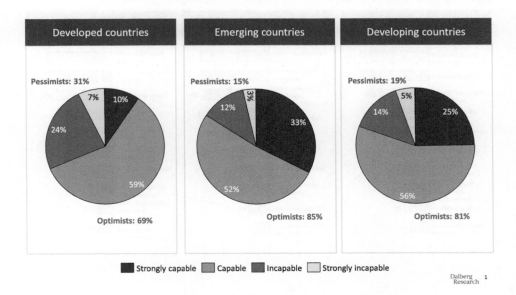

Figure 8. To what extent is the UN Development System capable of significant reform?
Source: FUNDS 2014, Global Survey.

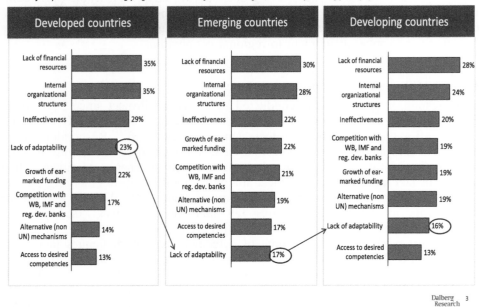

Figure 9. What are the key challenges for the UN in development?
Source: FUNDS 2014, Global Survey.

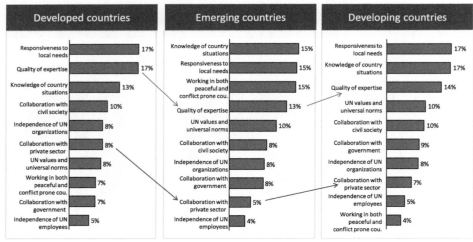

Figure 10. Which factors would be most significant in improving the UN's effectivess in development?
Source: FUNDS 2013, Global Survey.

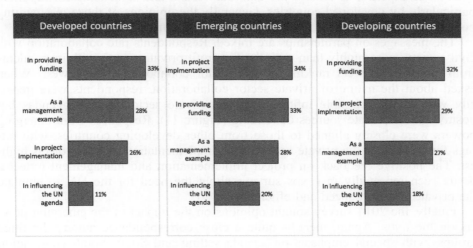

Figure 11.   How do you consider the private for profit sector as a partner for the UN in development?
Source: FUNDS 2013, Global Survey.

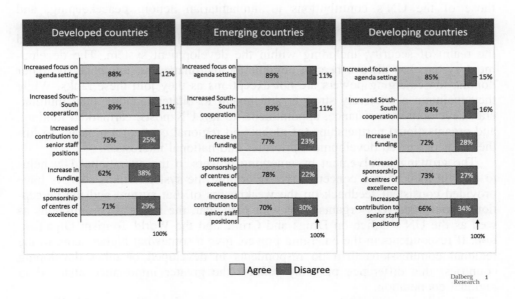

Figure 12.   What will be the future impact of the emerging economic powers on UN development organisations?
Source: UN FUNDS 2014, Global Survey.

Quality of expertise is among the top four factors and is considered important particularly by developed countries. Generally the opinions of those in emerging powers are similar to those in other developing countries.

The messages on partnerships are mixed. Respondents rate collaboration with civil society more highly than with the for-profit private sector, with respondents from emerging powers ranking private sector collaboration the lowest. When asked about the nature of private sector collaboration, respondents were generally wary of the possible influence of the private sector on UN agendas but positive about private sources of funding (Figure 11). Responses from emerging powers were closely aligned to those from other developing countries, with ratings for the role of the private sector in the implementation of UN projects highest. The positive feedback on project implementation and management reflect a desire seen repeatedly in FUNDS surveys about the need for the UN to emulate the private sector in speed and efficiency.

Finally, the 2014 survey sought opinions on the impact of the emerging powers on the UNDS. Again, there is quite a close correspondence among the three groups, with special emphasis on agenda setting and South–South cooperation (Figure 12). The main differences are over funding. Interestingly the likelihood of increased funding is ranked much higher by those in emerging powers than among developed country respondents.

Conclusion

Notwithstanding the lower ranking of development activities when compared to those of the UN's contributions to humanitarian action, peacekeeping, and human rights, the emerging powers – particularly the largest among them – have begun to take initiatives to enhance their operational influence in the UN beyond the realm of security, including within the development system. The development system has always been a conduit for patronage and influence by major donors; the emerging powers are not exceptions as they join these ranks. While they maintain a relatively stronger attachment to bilateral, rather than multilateral, development assistance, appointments to top UN posts, earmarked funding, and organisational partnerships (of global and regional centres) are means to further their perceived development priorities and national interests.

The growing involvement by emerging powers in the operational UN helps to explain their shared concerns over reforming the system. FUNDS surveys have provided consistent feedback on the weaknesses of that system and the perceptions about many UN organisations – in particular, the regional commissions as well as the UN's Office on Drugs and Crime and the World Tourism Organization. If respondents in the emerging powers give a somewhat higher score to the regional commissions than do respondents in developed or other developing countries, this difference probably reflects the greater importance attached to regional cooperation.

The influence of the emerging powers in agenda setting – including the ongoing debates on the post-2015 agenda – is anticipated but is less apparent; several reasons can be adduced. First, global negotiations through the UN subsume (much more than operations) the interests and agendas of 193 member states. Second, the large ideological blocs of North versus South still prevail. Despite the calls for a universal agenda to succeed the MDGS, and despite the steady graduation of countries from lower-income status, the so-called North and the so-called global South still pursue positions based on perceptions of their own national interests. Currently the emerging powers, with their own differentiated interests, are unlikely to form a cohesive bloc. In light of long-standing links in various negotiating forums, they are more inclined to continue to align themselves with the G77 than to strike out on their own path. Their growing economic and commercial power and political influence are yet to rival and threaten developed countries. As long as UN debates are centred on a struggle to undermine the *traditional* hegemony (commercial, economic, and political) of industrialised countries – and increasingly their private corporations are coming in for greater scrutiny and criticism in the global South – the Manichean or black-and-white character of global negotiations will remain. The growing influence of the emerging powers is likely to be manifested through the strengthening of the common positions of the global South. The surveys reveal some of the areas where the emerging powers appear closer to other developing than to developed countries.

The outcome of the post-2015 debate will help determine the nature of global negotiations in the future and the role of emerging powers within them. The more genuinely inclusive and universal the new agenda to 2030 – which, in addition to providing new development targets, emphasises the importance of partnership across all income groups to generate global public goods – the more influential will be the emerging powers.

Notes

1. Nayyar, *Catch Up*; Mahbubani, *The Great Convergence*; and UNDP, *Human Development Report 2013*.
2. Weiss et al., "The 'Third' United Nations."

3. FUNDS, *Global Perception Survey* 2013.
4. For comparative purposes, the project decided to concentrate on developing-country members of the BRICS grouping and exclude the former 'superpower'.
5. FUNDS, *FUNDS 2013 Expert Survey.*
6. FUNDS, *2014 Future United Nations Development.*
7. UNDP, *UNDP Annual Report 2012–13*, 40.
8. Browne and Weiss, *Emerging Economies.*
9. See Browne and Weiss, *How Relevant are the UN's Regional Commissions?*
10. Browne and Weiss, *Making Change Happen.*

Bibliography

Browne, Stephen, and Thomas G. Weiss. *Emerging Economies and the UN Development System.* FUNDS Briefing 10. New York, September 2013. http://www.futureun.org/media/archive1/briefings/Funds_Briefing_10. pdf.

Browne, Stephen, and Thomas G. Weiss. *How Relevant are the UN's Regional Commissions?* FUNDS Briefing 1. New York, February 2013. http://www.futureun.org/media/archive1/briefings/FUNDS_Brief1.pdf.

Browne, Stephen, and Thomas G Weiss. *Making Change Happen: Enhancing the UN's Contribution to Development.* New York: World Federation of United Nations Associations, 2012.

Future of the UN Development System (FUNDS). 2014 *Future United Nations Development.* http://www.futu reun.org/en/Publications-Surveys/Article?newsid=34.

FUNDS. *FUNDS 2013 Expert Survey.* November 2013. http://www.futureun.org/media/archive1/surveys/ 131126_GlobalExpertPanelSurvey1.pdf.

FUNDS. *Global Perception Survey* 2013. March 31, 2013. http://www.futureun.org/media/archive1/surveys/ FUNDS2013GlobalPerceptionSurvey-EmergingEconomies.pdf.

Mahbubani, Kishore. *The Great Convergence: Asia, the West, and the Logic of One World.* New York: Public Affairs, 2013.

Nayyar, Deepak. *Catch Up: Developing Countries in the World Economy.* Oxford: Oxford University Press, 2013.

UNDP. *Human Development Report 2013: The Rise of the South.* New York: UNDP, 2013.

UNDP. *UNDP Annual Report 2012–13.* New York: UNDP, 2013. http://www.undp.org/content/dam/undp/library/cor porate/UNDP-inaction/2013/English/UNDP_AR2013_english_WEB.pdf.

Weiss, Thomas G., Tatiana Carayannis, and Richard Jolly. "The 'Third' United Nations." *Global Governance* 15, no. 1 (2009): 123–142.

War-torn countries, natural resources, emerging-power investors and the UN development system

Graciana del Castillo

Ralph Bunche Institute for International Studies, The City University of New York Graduate Center, USA

The unsustainable aid dependency of war-torn countries – most of which are rich in natural resources – makes it imperative to start gradually replacing aid with foreign direct investment (FDI) and exports. This article identifies ways in which stakeholders – governments, the international community, including the UN development system, foreign investors, and local communities – could work together in a 'win-win' situation. Most crucial is avoiding conflict-insensitive policies that fuel discord by putting governments and foreign companies, often from emerging markets, in direct confrontation with local communities. The control of natural resources is often a root cause of conflict, and the latter's exploitation can become a major challenge as wars end. The peculiarities of war-torn countries are discussed along with the specific impediments to attracting FDI into the exploitation of natural resources. An effective and fair legal framework is necessary to ensure that investors do not operate as 'enclaves', creating new conflicts.

Countries at low levels of development coming out of civil war or other chaos – following peace agreements or military intervention – find it particularly difficult to foster domestic savings or attract foreign direct investment (FDI) in the short run. This is true despite the fact that many of these countries have large endowments of natural resources that are much sought after by investors worldwide. At the same time the so-called peace dividend with which countries often experiment after wars is negligible in countries where military expenditure was largely foreign-financed. In fiscal terms this means that, as the need for military expenditure drops, there is little room for diverting domestic resources to non-military purposes.

Thus, war-torn countries rely primarily on official aid flows – from both bilateral and multilateral donors, including the United Nations development system (UNDS) – to finance their humanitarian needs as well as their basic operational and development expenditures. Financing is unquestionably a critical ingredient of, and constraint on, economic reconstruction – or the economics of peace – in these countries.

The economics of peace is an intermediate phase between the economics of war and the economics of development. During this phase the main objective should be that the country does not relapse into conflict. Because there cannot be sustained development without peace, the political (or peace) objective should always prevail over the economic (or development) one. For this reason best policies from a purely economic or financial point of view are not always possible or even desirable during this phase. This is what makes economic reconstruction so different from development as usual. Because control of natural resources was often the root cause of the conflict, the exploitation of such resources during this phase is particularly challenging and requires conflict-sensitive policies.[1]

As is well documented in the literature, aid to war-torn countries – which often accounts for a large percentage of these countries' GDP – has been mostly ineffective in helping them to stand on their own feet. In fact, it has often led to serious aid dependency. While 'humanitarian aid' to save lives and provide minimum levels of consumption given largely by foreigners – the UNDS, international NGOs, and bilateral donors – starts in the very early stages of the reconstruction process and has been rather effective, it does not wither soon enough to avoid the price distortions and the work disincentives associated with this type of aid.[2]

At the same time the provision – mostly by the UNDS and bilateral donors – of 'reconstruction aid' is often delayed pending elections, the establishment of institutions and policies, and improved governance, security, and human capacity that would make such aid more effective. In the meantime countries often revert to war. In fact, war-torn countries have shown roughly a 50% chance of relapsing into conflict. Moreover, those that succeed in maintaining the fragile peace often find themselves in an aid trap.[3]

Indeed, reconstruction aid has been largely ineffective in supporting the reactivation of agriculture, legitimate business activities, and other job-creating investment in basic services and infrastructure for the large majority of the population. While domestic and foreign elites often thrive in post-conflict situations, war-torn countries that fail to create a level-playing field for farmers and small entrepreneurs ignore the productive capacity and creativity of a large part of the population. To involve these much-neglected groups – including women – in productive and licit activities is critical to peacebuilding. Unless growth in these countries creates employment and contributes to food security and poverty alleviation, it can become a new source of conflict, often exacerbating existing political, ethnic, regional, and even community divisions.

Because spikes of aid to countries embarking on the transition to peace are often short-lived, war-torn countries have the difficult challenge of replacing aid with FDI and exports as sources of finance and foreign exchange. This task is indeed quite difficult in countries affected by insecurity and where parts of their territory may even be outside government control. Such countries often have undeveloped institutional and legal frameworks; weak financial sectors and an unfriendly business climate; weak infrastructure and services; and poor governance, all of which add to the problem.

Moreover, by failing to provide basic services and security, governments are unable to gain political legitimacy in the eyes of the population. At the same time governments have little ownership of domestic policies, which are mostly imposed by donors through conditionality or simply because donors often finance development projects outside the national budget and in projects that may lack governments' blessing. In turn, lacking legitimacy and ownership of domestic policies, national governments find it more difficult to negotiate with foreign investors.

The challenge of economic reconstruction is indeed overwhelming: to create the basis for a just, viable, and sustainable economy in the long run, under the serious constraints of reactivating the economy while maintaining a fragile peace, political stability, and security in the short run. Although short-term jobs are often created, a dynamic and sustainable reactivation of the economy, which is critical to establishing peace, stability, and prosperity has been thoroughly lacking in most war-torn countries.

Investment and job creation may sound like normal development challenges, but in the context of war-torn countries these tasks are fundamentally different, because the latter requires conflict-sensitive policies – even if not optimal from a purely economic or financial viewpoint. The main objective of economic reconstruction in the short run is to address the grievances of crisis-affected groups that have been the root cause of the conflict. It is important to ensure that these groups get an immediate dividend in the form of employment opportunities in the licit economy and better living conditions if peace is to be long lasting.

Looking at the global economy today, two things are clear. First, donor countries have not yet recovered from the aftermath of the 2008–09 global financial crisis and they continue to be affected by fiscal challenges and high unemployment. Together with increased reluctance on the part of taxpayers to fund aid in faraway countries that has led to corruption and waste – as donors' own oversight bodies and the international press have well documented – this situation has affected, and will continue to affect, donors' aid and other support to war-torn countries. Many of the highly aid-dependent countries will find it difficult to sustain such dependency, while those embarking on the transition to peace will find it more difficult to get support.[4]

Second, the rapid growth of emerging markets has led them to a wild search for commodities worldwide, including in high-risk, war-torn countries and, until recently, in marginal and unexploited areas such as the Amazon, populated by indigenous groups that have so far lived in isolation. In both locations investments have been an increasing source of conflict with national and local governments and with displaced or otherwise affected communities.[5]

However, emerging countries whose economies grew rapidly in the 2000s and have become the engine of global growth since the global financial crisis have experienced significantly decelerated rates of growth, which is having an impact on the price of commodities (both as a result of decreased demand and high inventories). This situation may reduce companies' appetite to invest in natural resources in war-torn countries or may affect the terms of their investments, making them less attractive and more challenging to host countries.

The process of economic reconstruction – involving national governments and local communities as well as their foreign supporters – has proven to be mostly fragmented, chaotic, and wasteful, and has often-required large expenses in terms of peacekeeping operations or military forces to keep the peace. Hence there is a need for stakeholders to find ways to work together in the design and implementation of a simple, well-thought out, and integrated strategy for the reconstruction of war-torn countries that can result in a 'win-win' situation for all involved.[6]

Many war-torn countries have great potential for the exploitation of natural resources that could help them come out of their aid dependency and set the basis for independence. In most of them, however, FDI in natural resources – both in minerals and agricultural plantations – and government policies to support them have been the source of new conflicts with the displaced communities whose lives and livelihoods are affected. Perhaps Liberia provides the best example of this problem, but there are lessons also from Mozambique, Afghanistan and places such as the Niger Delta, where investors and communities find themselves in a 'no-win' confrontation as a result of conflict-insensitive policies on the part of both the government and investors.

Old and new issues relating to natural resource exploitation

The control of natural resources has often been the root cause of war – and a serious impediment to peace. Diamonds, for example, were the main source of conflict in Angola, the Democratic Republic of the Congo (DRC), and Sierra Leone; oil was the disputed commodity in Sudan. Indeed, the plunder of natural resources has been a major source of conflict in Africa. Access to natural resources and the concomitant gain in political and economic power is one of the main targets of 'spoilers', who often act violently against peace initiatives. One of the government's challenges in such situations is to ensure that those who benefited from the spoils of war have a stake in the economics of peace so that they will not oppose it.[7]

Other well-documented issues relate to the so-called resource curse, which results because many countries that are rich in national resources mismanage them to such an extent that they derive little economic benefit, not least because of the corruption and instability that their exploitation and trade facilitates. Although corruption in that environment is often rampant, some initiatives have been adopted to control it – and particularly to ensure that corruption does not fund violence.[8]

An area, however, in which research is still incipient relates to the way in which war-torn countries can get out of their aid dependency by effectively promoting FDI in the development, exploitation, and trading of natural resources. This presents a number of challenges. Perhaps the most pressing is the need to establish the right legal and regulatory framework to ensure that natural resources contribute to dynamic, equitable, and sustainable growth rather than to the infamous resource curse. Here the UN development partners can and should provide critical support to war-torn countries.

Donors in war-torn countries normally have an incentive to help these countries develop their natural resources. Such development would not only reduce their need to provide aid but also would increase supply and lower the price of natural resources, something that would normally benefit donors. Moreover, once production and exports increase, their import capacity would also grow, making them a larger market for foreign exports.

A remarkable feature of the past decade is that foreign investors are more diverse than in the past. With the rapid growth of emerging countries, there has been an increasing interest – notably from companies in China, Brazil, India and, to a lesser degree, Indonesia and Malaysia – in exploiting natural resources, even in countries plagued by insecurity, lack of infrastructure, and great uncertainty with respect to legal and regulatory issues. Despite data problems, it is clear that companies from these countries invest abroad under different modalities and with different levels of support from their own governments.[9]

Brazilian companies ventured abroad well before those from China and India. The stock of FDI abroad jumped from $50 billion in 2000 to $230 billion in 2012. Brazilian companies often operate from tax havens, which makes analysis difficult. Brazilian investment abroad is strong not only in mining and energy but also in food production. Although there are no institutionalised policy measures to support global investment by Brazilian firms, the Brazilian Development Bank has a 'Foreign Direct Investment' line of credit to stimulate investment by Brazilian firms abroad, offering preferential interest rates and covering the construction of new installations abroad, equipment purchases, mergers and acquisitions, turnover capital and export support. Brazilian companies have been active investors in Mozambique and Angola, the two largest Portuguese-speaking countries in Africa. The construction company Odebrecht, for example, is among Angola's largest employers, and the steel producer Vale has invested billions in coal mining in Mozambique.

By 2012 China's stock of FDI abroad surpassed $500 billion, as compared to about $5 billion in 1990 and about $30 billion in 2000. While Brazil's stock of $40 billion was eight times larger than China's in 1990, Brazil has now fallen behind. The 2011 Five-Year Plan reaffirmed China's 'going global' policy, and a large part of this is directed to developing countries. Mining, quarrying, and petroleum accounted for about half its new investments, and most of the top green-field investments in 2010 were in energy and raw materials. Some of China's largest global players are involved in war-torn countries, including several oil companies such as China National Petroleum Corporation (CNPC) and China National Offshore Oil Corporation (CNOOC), as well as major construction and railway companies. CNPC, for example, operates in Afghanistan and Sudan, CNOOC operates in Nigeria and Iraq, and the China State Construction Engineering Corporation also operates in Nigeria. China has also been a very active investor in natural resources in Latin America; war-torn countries should learn about this experience, which will help them negotiate with the Chinese.

Since 2000, when restrictions on Indian companies investing abroad were greatly relaxed, their investments have increased rapidly, with the stock of FDI abroad reaching $120 billion in 2012. While manufacturing accounted for the bulk of the investments in the first half of the 2000s, the second half shows a concentration in metals, energy, and natural resource investments. India's Oil and Natural Gas Corporation (ONGC) has invested in Iraq. Sudan was among the 10 largest recipients of Indian investment in 2002–09. Indian firms have explored agricultural and resource investments overseas because they face increasing resistance in India to large-scale projects involving displacement and environmental disruption.

FDI from emerging markets – often carried out by state-owned enterprises – raises a number of issues. Are these investors different from the more traditional ones and, if so, which ones are preferable, and why? Can investors from emerging markets bring technologies, know-how, and other expertise more easily adjustable to local conditions and to local inputs? Can these investors' cultural background and corporate practices be better for war-torn countries at low levels of development? Do their background and practices allow them to have better relations with local workers and supply providers? Are these investors more or less likely to create local jobs and adopt more conflict-sensitive policies? How do these investors behave in comparison with those from Western countries that have their own checks and balances at home with regard to their operations worldwide? How do they compare in terms of complying with national legislation and local practices in general, and with respect to transparency and corruption in particular?

It is perhaps too early to answer many of these questions, since much more research is necessary before we can draw definite conclusions. All of them, however, are important in terms of designing an appropriate legal and regulatory framework to ensure maximum impact, and also in terms of finding the appropriate monitoring system to ensure that the negative impacts of FDI in a war-torn country can be minimised.

What is clear, however, is that investments from companies located in emerging markets, particularly in China, will be packaged differently from those from Western countries. The latter's involvement in war-torn countries has been multifaceted: governments in donor countries provide economic aid and technical assistance. Part of the aid goes to building the physical and human infrastructure necessary for natural resource production and trade. At the same time these countries' military forces may be involved in providing security, either separately, or as part of North Atlantic Treaty Organization (NATO) or UN peacekeeping operations. Finally, private investors from these countries – over which the government has no direct control and, in fact, has restrictions in supporting – independently bid for natural resources.

The involvement of emerging market countries in war-torn ones is often quite different. China provides perhaps the most striking contrast to Western countries' involvement. It is neither a major financial supporter nor a contributor of military personnel, although there have been recent increases in resources and police. Furthermore, investors are often state-owned enterprises and, even if 'private-sector' companies are set up for specific purposes (such as building urban and rural roads in Liberia), they are clearly controlled and supported by the government. Some may even receive long-term financing from their government or development banks at preferential terms.

Although China is not a major donor, state-owned companies have flexibility to offer aid as part of their bidding. Moreover, China is willing to provide aid and concessional loans, which are not attached to economic conditionality, like that imposed by other donors and creditors, particularly the IMF and World Bank; nor are their aid and loans attached to conditionality with respect to human rights. The case of Angola is illustrative. As C. Alden describes it:

> The state-owned Indian oil company, ONGC 'thought it had secured a deal with Shell to assume the lease for Angola's block 18', but a last-minute decision by Angola's state-run oil company, Sonangol, gave the rights to China's Sinopec. Crucial to the turnaround was the Chinese government's willingness to provide a $2 billion loan to the Angolan government.[10]

This example also illustrates how even other emerging markets' companies find it difficult to compete with Chinese firms, given the different packages that the latter are willing to provide.

A big difference between Western and Chinese companies relates to over-sight and accountability. Both Western and Japanese firms have some degree of accountability to their shareholders and boards, are expected to demonstrate a degree of corporate responsibility, and need to make public their labour and environmental practices. They can also be sanctioned by the Foreign Corrupt Practices Act in the USA or by similar legislation elsewhere.[11] US companies in particular often find it difficult to compete with companies from other countries that have more flexibility to bribe local authorities to obtain economic conces-sions, a rather common practice in war-torn countries.

There is perhaps no better example of how Western and Chinese companies use different packages than the bidding for the Aynak untapped copper mine in Afghanistan in 2007.[12] Western countries and Japan were providing huge amounts of aid and technical assistance to the country, and NATO and US forces were providing security, but the bid from Western companies was significantly lower than that of the Metallurgical Corporation of China's (MCC) $3 billion bid for the mine itself. MCC also committed billions to infrastructure development to bring the copper to the market by rail to Pakistani ports.

The Aynak mine illustrates the difficulty for Western companies of compet-ing with Chinese companies in particular, which count with direct support from their government and put all the aid and investment that they are willing to pro-vide in the same package. It also suggests the danger to war-torn countries of getting less efficient, accountable, and conflict-sensitive investors because they do not compete on a level playing field. Western and Japanese aid, as well as NATO military assistance, continued in Afghanistan, despite the government allo-cation of the mining rights to a Chinese company. But what will happen after NATO combat troops withdraw? Had US companies been involved in this and other large investments in minerals and hydrocarbons in the country, would that have a different impact on foreign aid in the future?

Erica Downs argues that the Chinese ability to put in the same package invest-ment and infrastructure is consistent with a broader shift in the mining industry away from enclave private sector development and towards leveraging mineral development to benefit the broader economy.[13] Indeed, if one develops a copper mine in landlocked Afghanistan, or coal deposits in Tete Province in Mozambique, or iron ore in Liberia, which are far from the coast, it is necessary to worry about how to bring the product to markets. The issue to be investi-gated from the Aynak and similar investments, however, is whether linking infrastructure to a concrete project is a better and more cost-effective way of building the necessary infrastructure. It may well be. The fragmented approach that the international community – including the UNDS – has followed in these countries is often to build a road here, a bridge there, and an airport elsewhere, without linking infrastructure directly to the specific production and trade needs.

An oft-heard concern relates to Chinese firms' lack of transparency in the way they operate in a country, which extends to the way that they interact with local governments and communities. For example, in an attempt to bring transparency to a process vulnerable to corruption, and amid a bruising political battle over mining legislation in Afghanistan in 2012, the minister of mines, Wahidullah Shahrani, disclosed about 200 contracts for marble, coal, and other mines dating back to 2002. He reported, however, that he had requested the Chinese to make their Aynak contract public, but that the Chinese had legally negotiated a 'non-publication' agreement with the previous minister.[14]

Although more research is necessary before drawing definitive lessons for the effective exploitation of war-torn countries' resources, there is anecdotal evidence about specific conflict-insensitive policies of companies from emerging markets. This is particularly true of Chinese firms that follow the practice of bringing in labour from China rather than employing local workers, of disregarding labour and environmental codes, of using aid to outbid competitor firms in large projects often involving a large bribe to governments, and of being opaque in terms of the nature of their investments and companies. Not surprisingly, these practices often lead to conflict with the local communities. Joshua Kurlantzick, for example, notes:

> Chinese aid through infrastructure development and business projects lacks transparency. In Cambodia local activists accuse both the Cambodian government and Wuzhishan LS, a Chinese state-owned (plantation) firm, of forcing hundreds of villagers (in a northeastern province) off their land, repossessing the property, and then spraying the area, which includes ancestral burial grounds, with dangerous herbicides. Peter Leuprecht, the UN special representative for human rights in Cambodia, said in a statement, 'The government and the company have disregarded the well-being, culture, and livelihoods of the…indigenous people who make up more than half the population of the province'.[15]

Attracting FDI for natural resources in war-torn countries

War-torn countries rich in untapped natural resources face a number of challenges in exploiting them. First, while these countries cannot exploit their own resources because of a lack of technical capacity and financial resources, opening the sectors to global companies may create a dilemma for policymakers similar to the one that countries face with regard to privatisation. Countries may give large incentives to global companies to invest early in the transition from war, with the intention that this will help in the reactivation of the economy. Alternatively they may also wait until reconstruction has progressed and the economy has reactivated, in an effort to obtain a better deal from private investors. In many cases, however, countries will not be able to muddle through until the second alternative becomes feasible, and thus they are forced to part with their resource assets at bargain prices.

In the DRC, for example, in exchange for investment to upgrade the capacity of the country's diamond production, the government had to agree to future commodity-supply contracts, and at prices well-below market prices and for many years to come. The UN and others have denounced these contracts as unfair. However, only risk-prone investors would put down cash early in the peace transition. This is because of the high probability that the country will relapse into conflict or that future governments may reverse former contracts. To invest under such risky conditions, investors obviously expect a commensurate return.[16] Eventually, however, many governments have had to renegotiate resource contracts with private investors entered into by previous governments, just as countries in the normal process of development in Latin America and elsewhere have also done.

Second, infrastructure linked to richly endowed resources is often at risk of attacks. Thus, the provision of security for such infrastructure is important and often expensive. In 2005 Iraq's oil ministry suffered losses of more than $6 billion from about 200 attacks by armed groups on various oil installations throughout the country.[17]

Third, countries that rely heavily on exports of one or two commodities are vulnerable to Dutch disease – that is, they are likely to have appreciating real exchange rates that distort the price of non-tradable goods and services and undermine export competitiveness. In war-torn countries pressure for a real appreciation of the domestic currency early in the transition also stems from large inflows of aid and other financial resources. In countries such as Afghanistan and Liberia, however, a large part of the aid has been spent abroad (through imports), and Dutch disease has not been a problem. Since real appreciation may become a serious problem to a country's export competitiveness, this could be an issue of policy concern as commodities exports increase.

Fourth, economies that are heavily dependent on production and exports of one or two commodities are also highly vulnerable to changes in international demand and prices. Thus, a 'resource fund' (or stabilisation fund) for these commodities may be the most effective way for the government, which accumulates funds during booms and draws on them during recessions, to attenuate the impact of pro-cyclical fiscal policies. It is best practice to save for a rainy day but, in post-conflict transitions, it pours every day and what is best practice under normal development may be a wasted opportunity during a post-conflict transition.

An issue that requires fuller debate is whether resource-related income should be saved for the benefit of future generations in a fund giving a financial return, or whether it should be invested in human and physical infrastructure to improve the country's future productive capacity and the welfare of the population at the same time. The latter – if effectively and transparently invested – would probably have a higher rate of return than the former. Moreover, investment in infrastructure, by creating productive employment, will probably minimise the high chance that a country in transition to peace will revert to war. This is an area where the UNDS could play a critical role in supporting governments to ensure that resource proceeds are effectively and productively utilised.

Adopting in 2004 a best-practice resource fund modelled after the one created in Norway – a developed country with one of the highest incomes per capita and aging populations – did not serve East Timor well. It had a largely illiterate population and collapsing infrastructure, along with one of the fastest population growth rates and lowest per capita incomes in the world. Utilising those funds productively in the country's reconstruction could have served future generations well and at the same time may have avoided the country's relapse into conflict as well as the need for a new peacekeeping operation in 2006.

Adequate legal framework for natural resource exploitation

Perhaps one of the greatest challenges for war-torn countries is establishing the appropriate legal and regulatory framework, often from scratch, to allow them to attract foreign investment for natural resources, including hydrocarbons, mining, and agricultural sectors. Such a framework needs to reaffirm the fact that resources belong to the state for the benefit of all the people in the country. Thus, there is a need to establish a fair revenue-sharing mechanism among regions and provinces based on population and on the amount of resources that each produces. Despite the difficulties, establishing a fair legal framework for the use of natural resources has proved key in improving the prospects for peace and stability in resource-rich countries, though more often in derailing the prospects for them.

Negotiating such laws and having them ratified by parliaments is often extremely difficult politically. The experience of two war-torn countries – very different in terms of their past performances with regard to natural resources – is illustrative of the problems involved. In Iraq, for example, the oil industry was nationalised in the early 1970s. Twenty years later Russian and Chinese companies signed production-sharing agreements with the Iraqi government. In exchange these companies turned about 10% of their profits over to the government. In 2007 the Iraqi cabinet approved an oil bill that was highly unpopular among the Iraqi people. Over 60% of the population believed that oil should be developed and produced by Iraqi state-owned companies rather than by foreign investors.

The law was drafted with support from BearingPoint, a Washington consultancy firm that has major contracts with the US government in Kosovo, Afghanistan, and Iraq. The Iraqi population largely perceived the law as designed 'for the benefit of US oil companies'.[18] Luring contracts for economic reconstruction and investments in the oil sector was not far from the minds of those planning the US occupation. Iraqis reacted negatively to what they saw as an American effort to disempower them by giving contracts to as many as 5,000 foreign contractors, who would take over their oil wealth.[19]

This partly explains why the bill still languishes in parliament. The other major blockage is that the Kurds want to control Kirkuk and the fields around it, which account for about 10% of proven reserves, while the Sunnis live in an oil-poor part of the country, which makes distribution by the Shi'ite government a particularly difficult issue to settle in a way that is agreeable to all.

The Iraqi oil situation illustrates another issue with natural resources in war-torn countries. Indeed, with one of the largest oil reserves in the world, Iraq continues to attract foreign investors and to produce increasing amounts of oil, despite the failure to establish the proper legal framework. In the south of the country, where the security situation is calmer, Western oil companies continue to operate under service contracts, and Russia's Lukoil is expected to start soon operating a field considered the world's second-largest untapped oil deposit.[20] It is often the case in resource-rich countries that greed prevails over security and other concerns, particularly when the resources are in areas of relative calm. Although these companies may take advantage of oil opportunities in Iraq, peace and stability in the country will continue to be elusive if there is no framework to allocate revenue equitably.

In Afghanistan extensive geological surveys in the 1950s and 1960s done by Soviet mining experts had identified deposits of copper, iron ore, coal, gold, barite, dolomite, limestone, talc, beryl, lapis lazuli, and emeralds. Natural gas deposits were exploited, and gas was piped to the USSR, which was the main way of servicing Soviet loans, particularly during the Soviet invasion in the 1980s. In 2006 the *Mining Journal* reported additional deposits of lead and zinc, chromite, cobalt, platinum-group metals, uranium, and various gemstones, which have been exploited in the past or could provide opportunities for green-field investments. Based on a 2010 memo from the Pentagon, the *New York Times* reported that the value of Afghanistan's untapped mineral resources could amount to nearly $1 trillion, 'far beyond any previously known reserves and enough to fundamentally alter the Afghan economy and perhaps the Afghan war itself '.[21]

Moreover, Afghanistan also has industrial metals and perhaps one of the world's largest deposits of lithium, used in laptop batteries. Geologists have been exploring the dangerous southern desert in Afghanistan for rare earth elements and suspect that actual quantities may be significantly larger than earlier estimates. These elements are used to manufacture many modern technologies from electric cars to solar panels. Security is a major constraint but, if it were to improve, experts believe that 'Afghanistan could provide an alternative source of rare earth elements for industrial countries concerned with the fact that China currently controls 97% of the world's supply'.[22]

Despite the great potential, little foreign investment has materialised so far, notwithstanding the tremendous publicity over bidding by Chinese and Indian companies for the Aynak copper mines in 2007 and the Hajigak iron-ore deposits in 2011. Investors' greed over two of the world's largest mines prevailed over their security, infrastructure, and other business-climate concerns. But, despite these projects' reported billion-dollar price tags and high expectations about related investments in infrastructure, the investments have shown little progress. While the development of the Aynak mine has been delayed by the discovery of Buddhist treasures that are being rescued by a team of French archaeologists, and despite investors' desire to renegotiate the contract, Hajigak investors are still waiting for the revised mining law that was approved by the cabinet and sent to parliament for approval in 2013.

The lack of an adequate mining and hydrocarbon law, and a series of other impediments typical of war-torn countries, led to a fall in FDI in Afghanistan starting in 2006. A sharply deteriorating security situation, a continued lack of electricity and adequate infrastructure, a shortage of skilled labour, inefficient bureaucratic procedures, and the need to renew companies' licences annually were major factors impeding foreign investment. Land grabs, chronic corruption, impunity, the inability to enforce contracts, and the fragmentation and ineffectiveness of aid deterred foreign and domestic investment further. As a result, FDI collapsed to less than 0.5% of GDP annually in 2011–12, from over 4% in 2005. The difficulties in translating interest into investment in natural resources is illustrated by IMF revenue projections from mining amounting to only 2% of GDP by 2025.[23]

In addition to facilitating FDI and ensuring that there is a fair distribution of government revenue from those resources, the legal and regulatory framework for concessions for the exploitation of natural resources should ensure that they do not operate as 'enclaves' and that the country as a whole benefits from the links they create to the domestic economy. In particular, the framework should ensure that there is fair treatment of local communities affected by the concessions.

As an example, concessions in Liberia renegotiated or signed since the 2005 elections differ in the way that they address the corporate responsibilities of foreign investors with regard to workers in the concessions, as well as to indigenous peoples displaced by them. It is important to distinguish between what the concessions contemplate for the displaced and affected groups from what these groups actually get.[24]

Many of the concession contracts include investors' commitment to create clinics, schools, roads, and other infrastructure within the concessions for their workers. They do not, however, require the provision of such services to those groups displaced by the concessions. Some contracts include the creation of financial funds to support displaced populations and may also contain some vague language with regard to compensation for their lost livelihoods. The lack of specificity in this regard has become a source of contention, because companies have often offered to pay for a crop rather than compensating for the sustained loss of livelihoods. Most of the concessions are likely to create environmental problems and are often a threat to the local biodiversity and ecosystems. Although concessionaires are responsible for environmental studies, the real impact is not always monitored and standards are not enforced because of lack of expertise and of the financial means to do it at the local level.

Thus, in addition to the displacement and loss of livelihoods for affected communities, and to the environmental and biodiversity costs associated with many concessions, these often create risks to human security beyond the economic and environmental. This is because of the lack of consultation with local communities about the projects involved and about compensation for the lost livelihoods and other social impacts that affect them dearly. The road can easily lead back to armed conflict.[25]

At the same time, the legal and regulatory framework for natural resource development should include specific requirements for foreign investors detailing that, as a quid pro quo for the preferences granted in terms of land or any tax or tariff exemptions, the government expects foreign investors to pay local workers fair wages and benefits; to establish basic security, human rights and other adequate working conditions; and to achieve minimum levels of investment and/or local employment. The government also expects foreign investments to set up links between their export activities and the local economy by using competitive local inputs and services and increasing other local procurement; to contribute to *in situ* training of local workers and transfer of technology and managerial capacity; to train local workers (in the country and abroad) in administrative and managerial jobs so that they can assume more responsible and higher-paid jobs in the concessions; to establish agreements with local technical schools and universities to create specialised courses, internship programmes, and other arrangements to promote transfers of technology and capacity building of the local labour force; and to exercise corporate responsibility in social and environmental areas (ie create local parks, schools, clinics, and other such projects).

International experts will have to be involved in drafting the legal and regulatory framework for the concessions, and the local governments will need to develop capabilities to monitor and enforce it. The latter will be difficult because of the complexity of the contracts and the limited capacity of national and local governments in war-torn countries. Both in drafting the legal framework and its monitoring, the UNDS could play an important and constructive role so that these countries can move away from enclave production. The latter not only limits the impact of FDI on the domestic economy but has also proven to be a source of conflict with the communities.

Conclusion

The problems with economic reconstruction of war-torn countries have been extensively analysed. They often grow fast (albeit from a low base) as a result of large volumes of aid and of the presence of the international community, including foreign troops or large UN peacekeeping operations. This leads to large and unsustainable growth in construction and services. At the same time the rural sector, which provides for the lives and livelihoods of the great majority of people, is neglected. This has clearly been the case in Liberia and Afghanistan.

War-torn countries may also grow fast because of 'enclave-type' production and export of natural resources, including hydrocarbons, mining, and agricultural products. Iraq and Angola are good examples and so is Liberia, where the IMF has estimated that roughly half the rapid growth of recent years is related to this type of activity, mostly in mining, rubber, and palm oil.

Concessions to foreign investors for the exploitation of natural resources, together with ineffective aid policies, have led to 'growth without development', a term coined by Robert Clower in connection with Liberia, where growth benefits mostly foreign investors and domestic elites and increasingly becomes a threat to human security. Enclaves are generally a source of labour exploitation and often displace indigenous communities and endanger their livelihoods, as well as destroying forests and wildlife.[26]

Perhaps Siakor and Knight best articulated the threat to human security in Liberia, when they wrote in a *New York Times* article in 2012 that 'unbeknown to many outside Liberia, Mrs. Johnson Sirleaf's government may now be sowing the seeds of future conflict by handing over huge tracts of land to foreign investors and dispossessing rural Liberians'.[27]

While governments are willing to give large extensions of land to foreign investors, donors – including the UNDS – are willing to finance a large part of the infrastructure that these investors need to exploit natural resources. Yet there has been very little interest on the part of donors or investors to finance the infrastructure needs of small farmers and other micro-entrepreneurs, particularly in the communities that have a claim on those resources.

It is thus that the promise of natural resource development for many communities remains just a promise, in part because of overall insecurity in the country that discourages FDI, but in part because of problems with the communities that place the investors and the communities in a 'no-win' confrontation.

The case, for example, of the Niger Delta in Nigeria is illustrative because communities sabotage oil pipelines, capture part of the oil, and put oil workers at risk, raising the cost of production and leading to waste and pollution. In his fascinating book *Untapped: The Scramble for Africa's Oil*, John Ghazvinian describes the details relating to the practice of tapping into a pipeline (oil or natural gas), known as 'illegal bunkering', the problems it creates for all concerned (companies, communities, governments), and how, the more profitable this becomes, the more it attracts the involvement of mafias.[28]

Given the importance of natural resources to the peace, development, and prosperity of many war-torn countries, there is a need for a broad-based debate on how foreign investors can assist in the development and trade of natural resources. At the same time means should be found so that investors can create links to the rest of the economy, including to the communities directly affected by them. It is imperative that governments (at the national and local level), together with foreign investors, donors, and local communities, work in a 'win-win' situation to ensure that the gains from such resources are justly distributed and that aid can be gradually allowed to wither. The UNDS does indeed have a crucially important role to play in supporting governments and local communities in such efforts.

Notes

1. See del Castillo, *Rebuilding War-torn States*.
2. For a detailed discussion, see ibid; del Castillo, *The Economics of Peace*; and del Castillo, *Guilty Party*.
3. del Castillo, *Rebuilding War-torn States*, 30.
4. For a comparison of aid levels, see del Castillo, "Is the UN System up to the Challenge?"
5. The term 'indigenous communities' is used in a broad sense to include not only indigenous peoples but also other farming communities that live near the natural resources and are dependent on them.
6. For proposals on how the different stakeholders might work together in Afghanistan and Liberia, see del Castillo, *Reconstruction Zones;* Castillo, *Aid and Employment Generation*; and Castillo, *Guilty Party*.
7. See Doyle, "Strategy and Transitional Authority," 82.
8. See Humphreys et al., *Escaping the Resource Curse*.

9. UNCTAD data are used for FDI outflows; information about the different modalities in which these companies operate is from the FDI Investment Profiles of the Columbia Center for International Investment.
10. Alden, "China's New Engagement with Africa," 22.
11. Kurlantzick, "China in Southeast Asia," 207.
12. See Gilpin, *Improving High-value Resource Contracting.*
13. Downs, "China Buys into Afghanistan."
14. See Bowley and Rosenberg, "Mining Contract."
15. Kurlantzick, "China in Southeast Asia," 207.
16. See, for example, the three reports of the United Nations Panel of Experts on the Illegal Exploitation of Natural Resources and Other Forms of Wealth in the DRC.
17. Reported by Agence France-Presse in 2005.
18. Janabi, "Row over Iraqi Oil Law."
19. See Baker and Hamilton, *The Iraq Study Group Report.* See also del Castillo, *Rebuilding War-torn States,* chap. 10.
20. Lawler and Mackey, "Iraq Returns."
21. For detailed information and data sources on Afghanistan in this and the following paragraphs, see del Castillo, *Guilty Party.*
22. Posted by *wadsam*, Afghan Business News Portal, April 25, 2013.
23. See also del Castillo, "Leveling the Afghan Playing Field."
24. Lorenzo Cotula points out that the lack of transparency and of checks and balances in contract negotiations creates a breeding ground for corruption and deals that do not maximise the public interest. Cotula, *Land Grab.*
25. For a thorough analysis of concessions in Liberia, two in the mining sector and two in the agricultural sector, and their impact, see Lanier et al., *Smell-No-Taste.*
26. Clower et al., *Growth without Development.* For a detailed analysis and data sources on Liberia's economy and why Clower's term applies to the post-conflict period, see del Castillo, *Aid and Employment Generation.*
27. Siakor and Knight, "A Nobel Laureate's Problem."
28. Ghazvinian, *Untapped.*

Bibliography

Alden, C. "China's New Engagement with Africa." In *China's Expansion into the Western Hemisphere*, edited by R. Roett and G. Paz, 213–237. Washington, DC: Brookings Institution Press, 2008.

Baker, J. A., and L. H. Hamilton. *The Iraq Study Group Report.* New York: Vintage Books, 2006.

Bowley G., and M. Rosenberg. 2012. "Mining Contract Details Disclosed in Afghanistan." *New York Times*, October 15.

Clower, Robert, et al. *Growth without Development: An Economic Survey of Liberia.* Evanston, IL: Northwestern University Press, 1966.

Cotula, Lorenzo. *Land Grab or Development Opportunity? International Farmland Deals in Africa.* Columbia FDI Perspectives 8. New York: Columbia University, June 22, 2009.

del Castillo, Graciana. *Aid and Employment Generation in Conflict-affected Countries: Policy Recommendations for Liberia.* Working Paper 2012/47. Helsinki: UNU/WIDER, 2012.

del Castillo, Graciana. *Guilty Party: The International Community in Afghanistan.* Bloomington, IN: XLibris, 2014.

del Castillo, Graciana. "Is the UN System up to the Challenge?" In *Post-2015 UN Development: Making Change Happen,* edited by Stephen Browne and Thomas G. Weiss, 144–159. London: Routledge, 2014.

del Castillo, Graciana. *Rebuilding War-torn States: The Challenge of Post-conflict Economic Reconstruction.* Oxford: Oxford University Press, 2008.

del Castillo, Graciana. *The Economics of Peace: Five Rules for Effective Reconstruction.* Washington, DC: United States Institute of Peace, 2011.

del Castillo, Graciana. *Reconstruction Zones in Afghanistan and Haiti: A Way to Enhance Aid Effectiveness and Accountability.* Special Report 292. Washington, DC: United States Institute of Peace, 2011.

del Castillo, Graciana. 2013. "Leveling the Afghan Playing Field." *Project Syndicate*, August 8.

Downs, Erica. "China Buys into Afghanistan." *SAIS Review* 23, no. 2 (2012): 65–84.

Doyle, Michael. "Strategy and Transitional Authority." In *Ending Civil Wars: The Implementation of Peace Agreements*, edited by Stephen John Stedman, Donald Rothchild, and Elizabeth Cousens. Boulder, CO: Lynne Rienner, 2002.

Ghazvinian, J. *Untapped: The Scramble for Africa's Oil.* New York: Harcourt, 2007.

Gilpin, Raymond. *Improving High-value Resource Contracting in Afghanistan.* Washington, DC: United States Institute for Peace, 2010.

Humphreys, Macartan, Jeffrey D. Sachs, and Joseph E. Stiglitz. *Escaping the Resource Curse.* New York: Columbia University Press, 2007.

Janabi, Ahmed. "Row over Iraqi Oil Law." *Aljazeera*, May 8, 2007. http://www.aljazeera.com/news/middle east/2007/05/200852518577734692.html.

Kurlantzick, Joshua. "China in Southeast Asia." In *China's Expansion into the Western Hemisphere*, edited by R. Roett and G. Paz, 193–212. Washington, DC: Brookings Institution Press, 2008.

Lanier, Frazer, Ashoka Mukpo, and Frithiof Wilhelmson. *Smell-No-Taste: The Social Impact of Foreign Direct Investment in Liberia*. New York: Columbia University, 2011.

Lawler, Alex, and Peg Mackey. 2014. "Iraq Returns as World's Fastest-growing Oil Exporter." Reuters, March 5. http://www.reuters.com/article/2014/03/05/iraq-oil-idUSL6N0M22P120140305.

Siakor S. K., and R. S. Knight. 2012. "A Nobel Laureate's Problem at Home." *New York Times*, January 20.

Index

Text in **bold** denotes tables and boxes; text in *italics* denotes figures.